THE ABILITIES OF BABIES

FRONTISPIECE. PLATE I

This twenty-months' boy is about to do item D 49 (Chapter XIV). Note the attentive expression. This boy plays constructively with materials. Note the low stool and comfortable position at the table. The Examiner sits also at the low table opposite to him, and the apparatus can be seen arranged on the trolly at the Examiner's right until needed. The nurse is seated behind the child, but near to him to give him reassurance.

THE ABILITIES OF BABIES

A STUDY IN MENTAL MEASUREMENT

RUTH GRIFFITHS
M.A., Ph.D., Dip.Ed., F.B.Ps.S.

UNIVERSITY OF LONDON PRESS LTD

ISBN 0 340 08505 3

Fifth impression 1970

University of London Press Ltd
St Paul's House, Warwick Lane, London EC4
Printed in Great Britain by
Lowe & Brydone (Printers) Ltd., London

PREFACE

THIS book is the outcome of a long experience of testing children of all ages and types and also of considerable experience of educational and psychotherapeutic work among children. It is based upon extensive research that had its origins in work among mentally handicapped persons in the years before the war. From this I built up my own provisional Scale of Tests, based partly on the needs of mentally defective persons and partly on tests and observations of normal children of the younger ages. The work was for years incidental to other activities, but during the war it was stimulated by my experiences as a psychologist working among evacuated children. It was not until after the war that I found opportunity to standardise this first part of my scale on a population of normal babies.

In constructing a scale of this kind for the early period of life it is essential that it should measure only those trends (or sequences) of development that are significant for intelligence or indicative of mental growth. It is inevitable, therefore, that every worker in this field will find his schedules overlapping in detail with those of other workers. All the early scales contain items common to one another, and my own scale is no exception; there is, however, much in the scale as it now stands that is new. It is constructed in a somewhat novel manner, as described in the text, and there is a new set of standardised apparatus for use in applying the tests. Over 1,000 infants between two weeks and two years of age have now been tested by this method, and the scale itself was standardised on a representative sample of 604 London babies.

I am indebted to works by Mary Shirley, Charlotte Bühler, Arnold Gesell and others, from whom I have learnt much. I should particularly like to thank Dr. Arnold Gesell for his numerous and illuminating books and observations about mental growth, and for permission to include in my scale a number of items from his early schedules. My thanks are also due to Messrs. John Wiley & Sons Inc., New York, for permission to include references and brief quotations from articles in their book, *A Manual of Child Psychology*, edited by Leonard Carmichael.

I must thank most warmly Professor Sir Cyril Burt for his careful reading of the book, and for his numerous helpful suggestions. I am most grateful to Professor P. E. Vernon, Professor of Educational Psychology, University of London, who very kindly read the statistical sections at an early stage and made several valuable comments and suggestions.

I must thank Dr. Emanuel Miller, of St. George's Hospital, not only for his kindly interest in the whole project but also for reading the book in manuscript, and for his encouraging and helpful comments. I am gratefully indebted to Professor D. W. Harding and Miss Monica Lawlor and her assistants of the Psychology Department, Bedford College, University of London, for all (except one) of the photographs. I am glad to acknowledge the assistance of Dr. M. E. Hebron, of the Psychology Department, University of Hull, who arranged for much of the statistical work in Chapters V and VI to be checked by the computation service of that department.

I am indebted to the following people for their co-operation and practical assistance: the late Mrs. E. Nathan for carrying out a number of preliminary tests; Mrs. Sedgley, Psychologist at Stoke Park Colony, Bristol, and Mr. Terence Moore of the Child Study Department, University of London, for useful comments; Dr. J. A. Scott, Medical Officer of Health, London County Council, and Dr. Violet Russell, Senior Assistant M.O.H., Kensington, for permission to carry out extensive testing work in the institutions in that area; Dr. Rosemary Bradmore for allowing her son to be photographed for the Frontispiece of this book; the staffs of the institutions in Kensington who so patiently permitted me to invade their places of work over a period of years, and in particular, Miss Carter and her staff of the South Kensington Infant Welfare Centre, where special arrangements were made for a large number of children to be tested; my friend, Miss Tothill of Perth, for the photograph of a child "writing a letter" (Plate 23); and finally, my friend Miss Vida R. Hume, M.A., for typing the manuscript and for her unfailing help, without which this work might never have been written.

In conclusion, I must thank my Publishers, The University of London Press, for the great care they have taken in the preparation of the book.

RUTH GRIFFITHS.

146 *Harley Street, London, W.1*
July, 1960

CONTENTS

LIST OF TABLES, FIGURES AND PLATES

TABLES

FIGURES

PLATES

CHAPTER I

INTRODUCTION

MEASURING intelligence or assessing degrees of ability in babies is a comparatively recent development in applied psychology. The attempt to extend testing procedures to include children below two years of age follows logically and necessarily upon the testing of older children.

In view of their extreme immaturity, the testing of such young subjects may well appear a difficult or impossible task. In this book, however, a fresh approach to the problems involved in testing the very young will be described, and a new scale of tests will be presented. The justification for this work lies in the urgency of the need for early diagnosis of mental condition in special cases.

Psychological testing of older children has now been long established, and tests of many kinds have been successfully applied to large populations of children. The Binet-Simon Scale (Binet 1903, 1908, 1911, 1915) [1] is well known and is one of the most useful instruments so far placed in the hands of psychologists. It was first devised as the result of researches into intelligence carried out by Galton and others during the closing half of last century, and has been revised and modified several times, in America by Goddard (1911) and Terman (1916), and in this country by Professor Sir Cyril Burt (1921). The latest American revision by Terman and Merrill (1937) was based on a total sample of 2,757 children. This revision has extended the range of the tests so as to make the testing of older children (and adults) more accurate, and has also carried the work down to the latter part of the second year of life.

For the purpose of measuring development (including intellectual progress) in children *below* this age level, several scales have been devised. The extensive work of Gesell (1925), Gesell and Amatruda (1941), Shirley (1933a, 1933b), Stutsman (1931), Bayley (1933, 1940), C. Bühler (1930, 1935), P. Cattell (1940) and others is well known. In this country the scale of intelligence tests has

[1] Dates are placed after authors' names as references to the Bibliography which will be found at the end of the volume.

been extended backwards below the age of two years by Professor Burt (1929)[1] and by Professor Valentine (1945). The scales differ considerably from one another in regard to selection of test items, weighting and classification, in spite of certain basic similarities between them (Chapter III).

There are certain difficulties inherent in the nature of this work of testing babies that make it different from work with older children. The problems of sampling, of test construction and of standardisation are considerable (Chapter V); and the management of the test situation itself involves the application of what is virtually a new testing technique (Chapter X).

In this research an attempt has been made to solve these problems. The work has extended over several years, and has involved a detailed study of the mental development of several hundred babies, ranging in age from two weeks to twenty-four months. Tentative norms of development have been established over a wide range of activities. From these the new scale of tests has been derived. Moreover, a new diagnostic technique (differential diagnosis of mental status), for studying development in special cases, has become possible. This method is demonstrated by means of "profiles" (Chapters VII and VIII). Naturally further work will need to be done on the use of this scale, for both normal and handicapped children, before its reliability or validity can be finally established, but the indications so far are encouraging (Chapter VI).

In Part I of this book the various problems associated with this project will be taken up one by one and discussed in relation to the way the scale was constructed. In Part II the standardisation of the scale and preliminary statistical findings will be presented. In Part III the method of administering the scale and the standardisation of procedures will be described in detail.

[1] See *Report of Mental Deficiency Committee* (1929), Part IV, p. 218; Ages I and II.

Part I

CRITERIA FOR A NEW TECHNIQUE FOR TESTING INFANTS

CHAPTER II

OBSERVATION OF NORMAL INFANTS AND TEST CONSTRUCTION

THE twin themes of this report are test construction and psychological diagnosis. There is no intention of offering here any exposition of the general theory (or theories) of child psychology, although reference will be made to the findings and theories of other workers.

There were five sources or criteria by which the writer's attitude to the problem of test construction was influenced:

1. The approach to a test programme began with *observation*, that is, with detailed systematic observation of children.
2. It took into account previous test methods and existing tests (Chapter III).
3. It was based on a study of (*a*) trends that appeared significant for mental growth and (*b*) the interrelations between the basic avenues of learning.
4. It took into account the special needs of handicapped as well as of normal children in the test situation (Chapters IV and VIII).
5. It was necessary that the resulting scale of tests should fulfil certain statistical requirements (Chapters V and VI).

In the present chapter we shall deal with the first of these criteria, namely observation, this being the foundation on which the new scale was built. Other aspects of the approach (2, 3, 4 and 5 above) will be dealt with in subsequent chapters.

Observation

Systematic observation of infants and young children was regarded as the most useful preliminary study (quite apart from an extensive experience of testing children of all other ages) that could be made in preparation for research in this field. A great deal of detailed and precise information was needed concerning the behaviour of children of these young ages before the work of test construction could begin. Much information about individual children is available in the extensive literature, in particular in biographical studies of babies that have been published since the end of last century: Darwin (1877), Champneys (1881), Shinn (1893, 1900) and others; see summary by Dennis (1936).

The work of James Sully (1896) undoubtedly laid the foundations in this country of a scientific approach to the early years. In his *Studies of Childhood* he gives much detailed information about young children.

An important recent book representative of the biographical trend is *The Psychology of Early Childhood*, by Valentine (1942). Much valuable information and many relevant suggestions were found in these biographical studies, and also in other sections of the literature, to supplement personal observation.

Observational studies of babies of the relevant ages were undertaken in Infant Welfare Centres, Day Nurseries and other institutions. Such studies may be made in a variety of ways. They may involve cross-sections of the community or longitudinal studies. In the latter, as Shirley (1931a, 1931b) and others have found, light can be thrown on certain fundamental problems of growth and development by long-continued observations of the same individuals. Development proceeds rapidly in babyhood, and studies of individual children continuing over a period of time are undoubtedly rich in results. However, for the purpose of building up a scale of tests, large numbers of babies had inevitably to be included, and therefore, because of the time factor, the longitudinal method could be used in the present study only to a limited extent. This has so far been done (1) by retesting small samples of our normal subjects, and (2) by follow-up studies of a few children presenting special problems (Chapter VI).

As the subjects of these preliminary experiments were very young, and a broad study of infant development was envisaged rather than a study of some specific aspect of behaviour, it was decided to make protocols in some detail. In this way the spontaneous behaviour of individual infants was studied: their reactions to one another, to other people, to objects in the environment and to various test situations. They were observed at first individually and later in groups.

For individual studies the observer took a notebook, sat beside the young baby's cot and, commencing at a definite time and noting the time at regular intervals, took down everything that could be observed in, say, one hour, repeating the experiment

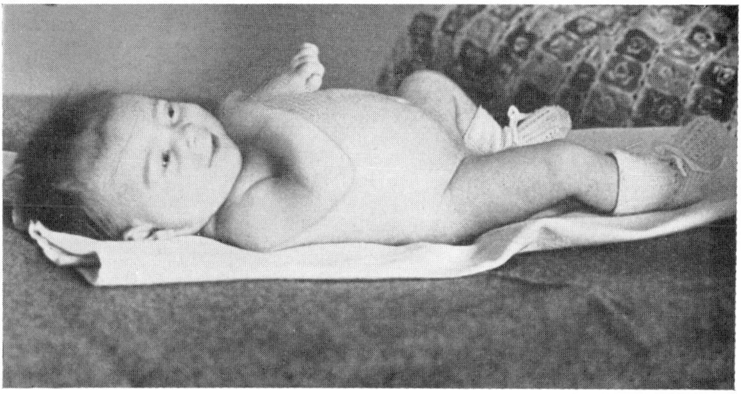

PLATE 2

This little girl is just six weeks old. She is tiny for her age (petite), but well nourished. She is bright and well-developed socially. Her happy smiling and also kicking and arm waving (which have slightly blurred the picture) are in response to her mother, who is sitting near by and talking to her.

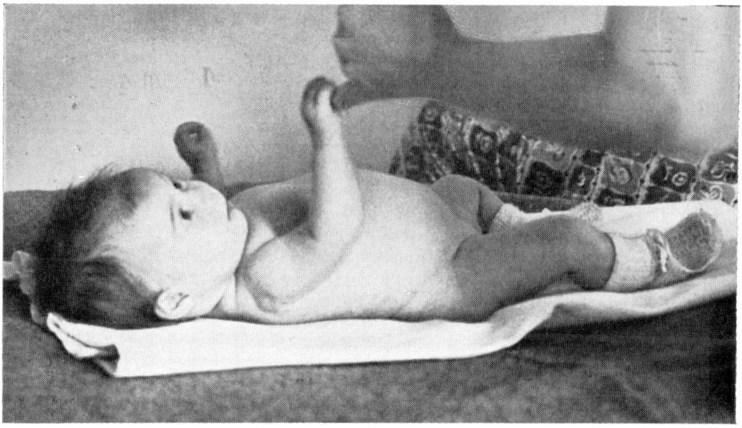

PLATE 3

She has stopped kicking now, and is looking up into her mother's face with wide-eyed interest while she hangs on firmly to Mother's little finger. She does not let go even when Mother's hand is moved strongly from side to side. It should be noted that the baby's left hand has also taken on the grasping position. The size of the adult hand and the tiny grasping hand of the baby are seen in contrast.

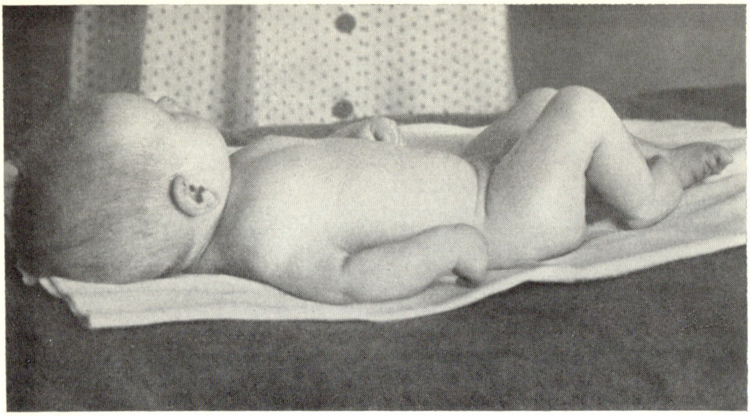

PLATE 4

Relaxed physically, this three months' boy is watching the ring which the Examiner swings slowly round in a circle above him. Note the curled-up hands and feet and relaxed body which accompany the concentration.

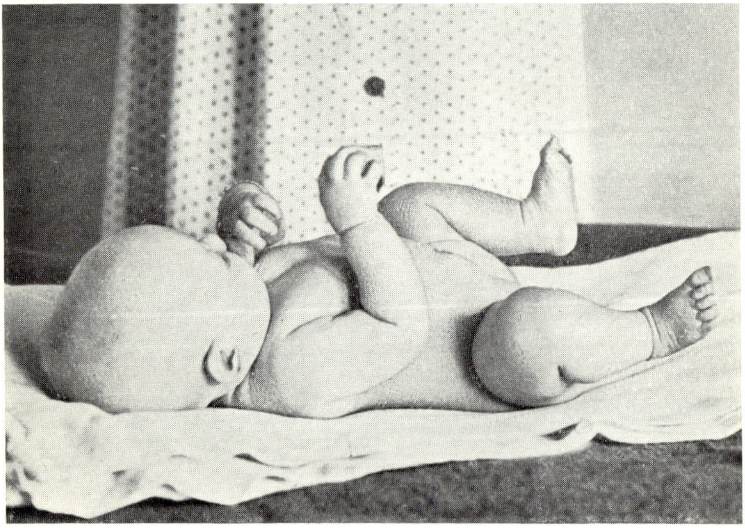

PLATE 5

This child is also three months old. She is kicking joyfully after successfully accepting a cube which the Examiner has placed in her hand. The left hand takes on a similar attitude to the right, but she could not yet hold a second cube; if she grasped it she would immediately relinquish the first one. Her span of attention is as yet too narrow.

from time to time. These protocols soon contained observations of a variety of activities. Of the youngest babies, whose reactions were less complex than was the case with the older ones, fairly complete studies could be made, but even here the material was extensive and cried out for some degree of classification. The notebooks soon became loaded with useful material such as descriptions of locomotor activities, hand and arm movements, murmured sounds, crying, facial movements, eye movements, "startling", as well as descriptions of waking, sleeping, feeding and so on.

With older babies the general protocol method is more cumbersome and difficult, and in practice it was found better to have some specific type of activity or trend of development to look for exclusively. These older children, when in action, move so rapidly that it is difficult to study their movements except with a ciné-camera. Note-taking is a limited method unless some degree of selection or specialisation is introduced. The attention of the child is liable to go rapidly from one object in the environment to another. Speech or babble frequently accompanies activity. Children of these ages, about nine months and older, can concentrate intensely for very short periods of time on anything that interests them, but the general picture is one of rapid exploration, quick interest in and as quick discarding of each successive source of stimulation. This rapid change of direction of interest is characteristic until about the middle of the second year. Naturally it varies from child to child. The mother says: "I don't know what to do with him, he's all over the place." This quality, this rapid flight of attention in the older babies, can actually be utilised in the planning of a scale and also in the test situation.

A condition such as this, involving the inability to concentrate for more than a few moments on a task, or even to keep for more than a very short time in any one place, is characteristic, and therefore quite normal, at these ages. It is, however, a symptom of severe retardation or abnormality in older children. Rapid flight of attention and excessive restlessness are frequent characteristics of older defectives. This fact may illustrate a truth that can be more widely applied, namely that certain symptoms that lead to the diagnosis of defect in older subjects may not be abnormal conditions in themselves, but merely indicate the degree of emotional immaturity or intellectual retardation that may be present in a particular patient. In infancy a restless exploratory attitude to environment is normal and must be taken into account in planning procedures.

The difficulties inherent in any detailed scheme of observation may not be apparent, but they are considerable. The most serious is the fact that a bias is liable to be introduced into the note-taking, simply because of the impossibility of noting everything that takes place, and the observer will tend to emphasise those aspects of the child's behaviour that most interest him and tend to neglect other trends that may be equally important. Thus, one person's record may be overweighted with speech items, another's with descriptions of manipulative skills, another's with the expression of emotional factors and so on. We have tried to guard against such possibilities.

Let us now summarise some of the results of this preliminary work and report some impressions.

In approaching the study of the first days, weeks and months of a baby's life, we are not only approaching the very beginnings of all branches of our subject (psychology), but also the very beginnings of individual experience. Here cognition in some form begins. A baby undoubtedly thinks. As to how he thinks and develops intellectually very little is actually known, but mentation would appear to proceed from birth, and indeed to be present to some extent even before birth, as has been suggested by experimental investigations (Carmichael, 1946, p. 43).

Simple awareness and early cognition are perhaps most easily inferred from the child's facial expression when actively listening and from those early murmured sounds that begin to be made soon after birth (Chapter XIII, "Hearing and Speech"). Quite soon the baby is able to respond vocally to the mother's voice speaking to him and to carry on a kind of monosyllabic conversation, e.g. "a-a-a" or "er-er-er", and soon certain guttural or labial sounds may be distinguished. Speech sounds gradually grow in number and complexity and involve a degree of *imitation*. The observed sequence is: (1) the baby quietens and then assumes an attentive listening expression, with eyes on the mother's face; (2) there is a pause during which the mother is talking softly to him; (3) then comes the vocal response. The imitative nature of this response becomes clearer as speech develops, and the sounds produced gradually approximate nearer to the sounds heard. There is frequently a considerable time-lag between a heard stimulus and the child's response. (See also M. M. Lewis, 1935.)

Most of the child's activity at this level is, however, motor in type, and suggests active striving to attain certain ends. The so-called random or mass movements of the young baby gradually give place to movements that appear purposive. The resulting locomotor series and developing hand and eye co-ordination can not only be observed but definitely tested for and assessed from the first month of life. (See Chapters XI, XIV and XV.)

At this level also can be easily distinguished the changing emotional tone of the child with changing conditions, and not only those most obvious changes that lead to crying. The child appears sensitive to the social situation almost from the beginning. The psychologist who spends much time testing very young babies himself becomes sensitive to the child's mood, and manipulates conditions to keep a positive relationship in being between himself and the child. The problem of "rapport" with these very young subjects in itself provides an interesting study. (See Chapter X.)

The human baby is very helpless when just born, more helpless than almost any other new-born creature. Yet he appears to be endowed (like other creatures) with a certain protective mechanism that enables him to respond to another of his kind. He is endowed at an instinctive level with the ability to move towards or accept the source of nourishment. He similarly demands and secures protection and attention. This comparatively simple situation, the early relationship between mother and child, constitutes the first simple social fact and, as the child grows, this relationship itself develops into the earliest true social relationship between two human persons. This first simple social fact would appear to be the most important and far-reaching circumstance in the whole of human development. It is, moreover, something on the effects of which the child is dependent, physically and psychologically, intellectually and emotionally, throughout infancy and childhood and for long afterwards. (See diagram, Fig. 5.)

Observations made by psychologists and also by analytic writers amply illustrate from their varying viewpoints and in many different contexts the importance and significance of this early relationship and its effect upon later development.

James Sully long ago (1896) stressed the importance of the early stages of development and the training of young children in the home. Professor Burt in his *The Young Delinquent* (1925) refers to early experiences in the home and to environmental factors in his studies of delinquency. The recent work of Bowlby (1949) describes the families and home life of delinquent children. Professor Flügel (1921) in *The Psycho-analytic Study of the Family*, Bernfeld (1929) in *The Psychology of the Infant*, Klein (1932) in *The Psycho-analysis of Children* and Anna Freud (1934, 1946), all stress from different viewpoints the importance of early influences on later development. The direct study of the phantasies and imaginings of young normal children also throws light on early experiences and their relevance to intellectual development (Griffiths, 1932, 1935). Studies of play activities provide similar evidence (Lowenfeld, 1935). Studies of the social and emotional development of young children are relevant also (Bridges, 1931, 1932; Bühler, 1930, 1940); and the extensive work of Susan Isaacs, who wrote from both the educational and psycho-analytic points of view, must be referred to in conclusion (Isaacs, 1930, 1932, 1933, 1948, etc.).

These writers may be cited among many others. The weight of the evidence shows that a young child can be expected to develop normally only when surrounded from birth by an aura of affectionate understanding and emotional security, and that he also needs a stable home life from the beginning, and suffers if deprived of this.[1] Too many changes of environment may seriously affect a young child's intellectual development also, especially if accompanied by other forms of deprivation or hardship.

So dependent is the young baby on the maintenance of a normal relationship with his milieu that his whole developmental progress may become distorted or slowed down if this normal relationship should be disturbed or destroyed. There is, then, a sense in which the whole of the child's development may be regarded as social. Imitative speech may disappear altogether when the mother is for a period unable to care for her child. Similarly, other aspects of development may be impaired, at least during the period of separation. A baby just beginning to walk may return to the crawling phase. Special cases among young children could be quoted who still showed retardation in one of these directions, following upon early separation from the mother's care, long after the period of deprivation.

It is therefore important for the psychologist to know something of a child's home circumstances and previous history before a

[1] See *Report of Care of Children Committee*. Chairman: Myra Curtis. H.M. Stationery Office (1946).

psychological diagnosis in any special case is arrived at, or regarded as conclusive.

The *social factor* is therefore one that cannot be ignored in the test situation, and there is a sense in which all test items may be regarded as social items. There are, however, a number of directions in which it is possible to test deliberately for the child's level of learning social ways and acquiring habits that are indicative of his stage of personal social adjustment. (See Scale B, Chapter XII.)

The creative activity of the normal healthy baby goes forward happily when the social situation is satisfactory. He explores and investigates his total environment in a piecemeal manner, observing, demanding, handling, imitating, struggling in all manner of ways to come into relationship with and gain some command of his environment. He expends energy for short periods at a tremendous rate, then lies quiescent or murmuring to himself until he falls asleep. His energy is limited and he is easily fatigued.

In any attempt to test very young babies, account must be taken of their extreme immaturity. Neither their intellectual nor their emotional stability are as yet established. Illness can disturb or retard progress in any or every direction, and general response to environment may be much lessened. In a case of illness, the lack of response may be in the nature of a regression, usually temporary and associated only with the period of illness. The psychologist must therefore expect a delicate infant to show fluctuations in his mental progress as reflected in successive test results, just as the physician finds fluctuations in his physical progress. The obvious corollary is that the psychologist must be prepared to test and retest children who present low results when first seen, before it is assumed that a test result is final. It may be advisable sometimes to postpone or abandon the examination.

A certain orderliness exists in the way a baby develops. He must sit before he creeps and (usually) creep before he walks. He must vocalise and then babble before he talks (though there are some exceptions to this). He understands speech before he uses it. These things are somehow laid down in his physical and nervous constitution. Thus, to quote from Gesell[1] "The maturation mechanisms are so firmly entrenched that they are not readily transcended by training", and again: "The basic ontogenetic

[1] See Gesell's article, "The Ontogenesis of Infant Behaviour", in Carmichael, L. (Ed.) (1946), *A Manual of Child Psychology*, pp. 314 and 315.

forms of individuation are the result of maturation. Conditioning is superimposed, as it were, upon a maturational substrate." And again: "Environmental factors support, inflect and modify, but they do not generate the progressions of development."

However, it is the *rate* at which development takes place that determines the child's mental status at any one time, and this, the rate at which he develops, appears very largely dependent in the earliest stages upon the social background and related circumstances of the child. Maturation reaches its fullest potentialities (for that particular child) only under favourable socio-psychological conditions. Thus, a happy child lifts its arms to be taken up, strains to lift head from pillow, crawls after toy or ball when rolled towards him by the parent. (These are all test items.) The depressed, unhappy baby lies inert, inactive, his "maturational" processes in abeyance, slowed down, delayed. The same applies to hand and eye development, to speech development and to all the interwoven skills of infancy. A study of special cases throws these facts into relief.

To recapitulate briefly so far, the young baby is found to be dependent in a significant and intimate manner upon the several members of the family group for that background which makes normal development possible. He responds in a threefold manner to this environment. He thinks, feels and acts, gradually gathering up the ideas of those amongst whom he lives, imitating their actions, learning their speech and responding actively to the stimulus of his environment. He is immature, dependent, with a tendency to alternate between active and passive moods, and even to retreat or regress when ill or overstimulated. He reacts to people both positively and negatively, and is liable to be apprehensive of strangers and new situations. In the early weeks and months he is peculiarly dependent upon the mother for his sense of personal security.

For these and other reasons the attempt to measure *intelligence* in babies may cause some scepticism. This is to be expected. The infant is so very immature, insecure, and limited in his means of self-expression that he is in fact difficult to test. But actually every attempt to measure general intelligence has similarly in the past been resisted by earlier generations of critics, and yet has proved successful. Intelligence is usually defined as "innate, general, cognitive ability", and this definition may be tentatively accepted in relation to the new scale. Whether in fact the test procedure described in detail in the following chapters can claim to measure this innate ability as efficiently as tests for older subjects must wait until further research has been carried out (1) in applying the scale to subjects at different ages (see "Retest Studies" in Chapter VI), and (2) in comparing results on this test with results on other scales. This question is intimately related to the question of constancy of the I.Q. to be discussed in Chapter IV ("Predictive Value of the New Scale"). Moreover, testing ability in this early period involves measuring many skills of a motor type that are basic to intellectual growth in this period, and the general character of the scale necessarily differs somewhat from tests applicable to older children.

We must now turn to a further aspect of this problem, and to consideration of the essential sequences that must be measured. There would appear to be three main directions in which human development as such differs from that of the higher animals. First of all, man has attained the erect posture.

By the end of the first year of life the baby normally achieves the upright posture, although the average child does not actually stand and walk alone until about two months later. This matter of achieving the upright posture does not appear to happen as the result of a mere maturation of function, although of course there is for the vast majority of children an orderly sequence of events. There are considerable individual differences in the *rate* of progress towards walking, and also considerable variations, as Gesell himself has amply shown, in the methods used by different babies. Some, for example, soon learn to creep on hands and knees, others do a sort of bear walk, some shuffle along on one hip or career about in a sitting position before they develop courage enough to grasp some piece of furniture and pull themselves up. The child's ability to rear himself up at last and walk like a man does not appear to be the *mere* result of the unfolding of an inborn function; it is here, in a study of the actual rate of development and divergence of method of individual children, that the problems of inheritance and environment meet, and the old controversy can perhaps be seen in a new light. It would appear to be that vital energy, that persistence, that determination, the expression of a fundamental will to grow and develop, superimposed upon an inherited predisposition, which brings about the result. The baby *wants* to walk, although he may not have a clearly defined or final end in view. He first struggles to sit, then to secure a toy beyond his reach, then to see what is above the table top, and so on, building up in successive stages a highly complex series of skills. (See Scale A, Chapter XI.) He puts forth effort and eventually he succeeds. How shall this fundamental drive be described? Is it mere maturation? Is it the expression of an "élan vital"? Is it libido? Or are we justified in regarding it as one aspect of mental effectiveness at this level, in fact as "*g*" or general intelligence (Spearman, 1923, 1927), conceived as the energy of the total organism, finding its outlet through the specific ability of learning to walk?

Having through inheritance the capacity to learn to free his hands from their earlier function (of helping him to creep and climb), the human child goes ahead with *manipulative skills*, and develops more rapidly the use of his hands after he has learnt to walk. (See Scales D and E, Chapters XIV and XV.) This second capacity in which man differs from the higher animals is clearly related to the first. This is plain when consideration is given to what this emancipation of the hands from their more primitive function has meant in man's development, making possible all the varying manipulative skills of the craftsman, the artist, the engineer, the surgeon throughout history.

The third and, from the point of view of intellectual progress, the most important capacity that distinguishes man as man is, of course, the function of *speech*. (Scale C, Chapter XIII.) This is in the first place a motor skill of great delicacy and complexity, usually acquired in infancy. It is also a means of social communication and necessary for life in the community. It is a symbolic means of expression that forms the basis of intellectual life. More will be said about the acquisition of speech elsewhere. (See also M. M. Lewis, *Infant Speech* (1936).)

These three aspects of man's essentially human development do not grow up separately. Only logically, by abstraction, can they be separated. The child's mental and physical growth is a unified process, a total organic growth. These are three facets of one central process and, in studying babies, it is to these aspects of growth that we are bound to turn our attention. Moreover, consideration of special cases of handicapped and maladjusted children makes clear the need to include these aspects of development in assessing ability, for it is largely in these directions (and in general social inadequacy) that they differ from normal children. (See Chapter IV.)

Every case history that is taken by a psychologist, doctor, or social worker contains some description of the patient's early life, founded upon such questions as: "When did he first sit up?"; "How early did he walk alone?"; "When did he begin to talk clearly?"; "When did he learn to use a spoon?" For these represent significant stages in development essential to diagnosis of mental condition. But such questions need to be related to exact knowledge of when the average child achieves the various stages involved. The whole of this developmental process needs to be very exactly catalogued. Part III contains such an exact inventory worked out upon a fairly representative population of individuals.

The arresting fact is that all these three aspects of development, achieving the upright posture together with learning to walk, learning to use the first simple tools (spoon, cup, etc.) and the speaking of the first clear words, are all achieved by the average baby within the short span of the first fifteen months of his life. This is an enormous achievement, many-sided and comprehensive, which lays the foundations of all that comes afterwards. This is the significance of these early stages of life, for it is clearly here that the foundations of mental health and efficiency are laid. There is no lack of evidence of the active searching after and initiating of experience that prepares the way for each advance, in response both to internal drives and to external stimulation. Perhaps the writer's position here comes nearest to the convergence hypothesis of William Stern (1930), which stresses the dynamic view of the child as an active being, at the same time recognising that he can only act at all within the actual environment and within the limitations of inheritance.

All this development to which reference has just been made takes place in the baby with amazing *rapidity*, especially in the earliest stages. A child at three months is scarcely recognisable as the baby who so short a time ago was six weeks old! But even at six weeks he is very different from what he was at three weeks. The extent of this rapidity of development can be demonstrated in many ways. Here it is best observed in a study of test results. We shall therefore conclude and illustrate this chapter by a study of the test sheets of several average and very young babies, and by the following descriptions of their stages of development. (Figs. 1–3.)

In the first-year tests of the new scale, there are as many as *three* test-items for each *week* of age. Thus at this early age, where the development is most rapid, the test is capable of providing a very

Months of Age	A		B		C		D		E		Name: T. H.
	Locomotor		Personal—Social		Hearing and Speech		Eye and Hand		Performance		Age: $6\frac{2}{3}$ weeks
1	Lifts chin when prone.	1 ✓	Regards person—momentarily.	1 ✓	Startled by sounds.	1 —	Follows a moving light with the eyes.	1 ✓	Grasps examiner's finger.	1 ✓	*Notes and Comments*
	Pushes with feet against examiner's hands.	2 ✓	Quieted when picked up.	2 ✓	Quieted by voice.	2 ✓	Looks at ring momentarily.	2 ✓	Reacts to paper. I—Generalised physical movements.	2 ✓	
	Holds head erect for a few seconds.	3 ✓	Enjoys bath.	3 ✓	Vocalisation other than crying.	3 ✓	Looks steadily at ring held still.	3 ✓	Hand goes to mouth.	3 ✓	Very active baby.
2	Lifts head up when prone.	4 —	Smiling.	4 ✓	Listens to bell.	4 ✓	Follows moving ring horizontally.	4 ✓	Shows energetic arm movements.	4 ✓	Moves about a lot.
	Kicks vigorously.	5 —	Visually recognises mother.	5 ✓	Cooing—one syllable.	5 —	Follows ring vertically.	5 —	Reacts to paper. II—Vigorous head turning.	5 —	Sociable smiling child.
3	Active in bath—kicks.	6 ✓	Vocalises when talked to.	6 —	Searches for sound with eyes.	6 —	Glances from one object to another.	6 —	Holds doll.	6 —	Appears healthy.
	Lifts head when in *dorsal* position.	7 —	Follows moving persons with eyes.	7 —	Listens to music.	7 —	Follows moving object in a circle.	7 —	Plays with own fingers.	7 —	
	Rolls from side to back.	8 ✓	Returns examiner's glance with smiling or cooing.	8 —	Makes 2 + different sounds.	8 —	Watches object pulled along by string.	8 —	Looks at cube or toy on table.	8 —	Total score: 21 items.
4	Back firm when held in sitting position.	9 —	Friendly to strangers.	9 —	Searches for sound with head movements.	9 —	Grasps ring when given.	9 —	Resists doll withdrawal.	9 —	
	Lifts head and chest when prone.	10 —	Resists adult who tries playfully to take ring.	10 —	Laughs aloud.	10 —	Visually explores new environment.	10 —	Clasps cube put in hand and holds it.	10 —	M.A. $\frac{21}{3} = 7$ weeks.
	Totals. *A*	5	*B*	5	*C*	3	*D*	4	*E*	4	

FIG. 1.—Test sheet showing details of test of baby, aged $6\frac{2}{3}$ weeks.

Months of Age	A		B		C		D		E		Name: *M. H.*
	Locomotor		*Personal—Social*		*Hearing and Speech*		*Eye and Hand*		*Performance*		*Age:* $13\frac{3}{8}$ *weeks*
1	Lifts chin when prone.	1 ✓	Regards person—momentarily.	1 ✓	Startled by sounds.	1 ✓	Follows a moving light with the eyes.	1 ✓	Grasps examiner's finger.	1 ✓	*Notes and Comments*
	Pushes with feet against examiner's hands.	2 ✓	Quieted when picked up.	2 ✓	Quieted by voice.	2 ✓	Looks at ring momentarily.	2 ✓	Reacts to paper. I—Generalised physical movements.	2 ✓	
	Holds head erect for a few seconds.	3 ✓	Enjoys bath.	3 ✓	Vocalisation other than crying.	3 ✓	Looks steadily at ring held still.	3 ✓	Hand goes to mouth.	3 ✓	
2	Lifts head up when prone.	4 ✓	Smiling.	4 ✓	Listens to bell.	4 ✓	Follows moving ring horizontally.	4 ✓	Shows energetic arm movements.	4 ✓	
	Kicks vigorously.	5 ✓	Visually recognises mother.	5 ✓	Cooing—one syllable.	5 ✓	Follows ring vertically.	5 ✓	Reacts to paper. II—Vigorous head turning.	5 —	
3	Active in bath—kicks.	6 ✓	Vocalises when talked to.	6 —	Searches for sound with eyes.	6 ✓	Glances from one object to another.	6 —	Holds doll.	6 ✓	
	Lifts head when in *dorsal* position.	7 —	Follows moving persons with eyes.	7 ✓	Listens to music.	7 —	Follows moving object in a circle.	7 ✓	Plays with own fingers.	7 ✓	
	Rolls from side to back.	8 ✓	Returns examiner's glance with smiling or cooing.	8 ✓	Makes 2 + different sounds.	8 ✓	Watches object pulled along by string.	8 ✓	Looks at cube or toy on table.	8 ✓	Total score: 44 items.
4	Back firm when held in sitting position	9 ✓	Friendly to strangers.	9 ✓	Searches for sound with head movements.	9 —	Grasps ring when given.	9 ✓	Resists doll withdrawal.	9 ✓	M.A. $14\frac{3}{8}$ weeks.
	Lifts head and chest when prone.	10 ✓	Resists adult who tries playfully to take ring or toy.	10 ✓	Laughs aloud.	10 ✓	Visually explores new environment.	10 —	Clasps cube put in hand and holds it.	10 ✓	
	Holds head erect continuously.	11 ✓	Frolics when played with.	11 —	Turns head deliberately to bell.	11 —	Reaches for ring and grasps.	11 —	Drops first cube for second.	11 —	
5	Lifts head and shoulders, *dorsal*.	12 —	Stops crying when talked to.	12 —	Listens to tuning fork.	12 —	Carries ring to mouth.	12 —	Reacts to paper. III—Pulls it away.	12 —	
	Rolls from side to side.	13 —	Turns head to person talking or singing.	13 —	Coos or stops crying on hearing music.	13 —	Clutches at dangling ring.	13 —	Shows interest in box.	13 —	
6	Plays with own toes.	14 —	Anticipatory movements when about to be lifted.	14 —	Talks (babbles) to persons.	14 —	Secures dangling ring.	14 —	Takes cube from table.	14 —	
	Totals. *A*	10	*B*	9	*C*	8	*D*	8	*E*	9	

FIG. 2.—Test sheet showing details of test of baby, aged $13\frac{3}{8}$ weeks.

Months of Age	A		B		C		D		E		Name: L. G.
	Locomotor		*Personal—Social*		*Hearing and Speech*		*Eye and Hand*		*Performance*		*Age: $25\frac{2}{3}$ weeks*
1	Lifts chin when prone.	1	Regards person—momentarily.	1	Startled by sounds.	1	Follows a moving light with the eyes.	1	Grasps examiner's finger.	1	*Notes and Comments*
	Pushes with feet against examiner's hands.	2	Quieted when picked up.	2	Quieted by voice.	2	Looks at ring momentarily.	2	Reacts to paper. I—Generalised physical movements.	2	
	Holds head erect for a few seconds.	3	Enjoys bath.	3	Vocalisation other than crying.	3	Looks steadily at ring held still.	3	Hand goes to mouth.	3	
2	Lifts head up when prone.	4	Smiling.	4	Listens to bell.	4	Follows moving ring horizontally.	4	Shows energetic arm movements.	4	
	Kicks vigorously.	5	Visually recognises mother.	5	Cooing—one syllable.	5	Follows ring vertically.	5	Reacts to paper. II—Vigorous head turning.	5	
3	Active in bath—kicks.	6	Vocalises when talked to.	6	Searches for sound with eyes.	6	Glances from one object to another.	6	Holds doll.	6	
	Lifts head when in *dorsal* position.	7	Follows moving persons with eyes.	7	Listens to music.	7	Follows moving object in a circle.	7	Plays with own fingers.	7	
	Rolls from side to back.	8	Returns examiner's glance with smiling or cooing.	8	Makes 2 + different sounds.	8	Watches object pulled along by string.	8	Looks at cube or toy on table.	8	
4	Back firm when held in sitting position.	9 ✓	Friendly to strangers.	9 ✓	Searches for sound with head movements.	9 ✓	Grasps ring when given.	9 ✓	Resists doll withdrawal.	9 ✓	
	Lifts head and chest when prone.	10 ✓	Resists adult who tries playfully to take ring or toy.	10 ✓	Laughs aloud.	10 ✓	Visually explores new environment.	10 ✓	Clasps cube put in hand and holds it.	10 ✓	
	Holds head erect continuously.	11 ✓	Frolics when played with.	11 ✓	Turns head deliberately to bell.	11 ✓	Reaches for ring and grasps.	11 ✓	Drops first cube for second.	11 ✓	
5	Lifts head and shoulders, *dorsal.*	12 ✓	Stops crying when talked to.	12 ✓	Listens to tuning fork.	12 ✓	Carries ring to mouth.	12 ✓	Reacts to paper. III—Pulls it away.	12 ✓	

	Rolls from side to side.	13 ✓	Turns head to person talking or singing.	13 —	Coos or stops crying on hearing music.	13 ✓	Clutches at dangling ring.	13 ✓	Shows interest in box.	13 ✓	
6	Plays with own toes.	14 ✓	Anticipatory movements when about to be lifted.	14 ✓	Talks (babbles) to persons.	14 ✓	Secures dangling ring.	14 ✓	Takes cube from table.	14 ✓	
	Crawling Reaction (I) Draws up knees, etc.	15 ✓	Holds a spoon.	15 —	Manipulates bell.	15 —	Hands explore table surface.	15 —	Holds two cubes.	15 ✓	
	Sits with slight support.	16 ✓	Stretches to be taken.	16 —	Makes 4 + different sounds.	16 ✓	Plays with ring—waving or banging, etc.	16 ✓	Grasps box.	16 —	Total score 77 items.
7	Can roll from back to stomach, etc.	17 ✓	Drinks from a cup.	17 —	Responds when called.	17 —	Reaches for and picks up string—any method.	17 —	Manipulates cube	17 ✓	*M.A.* $25\frac{3}{8}$ *weeks.*
	Stepping reaction (*a*): Dancing movements.	18 —	Manipulates cup or spoon in play.	18 —	Two-syllable babble.	18 —	Looks for fallen object.	18 —	Reacts to paper. IV—Reaches for and takes.	18 ✓	
8	*Crawling (II)* Tries vigorously to crawl.	19 —	Reacts to mirror image: I—Looks at.	19 —	Shouts for attention.	19 —	Strikes one object with another.	19 —	Passes toy from hand to hand.	19 —	
	Sits alone for a short time.	20 —	Knows strangers from familiar friends.	20 —	Listens to conversations.	20 —	Watches examiner scribble.	20 —	Drops one cube for third.	20 —	
	Stepping reaction (*b*): One foot in front of the other.	21 —	Prompt reaction to situations, e.g. at table.	21 —	Singing tones.	21 —	Secures ring by means of string.	21 —	Manipulates two objects at once.	21 —	
	Crawling (III) Can turn around when left on floor.	22 —	Displeased if toy is taken away.	22 —	Babbled phrases: 4 + syllables.	22 —	Forefinger and thumb partly specialised.	22 —	Reacts to paper. V—Plays with, crumples, etc.	22 —	
	Totals *A*	17	*B*	13	*C*	15	*D*	15	*E*	17	

FIG. 3.—Test sheet showing details of test of baby, aged $25\frac{3}{8}$ weeks.

fine discrimination between one performance and another. (In the second year there are two items for each week of age.) At each successive stage of development, the former stage has been completely or almost completely superseded, there being practically no overlapping of test items needing to be taken in successive examinations. Thus in a few weeks with the youngest babies, and in a few months with the older babies, the entire picture changes. A glance at the percentage table and graph given in Chapter V, and also the graphs shown on the page opposite (see Fig. 4), will show the rapid rise in the numbers of children passing each item from month to month. In the second year, where this progress is not quite so rapid, the rise in percentages is better seen when the results are arranged in two-monthly groupings. (See percentage table and graph in Chapter V.)

Six Weeks Old.—At six weeks an average baby can lie and kick, though not very vigorously yet. He can hold his head erect for a few seconds, and can lift his chin well up when lying in the prone position. He has just learnt to smile and to recognise his mother visually (see Plate 2). He vocalises a little when talked to, and produces murmured sounds, vague and inarticulate. He listens to a bell that is rung very gently near him, and vocalises happily when resting. He follows moving objects horizontally, but not yet in other directions. He looks steadily at bright objects. He holds objects for a short time, grasps the examiner's finger (see Plate 3), reacts to paper and shows much physical and exploratory activity. He weighs about nine pounds (see Fig. 1).

Thirteen Weeks Old.—At thirteen weeks old an average baby is much bigger and sturdier than he was at six weeks. His body is firm, his lower limbs have developed with the constant exercise of kicking. He is "alive" in his environment and thoroughly enjoying life. An average baby can now lift his head and chest well up when in the prone position and tries to push himself up on his hands. His back is firm when held in the sitting position and his head well balanced. He looks at people, chuckles and laughs aloud as well as smiles. He can now follow moving objects in all directions, and passes a test involving visually following a ring swung full round in a circle (see Plate 4). He likes interesting sounds, looks in all directions (eye and head movements) in search of the bell, although he does not yet turn his head deliberately towards it. When he has no toy to manipulate, he likes to bring his hands together and play with his fingers. He likes to be held up near the table, and watches

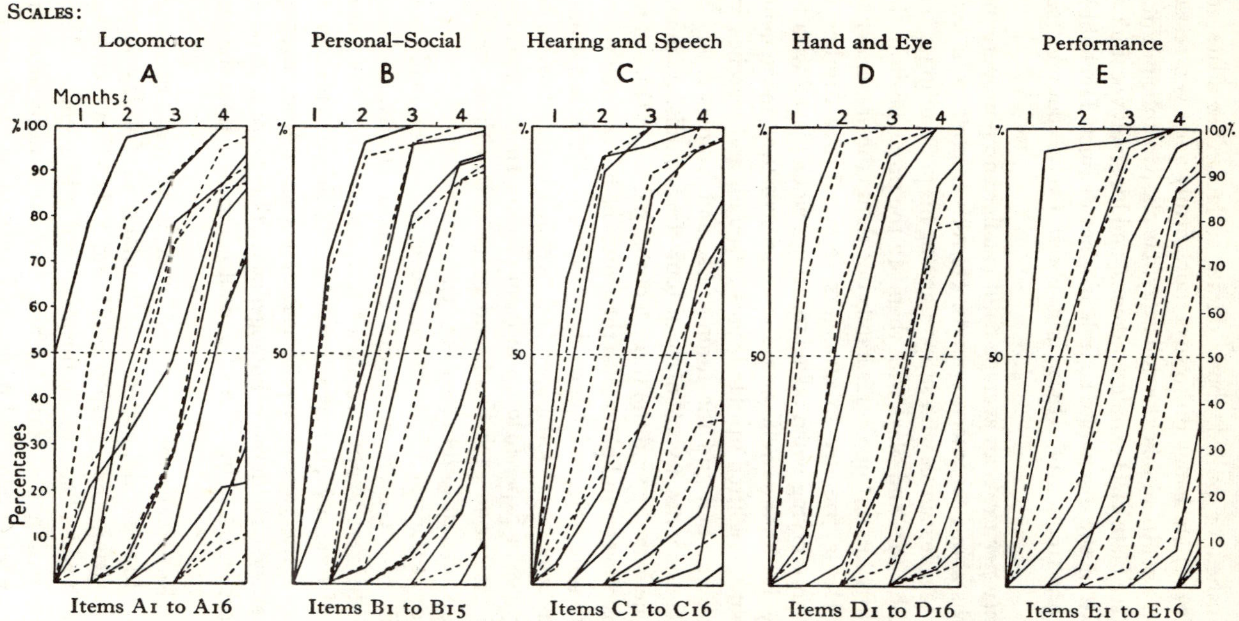

FIG. 4.—Showing rapidity of development in the early months of life in all five sub-scales. Raw percentages of babies passing items in each month of age during first four months.

objects pushed or pulled about on its surface. (See Plate 20, Chapter XIV.) He hangs on to toys more firmly and even resists when we try gently to take the doll away. He clasps a cube put into his hand (see Plate 5). He smiles and coos, and his small vocabulary of now two or three separate sounds is more distinct. His babble occurs more frequently. He weighs about twelve pounds (see Fig. 2).

By *twenty-five weeks* an average child is taller and plumper, and now weighs about seventeen pounds. He rolls himself right over from side to side, can sit with support among his pram pillows, and has found his toes and plays with them. In the prone position, he not only lifts himself up on his hands but shows the first crawling reaction. He is friendly to strangers (especially if Mother is present), stops crying when talked to, frolics when played with by somebody he knows well, and shows anticipatory movements when about to be lifted up. He listens to sounds and searches for them, likes the bell and the tuning-fork, and babbles freely to persons. He now has a vocabulary of four clear sounds. At manipulation, he is far beyond the three months' baby. He reaches for and grasps objects, and plays with them after he has secured them. He likes to send objects deliberately to the floor. He now not only takes away a piece of soft paper laid over his face but will also accept a piece of paper held up in front of him. He can hold two small objects one in each hand, and drops one of these when a third one is offered to him (see Fig. 3).

A glance at the test sheets given above (Figs. 1–3) will show the details of these characteristics even more clearly, and will illustrate the very slight overlap of test items taken after these intervals of time, which makes frequent retesting of children of these ages quite satisfactory. These test results from average children show considerable homogeneity. The more accurately the tests are arranged in order of difficulty, the more does this fact appear.

Nonetheless there are, in general, wide individual differences between child and child, not only in the total level of ability shown but also in detail. (See Chapters VII and VIII.) Some children show a much wider "scatter" in the total results than others. Moreover, even within the normal range very great differences are found in the levels achieved in different *types* of test, and the new classification of the test items, as well as the equality of difficulty of the sub-scales, serve to demonstrate these differences of type

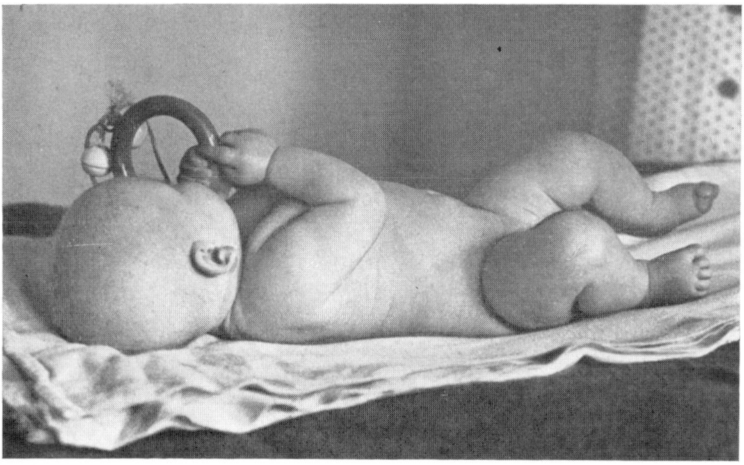

PLATE 6

This three months' little girl has accepted the bell-ring which was given to her, and is happily investigating this with both hands and also with her lips. She is not yet ready to reach out for an object, but can grasp and manipulate one that is given to her (D 9 and D 12).

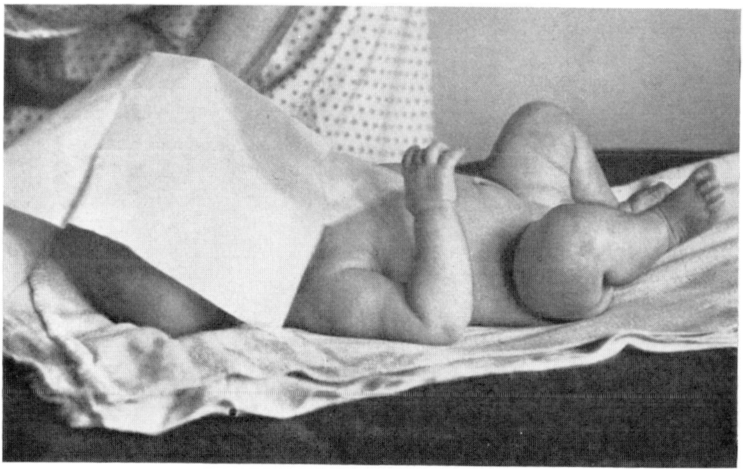

PLATE 7

(Same child as above.) Her face has now been gently covered with a soft handkerchief tissue. Her whole body is in motion in an attempt to dislodge it, both arms and legs going and head turning. Note the right hand approaching the paper which, however, she cannot quite pull away.

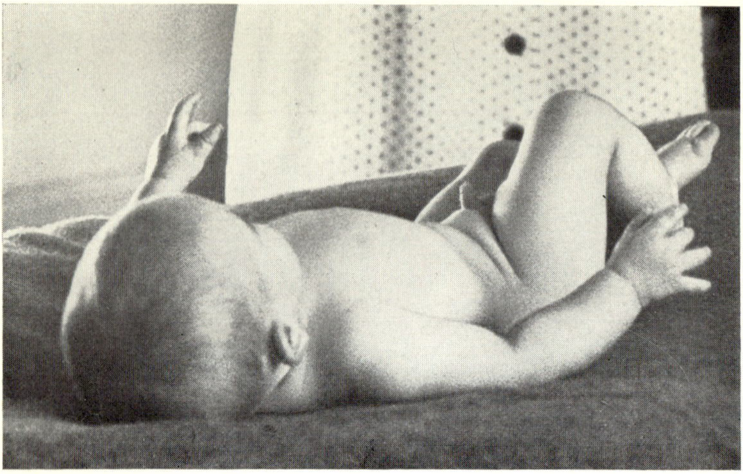

PLATE 8

Six months old. As soon as he was put down in the dorsal position, this boy began to kick and wave vigorously. He kicked with long, alternating, rhythmical "strides". There was style about this child's movements which were lovely to watch. Note the hands, with every finger expressive, both hands in similar position, the index finger almost pointing.

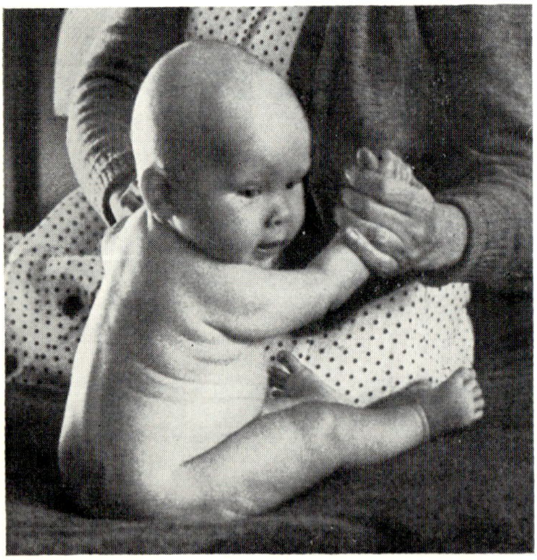

PLATE 9

This little girl is the same age as the boy above (Plate 8). She cannot quite sit alone, but is almost ready to do so. She has just pulled herself with slight help to the sitting position. Note the firm, straight back. Her balance is such that she can even give her attention elsewhere, and at the same time turn her head to look towards another person talking behind her.

between children. Naturally such differences are found in a more exaggerated way in special case studies. Yet some babies, and not only average ones, show a very even result across the five scales; others are more forward or more backward in one or more of the measured directions. (See Chapter VII.) The test has been deliberately designed to throw into relief these differences.

Thus, one child may be far ahead of others on the locomotor side, perhaps walking at eleven or twelve months, when the average age for walking alone is towards the end of the fourteenth month. But he may not yet be babbling much, or may not yet be interested in materials or toys at the level usual for his age. This need cause no concern; presently, when this child's walking is established, he will turn his attention in other directions, assuming of course that opportunity and normal stimulation are provided. His apparently one-sided progress is due to the variety of the demands for development made by his environment, and to the limited mental energy (span of attention) available to cope with them. These facts will be further illustrated in the profile studies of children.

In general, we can say that not only does the young child develop at a surprising rate, each stage rapidly superseding the last, but individual differences on the total result (as will also be seen when we come to the statistical sections) are at least as great as with older subjects.

In Figs. 1–3 we have shown the early test-items of the five sub-scales. The entire inventory of tests will be found in Appendix II.

CHAPTER III

A STUDY OF OTHER TESTS AND A NEW CLASSIFICATION

Other Tests

WE shall now consider the problem of the classification of test items in relation to other tests.

Gesell (1925) classified the items of his scale into four groups, namely: Tests of Motor Development, Language Development, Adaptive Behaviour and Personal–Social Development. A number of the items that he used in his original schedules are also included in a modified form in this new scale, as will be recognised, but with a different classification. Motor Development in Gesell's original schedules includes items of the locomotor sequence as well as some items testing manipulative skills. These together are apparently taken as representing a total "motor sequence".

Under the heading of Adaptive Behaviour we find in Gesell's scale a variety of tests of different types, some of them manipulative and others that would appear to be more like personal–social items. So varied is this group that it is not easy to discover what is intended by "adaptive" behaviour. Manipulative tests also occur in the personal–social scale, but here it is a matter of interpretation as to which of the two factors is the more important or relevant.

Shirley (1933) also groups manipulative items with locomotor items under the general heading "motor reactions". These she studies interestingly as a total sequence, finding evidence for the anatomical "law" of "developmental direction", namely the idea that development proceeds from the head of the organism towards the extremities; that is, cephalocaudal-proximodistally. This is a controversial question and the evidence is conflicting. McGraw (1933) gives some of the evidence to the contrary.

Charlotte Bühler (1935) presents an entirely different classification from other schedules. Her classification includes six groups of tests: Sensory Perception, Body Control, Social Responses, Learning, Manipulation of Materials and Intellectual Activity.

The last group, Intellectual Activity, under which any speech items are included, does not begin in Bühler's Scale until about the ninth month.

In the last chapter we discussed the differences that exist between the development of human babies and the higher animals, and found these differences significant for mental growth. Certain workers, interested in comparative psychology, discover many points of similarity between the development of the higher apes and that of man, and sometimes introduce into test scales for infants items that were previously used in studying apes.

In the writer's opinion such tests should have no place in a scale that tries to give a true picture of infancy and measure intelligence in human babies. If such a comparison could yield anything of value in connection with test construction, it would be because of the differences rather than the similarities that exist between human and animal behaviour. Charlotte Bühler introduced a few such tests into her scale. Karl Bühler, in his *Mental Development of the Child* (1930), refers to the belief that there is a phase of infant development near the end of the first year so similar to a stage of development in chimpanzees that it can be designated as "A Chimpanzee Age"!

To go to the evolutionary past in search of suitable items for measuring *intelligence* in human beings would seem to be a strange and cumbersome procedure. It is not so much that it sets the standard low, as that it deflects attention from what is essentially human. Rather should the observer be alert for those signs and indications of intelligence, even in babies, that have relevance for the *future* of man. Consider, for example, the delicacy and beauty of the process whereby the child during the first year of life learns by touching, grasping, manipulating to explore his material world; and note also how the useless thumb comes gradually into relationship with the other digits before the end of the first twelve months, the fine turning of the wrist in certain skills and the pointing of the index finger. There are also those later skills: the capacity to fold a piece of paper neatly, to build a high tower of bricks, to turn a screw, to throw and catch a ball, and many other varied skills of the child and later of the man throughout his life. Some of these the ape also learns, but quite early the child outstrips the animal.

It is significant, perhaps, to remember that those psychologists who would see in a child so much that is characteristic of a chimpanzee, such as his powers of imitation, interest in climbing and so on, are of the same school as those who tend to deny or ignore the earliest phases of speech development and who do not appear to find in early vocalisation and babble any introduction to or preparation for true speech, or any meaning in it for the child! We shall return to this important point. It surely is the *destiny* of the child, so different from that of the ape, that must give direction in this matter. Just as the human hand is framed for finer things, so is the human voice in infancy prepared for adult speech, both being instruments of thought emanating from a human brain. These abilities are largely developed through imitation, which, far from being the mere mimicry of the animal, is the main instrument of learning in the earliest stages in both the practical and verbal fields.

Because a baby does not use adult language in its first year, some workers leave practically all reference to items of speech until the second year. This makes the tests, from the writer's point of view, one-sided, in so far as one whole aspect of the child's mental development is omitted in the earlier period. The first year lays the foundations of mental development in *all* its aspects. Here are quite definitely to be found the beginnings of speech expression: objective imitation and subjective monologue, active listening to sounds and conversations, followed by vocalisation, repetition of single sounds and the development of babbled speech. There is, in fact, as much here to be observed and measured in the verbal as in any other field, and as speech is of such great importance for the intellectual aspects of development, it should be weighted in any valid scale at least as heavily as other abilities.

Let us look for a moment at speech items as included in other scales. In a valuable review by Dorothea McCarthy included in Carmichael's *Manual of Child Psychology* (1946), the speech items in eight scales are given. The reports are described as "major studies". The interesting point is that, although all these workers include speech items, they vary to a large extent in the number of such items they include, and therefore in the importance they attach to the acquisition of speech and our ability to measure it, during this period of life. To quote McCarthy (p. 481, Carmichael): "Many writers leave periods of several months, during which they evidently were more interested in motor, sensory, social, or emotional aspects of the children's development, and for which no language items appear in their scales." The number of items ranges from only five (Bühler and Hetzer, 1935) to twenty-four

(Bayley, 1933) and twenty-eight (Gesell and Thompson, 1934) for the total period of the first two years of life; most of these items belong exclusively to the second year. To quote further (p. 487, Carmichael): "Bayley does not have any language items from the twelfth to the seventeenth month, Shirley has none between the ninth and fourteenth months, and C. Bühler has none from the sixth to the ninth month or from the eleventh to the fifteenth month." It is difficult to understand how such an important matter as speech could be treated with such varying emphasis in these scales.

Summarised from Dorothea McCarthy, in Carmichael (1946) (pp. 476 et seq. See Table on pp. 482–5)

"*Number of verbal items listed in the first two years.*"

Bayley	1933	24
Shirley	1933	14
Bühler	1930	10
Bühler and Hetzer	1935	5
Gesell, Thompson and Amatruda	1938	17
Gesell and Thompson	1934	28
Gesell	1925	15
Cattell	1940	14

Bühler (1930, 1935) omits all reference to speech development in the early months. The first speech item in her scale occurs at nine months. There is no separate group of speech items in her classification; they are included under the heading "intellectual development". Although many of her subjects were babies in institutions, it is hard to believe that so little speech development was taking place during the first year as this scale would indicate.

Other workers have still other classifications. Emphasis varies from worker to worker. There is no generally accepted criterion as to what is to be included or to what extent. A new approach appears to be needed.

In the new scale described herein, the same emphasis is placed on speech as on other aspects of development. Speech development is exceedingly rapid in the first year of life. The Speech Scale contains fifty-two items altogether for the two years, and a few additional speech items occur in the personal-social scale.

If it is legitimate to include the first slight lifting of the chin from the pillow (locomotor scale) in the first month of life, then there is no reason why the baby's first murmured sounds occurring at the same period should not be included in the inventory. Thirty-one of the fifty-two items in Scale C belong to the first year. Only thus, in considerable detail, is it possible to study as it deserves this important function of speech development and grade the fine differences that exist between child and child in this aspect of development as in every other.

There is a point in work of this kind when, having studied the work of others, the investigator must leave all aside and go back to the human material itself and learn more about infant development from the infants themselves.

(*a*) Trends that appear Significant for Mental Growth, and (*b*) the Basic Avenues of Learning

Let us now turn our attention briefly to a consideration of certain significant trends of development and the basic avenues of learning, their inter-relationships and their origins. These will be shown diagrammatically (see Fig. 5). There is nothing new in what follows, but this particular way of relating together what appear to be the basic facts of experience may serve to illustrate the foundation on which the new scale is built.

It would seem that the earliest beginnings of mental development rest back primarily upon the physiological functions and the child's developing awareness of his physiological needs. The physiological functions are rhythmical, occurring regularly in time; for example, ingestion and digestion, waking and sleeping. From the moment of birth, with the onset of breathing and the beginning of a separate existence, the child must begin to adjust to the physical environment. Even before birth the child must have experienced at some level, probably mainly physiological, the various rhythms of life, for these are already laid down in his nervous system.

In earliest infancy the baby begins to adjust to the rhythms of experience, to come to expect certain happenings at certain times and in certain places. This ability to adjust is fundamental to habit formation, and with the child's growing awareness of his social environment he learns to react in a twofold way, now positively and now negatively, the whole complex of activities and retreats from activity being in a sense an outgrowth of the child's natural

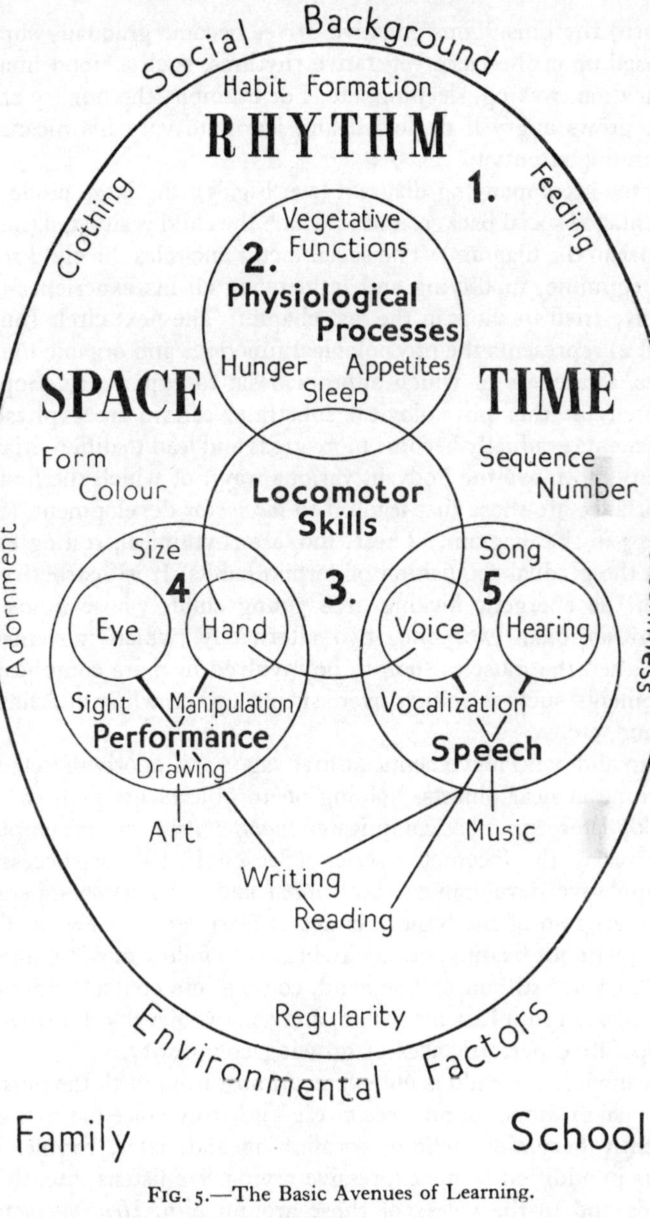

FIG. 5.—The Basic Avenues of Learning.

(inborn) rhythms. Thus conative drives become gradually superimposed upon the basic vegetative rhythms, such as food intake, elimination, waking, sleeping, etc. For example, the hungry child cries, grows angry if neglected and learns to vary his means of demanding attention.

In the accompanying diagram (see Fig. 5), the large circle represents the social background in which the child is situated (numbered 1 in the diagram). The social factor encircles the child from the beginning, modifying and influencing all his experiences, as we have tried to show in the last chapter. The next circle (numbered 2) represents the physiological functions and organic movements, awareness of which appears basic to experience. Superimposed on this physiological substrate, certain weak physical movements gradually become more gross and lead to differentiated attempts to move the body in various ways, of which the first in importance are those that lead on to *locomotor* development. (See circle 3 in the diagram.) These, too, are rhythmical, resting back upon the gradual acquisition of certain habits. It is instructive to watch the energetic kicking of a young child, whose limbs go vigorously one, two, one, two alternately, which movements strengthen the muscles soon to be involved in more complicated movements such as rolling over, sitting up, crawling and finally walking, etc.

Arm and hand movements, at first vague and poorly directed—clutching at near objects, holding on to objects grasped—which develop later into more complicated *manipulative* acts, accompany and overlay the locomotor series. (See circle 4.) For successful manipulative development, both *hand* and *eye* must co-operate. These are two of the basic avenues of learning. The eye, at first roving without fixating, gradually begins to follow moving objects and "look at" still ones. The hand, coming into contact with near objects, soon supplements vision, and the two develop together in manipulative performances of growing complexity.

Meanwhile the child is not silent. Almost from birth the normal baby makes vague sounds (see circle 5), hardly voiced at first but presently becoming definite vocalisation and, later, babble. All this is in addition to his expressive crying. He listens intently to sounds and to the voices of those around him. *Hearing* (active listening) and *voice* together result in vocalisation and babble, and the development of this is finally speech. Hearing and voice are two further basic avenues of learning.

All this development takes place in *Time* and in *Space*. The eye and hand co-operate in exploring the spatial surroundings, although even the blind child builds up his own conception of space and spatial relations out of his sense of touch and his concentration on manual exploration of environment. Hearing, then listening to a sequence of sounds, such as is involved in learning gradually to understand language, takes place in time rather than in space, and builds up in the child the expectation of meaningful sequences. A baby understands a great deal of the spoken language that flows around him long before his inexperienced vocal organs can frame a response.

These two broad sets of activities representing different types of experience—Performance (circle 4) and Speech (circle 5)—are the two main aspects of intellectual development, and together form the basis ultimately of formal education both practical and verbal. A more advanced stage in this developmental process is reached when the older child learns to read and write, for then all four main avenues of learning, *eye* and *hand* together with *voice* and *hearing*, all co-operate in the acquisition of this complex ability of understanding and reproducing written language. The new test therefore includes: assessment of locomotor development, personal-social adjustment, hearing and speech, hand and eye co-ordination, and performance.

Thus, very briefly, may be indicated the main aspects of individual development. Careful consideration of this diagram may show its further implications, which are too far-reaching to be further dealt with here; but this way of relating together the successive integrations of the growing child provides the basis for the new classification of test items that has resulted finally in the building of the Five-scale Test. But all these abilities form, as they develop, a complex and unified whole. The whole baby acts in everything he does, directing his attention, in rapid exploring and learning in relation to environment.

The Concept of Balance.—As has been implied throughout this discussion, a new conception of "balance" emerges from this way of regarding test construction. This provides the key to the vexed question of the classification of items in testing infants. At first a wide net must be cast to include a large number of different specific abilities, so that "*g*" or general intelligence can be measured in as many as possible of its manifestations. It has been the object of this work to develop a measuring instrument that shall be at once reasonably exact, well-balanced and comprehensive, so that those activities that later go to make an efficient person, or as many as possible of those skills that are measured in assessing intelligence in older subjects, shall be represented, as it were in embryo, in a valid test of the mentality of a baby.

This is, of course, but part of a wider question that concerns the testing of children of all ages. Psychologists know how valuable the Binet-Simon type of test has been. The Terman-Merrill Revision is in many respects more useful, whilst retaining the general character of the earlier scale. The main criticism that has frequently been launched against the Binet Scale is that it is too verbal, the critics realising the importance of that other side of the problem, the need for including tests that measure practical skills. It has therefore been customary to supplement the Binet Scale with performance tests whenever possible. Yet the ability to comprehend and use language normally, enabling man to reason verbally, is one of the main characteristics of human mentality; the other begins with manipulative skills and develops into the capacity to reason concretely, as the result of concrete experience.

Even that useful and comprehensive instrument, the Binet-Simon Scale, would, it seems, be still more useful if it were more evenly balanced in regard to these two main aspects of man's complex abilities.

In the administering of psychological tests to older children, psychologists are frequently desirous of suggesting in a report something of the type of ability a child possesses as well as giving his general ability level. It may be important, for example, to be able to give some indication as to whether the child is likely to succeed better at verbal than at practical tasks. Such indications may be of very great practical importance and have wide educational (and vocational) implications, solving, for example, the question of the type of secondary education that would suit a particular child or children. It is quite possible to get some help on this question from the Binet-Simon test alone, in spite of the above criticism, for fortunately it has always included a certain number of practical tests and practical reasoning items.

In testing babies, the psychologist needs to be in the position to be able to say: "This child is better at manipulative skills than he is verbally"; or "This baby is more backward at walking than he is at performance"; or again: "Speech level is far below (or above) the rest of his developmental level." For, although in general the total result is the most valuable single piece of evidence concerning the child's ability level that can be arrived at, a complete diagnosis of mental status, whether of normal babies or of special cases seen in clinics, will depend on such additional information. (See Chapters VII and VIII.) If such further pertinent information is to be extracted from the test results, not only must the scale be well balanced, but the classification of the items into five groups or sub-scales, that may be scored separately, must rest back on some degree of statistical exactness and equality between the five separate scales. On such a basis the five-scale test has come into being. Each of the sub-scales, as will be seen in the statistical sections, is very closely equal in difficulty, *at each month of age*, to each of the others. (See Chapter V.)

The five scales are:

A. *The Locomotor Scale.*—This has been evolved in some detail, first using items suggested by others (for example, by Gesell), and then supplementing these by further observations of children and by extensive testing.

B. *The Personal-Social Scale.*—As we have tried to show earlier, the whole progress of the child takes place within the social setting and is conditioned by that circumstance, so that there is a sense in which *all* items may be regarded as personal-social items. More narrowly considered there are, however, certain matters related to the child's personal-social learning, to his grasp of the *mores*, customs or folk-ways of his particular social group, that can give definite measurable evidence of his progress in social adaptation.

C. *Hearing and Speech.*—Hearing, in the sense of active listening, is studied here, together with the child's progress in acquiring first a vocabulary of sounds, vocalisation and babble or pre-speech, that are finally superseded by adult language.

D. *Hand and Eye Development.*—This is a graded scale for assessing the child's level at manipulation, and it includes a study of the development of the hand itself as well as certain manipulative activities.

E. *Performance.*—A scale of graded performance tests, drawing on the developing ability to reason in practical situations or manipulate materials intelligently, completes the test.

These separate scales can, if desired, be scored separately and separate quotients allotted. This would be advisable especially for detailed diagnosis of handicapped children or child guidance cases over two years of age. For normal babies under two years of age a study of the scores on the several scales, because of the degree of equality of difficulty existing between these scales, gives all the information normally required, in addition to the General Quotient (G.Q.). (See Appendix I.)

Each scale contains fifty-two finely graded items, arranged in order of difficulty (on the basis of the percentage of babies passing them month by month) in so far as the present data allows. There is thus a total of 260 items for the two years, three items for each week of life in the first year and two items for each week in the second year. But in spite of this unusually large number of items, because of the fine grading and because account has been taken of the child's inability to concentrate on lengthy tasks, the entire scale takes an average of only twenty to thirty minutes to administer. The youngest babies take even less time than this, and those who are approaching two years of age take a little longer.

The usefulness of such a method will be illustrated in the next chapter.

CHAPTER IV

CLINICAL IMPLICATIONS OF THE NEW SCALE

The Needs of Handicapped and Maladjusted Children in the Test Situation

ALTHOUGH little reference was made in the last chapter to the diagnostic needs of handicapped children, these have been an important consideration throughout this study. A clinical test should enable the examiner to distinguish readily and certainly between different groups of children, the normal and the handicapped, the deaf and the defective, the emotionally disturbed and inhibited and the permanently mentally disabled.

The clinical approach is based on the fundamental attitude that asks: "How can we explore in more detail the actual abilities of this particular handicapped child?"; "How can we give enough weight to those directions in which his effort is unimpaired, and be in a position to assess the effect of specific disabilities on the total test result?" It answers the difficult questions of what to include in a scale and how to classify the total items. The need for a detailed differential diagnosis of mental status in handicapped children makes consideration of the problem of balance, and the resulting question of equality of difficulty in the sub-scales, an essential feature of the clinical test. The scale must provide for the assessment of intelligence in children suffering from the following groups of handicaps, and yet be a useful test for measuring general ability in normal infants and also for studying individual differences within the normal range.

1. *Locomotor Handicaps.*—A child who fails to learn to walk at the usual age is not necessarily on this account to be regarded as a backward child, in spite of the fact that retardation in this direction is frequently associated with intellectual retardation. If it is possible to measure the several aspects of development separately, including the level of locomotor development, in a handicapped child, it will be seen at once whether the condition of retardation is specific or more general, and to what extent, if at all, manipula-

tion and speech are also involved. There are considerable individual differences among such children, and slowness at learning to walk may be quite specific and have little relevance to the main intellectual problem. A great deal will depend upon the cause of the condition. A detailed history is needed, beginning with the birth history.

Unfortunately, with birth-injured children, or with children who have suffered brain damage through subsequent accident or severe illness, poor locomotor development is frequently associated with some awkwardness at manipulation, or slow speech development, or both; and because of their handicaps, and possibly also as a result of parental attitudes, they are liable to show some degree of personal-social inadequacy. These are among the most difficult cases to assess. A profile can be drawn, in such cases, that will show the results on the various scales in relation to one another, and will give a basis for considering in what direction advice to the parents, or help to the patient (such as treatment, special educational measures, placement and so on), can best be given. For a recent report on the Educability of Cerebral Palsied Children, see Dunsdon (1952).

2. *Personal-Social Failure.*—Maladjusted children show great divergence in their ability levels on different types of test. They tend to present a wide "scatter" in the test results. Such divergences can be measured more accurately if dealt with in separate scales. Maladjusted children almost always drop in score on the Personal-Social scale and tend also to "scatter" within this scale, owing to specific items of failure that are out of relationship with their general ability level. Failure on the Personal-Social scale almost always indicates some degree of emotional maladjustment. It suggests that the child is not learning, at the expected rate for his general ability level, those items of behaviour that depend on his relations with his milieu. For example, perhaps he does not feed himself yet although he is quite good at manipulation of objects in the "D" and "E" scales; or he is found to be still "on the bottle" when he can take solid food. His total score on the Personal-Social scale is out of line with the rest of his ability level. Such conditions are frequently part of a general picture of maladjustment, which may be the subject of complaint in a case brought to the Child Guidance Clinic. Sometimes other scales are involved, the child being difficult in at least one other direction, even where there is evidence enough that he is not as backward as the results on Scale

"B" alone would suggest. Sometimes there is also difficulty with speech; shy children may be very slow at expressing themselves in speech although they may show evidence of understanding a great deal of what is said in their presence. Serious speech retardation may itself indicate deep-seated maladjustment, for the reason that it demonstrates a failure of one of the main functions of speech, i.e. for social intercourse and social expression, and such failure may therefore indicate a dislocation of normal social relationships. Maladjustment of this kind may have a varied causation. A full investigation of the child's relationships with his environment and with the various members of the family is indicated, such as is undertaken in a Child Guidance Clinic or by a child analyst. The condition may result from an over-protective attitude on the part of the parents or an unwise indulgence from an over-fond nurse or relative. On the other hand, unhappiness or deprivation, as we have seen (Chapter II), or factors such as neglect, lack of opportunity to learn through lack of toys or materials, or a too restricted environment, may lead to maladjustment. If the problem is of this type, the fact will show up in the detailed test results, for such children fail in specific directions and present characteristic profiles.

The shape of a child's profile may change when he is retested after having had treatment in a clinic or other therapeutic measures have been successfully undertaken to relieve the condition. (See Case 35, Chapter VIII.)

3. *Speech Cases.*—Where a child is backward at learning to speak or has a speech disorder, he is in danger, if the condition is not corrected, of being regarded as generally backward or even as defective. This tendency to regard backwardness at speech development as indicating a serious condition of retardation may even be applied when the child shows evidence of normal progress in other directions. For this group of handicapped children the new method of assessment will be a boon, for, if it can be demonstrated in certain of these cases that the defect is specific and not general, the diagnosis of defect, with all its serious consequences for a young child, can be avoided or at least postponed. The disability can then be regarded as something to be treated rather than as a symptom of something incurable. Of course, where the speech retardation is consistent with the child's general level on the rest of the examination, he can only be regarded as generally retarded; but, as we have tried to show elsewhere, every attempt should still

be made, especially with these young subjects, to treat the condition or plan some procedure that will be of help to the parents of a backward child, according to the individual needs of the case. It is impossible to generalise, for every case is different and, as will be realised, must be studied in some detail.

Speech cases are more varied than are any of the other groups. Backward children all tend to present speech problems; maladjusted children are frequently slow of speech; then there are those children who are deaf or who suffer from some degree of hearing loss. These last present a very characteristic profile, for they are frequently quite good at manipulation, and learning to walk is normal. Thus they have normal scores for their ages on Scales A, D and E, fail badly on Scale C (Speech), and also tend to do less well than might be expected on Scale B. This is probably because, not hearing clearly the mother's voice gently urging him in his training, to hold the cup, to come when called, to give up a toy and so on, the deaf baby tends to be slower in personal-social development than are hearing children. A deaf baby is also frequently lacking in normal confidence, less sure of going even about the room or house alone, and he tends to cling to the mother. This is natural when we consider that such a child does not hear what is going on around him as other children do. (Ewing and Ewing, 1938, 1944.) Nevertheless, even a child badly handicapped in this way can be readily distinguished from a defective child by his detailed results on the five-scale test; in spite of variations of intelligence and individual differences between deaf children, they still show a profile of characteristic shape. (See Case 33, Chapter VIII.) (See also Eichholz, 1932.)

Hearing, in one of these special cases, may be found to be quite normal, but yet the psychologist finds that the child cannot pass the verbal tests and may show some of these same characteristics of speech to which we have referred. There may even sometimes be complete aphasia. Causes are complex and differ from case to case. The staffs of speech clinics in hospitals know these children particularly well. Some of them are emotionally disturbed children, their lack of speech being bound up with unconscious motives or fears. Some may be only slightly maladjusted, and a course of psychotherapy or speech therapy or remedial tuition may be indicated. Some of these are highly intelligent children, others are severely retarded. A few are so severely disturbed emotionally that they are scarcely accessible to treatment. The new scale is designed to throw light on the mental status in such cases, and thus eliminate the doubt as to their mental level that surrounds them.

4. *Manipulative Handicaps.*—Gross manipulative failure is seldom specific, and is more likely to be an indication of a general handicap than any other disability. Milder degrees of failure, such as awkwardness at handling materials may, however, be associated with emotional disturbance as frequently as with any actual physical condition. Lack of confidence in handling materials, or, with babies, inexperience through lack of contact with suitable toys in the home, may contribute to this condition. Here again comparison of a child's result on this scale (Scale D) with his performance elsewhere will help diagnosis. Left-handedness may also contribute to a degree of retardation in this field, especially in Scale D, and the laterality of the child should always be noted as a routine. Whether right and left have been differentiated, and one side become dominant, can usually be observed early in the second year. This is one of the test items in Scale D.

Spastic children often test low on this scale and on Scale E. (See profiles in Chapter VIII, Fig. 16.) Defects of vision are also reflected in the results on Scale D, blind or partially sighted babies doing poorly on this scale, as would be expected. (Chapter VIII, Fig. 17.)

Modifications of the Binet Scale were used by Burt for testing the deaf and also the blind (1929).[1] More recently the Binet Scale has been further modified for the purpose of testing the blind by Langan (1945).

A further set of manipulative tests, which by the second year approximate closer in type to performance tests as used with older subjects, comprise *Scale E.* The tests of the first year in this scale supplement Scale D by drawing on the child's capacity to make use of that degree of eye and hand co-ordination that he has acquired. Thus many of the eye and hand items are observational (Chapter XIV), the examiner noting thumb opposition, fine prehension, left-handedness and so on. In Scale E, definite test situations are presented to the child, to see if he can respond at a level indicated by his stage of development (maturation) as disclosed by his result on Scale D, and to what extent he has realised certain space and form relations.

Certain children having defects of vision or other disabilities

[1] *Report of Mental Deficiency Committee* (H.M. Stationery Office, 1929), pp. 220 and 221.

affecting hand and eye co-ordination (Scale D) may yet manage to achieve a somewhat better result in definite test situations of the kind offered in Scale E. Conversely, the well-developed child with no specific defect of hand or eye may fail in Scale E because of a lack of experience in handling toys and materials, or through nervousness, or maladjustment, or inability to understand what is wanted in the solving of these simple practical tests. In these ways the separation of those tests that measure hand and eye development as such from more definite tests of the performance type can add usefully to the total diagnostic picture.

In the last few paragraphs we have been considering cases of more or less general retardation or specific mental or physical handicap, and the differentiation of these in the testing of infants and young children by the new method. It must not, however, be concluded that the scale is useful only for such cases. All children show individual differences in intelligence, and there is almost unlimited variety in the profiles obtained from different children. (See Chapter VII.) The actual differences in total performance are usually expressed in terms of the general intelligence quotient or G.Q.; and the differences of type, showing inborn or acquired specific abilities or disabilities, are measured on the sub-scales and expressed also in quotients. Those fine differences that exist between one child and another within the normal range are of interest to the educator, and become increasingly important as the child grows older and plans have to be made periodically for his passage from one educational institution to another. It will be found that these differences are present in as great a degree in infancy as they are later in the child's life. Babies differ from one another in all respects, especially in all traits that can be measured; they show wide differences of general intelligence level as well as wide individual differences in their reactions to different types of test.

Predictive Value of the New Scale.—In spite of these findings of considerable differences, both general and more detailed, between children of these young ages and their relevance to educational problems, it must be emphasised that the writer does not at the present stage of this work claim any great predictive value for the new test procedure. It has been compiled with care and on the basis of detailed study of other scales, and applied and revised in relation to the study of a large sample of children of relevant ages. Nonetheless, much further work will need to be done on the scale itself in applying it to further groups of children, and in particular to further test-retest studies, before its relation to tests for older subjects will be known. It will be of particular interest and importance to watch the shape of the profile, and to determine whether or not this remains constant, with repeated tests in normally developing children, and also under what conditions or for what types of children the profile changes. It would, for example, be expected that a trough in a profile indicating some specific disability might disappear or become less exaggerated, after treatment of the condition had brought about complete or partial correction of the trouble. This is, indeed, what has been found to happen in a few selected cases. Further research will show to what extent this kind of result can be generally looked for.

In regard to predictive value, it is not to be expected that tests applicable to and legitimate as tests in the period of infancy, are necessarily similar in type to, or individually highly correlated with, tests suitable for measuring intelligence in older subjects. The most that can be done at the present stage of knowledge is to measure as accurately as possible those activities that are characteristic of infancy, and yet intimately related to the development of those necessary fundamental skills and abilities that underlie human efficiency at later stages. If such a test or group of tests can indeed show in these fundamental directions significant differences, on the one hand between one individual and another in the general level of development attained, and on the other hand can differentiate between subtler differences of type of ability (or disability), there is then every reason to expect that the procedure outlined will also be of value not only in indicating the child's position in relation to his group at the time of test, but may also be of value in indicating future possibilities.

It has frequently been asserted that there is little statistical relationship between test results so far carried out on young infants and tests for older children. This may be due to a complexity of factors, some of which may be indicated. Consideration must be given to the way these earlier tests have been constructed, possible lack of sufficient emphasis on verbal factors, lack of balance between tests of different types, differences of classification, and possibly also a failure to include only those main trends that are indeed significant for development. There are also other considerations, such as the necessary correction for age that must be made in the first few months of life. (See Chapter VI.)

It is impossible at present to know to what extent the new scale will indeed be predictive. However, a small number of babies have already been retested on the new scale, with encouraging results. (See Chapter VI.) As time goes on and children tested as infants reach an age such that they can be tested on other scales, further studies can be undertaken of the new scale's predictive value.

The question is by no means simple. There would appear to be little value from the writer's point of view in pruning away from an infant scale ("like dead wood from a tree", as Bayley has suggested) those individual test items that do not bear high positive correlations with individual items in later scales. To do this in the present stage of knowledge might well be (to continue the metaphor) to cut away the growing shoots also. It is possible to concentrate too exclusively on the diagnostic value of individual items, which are only, after all, individual stages, isolated items extracted (very often in a haphazard manner) from a developmental sequence recognised or unrecognised as such! Passing or failing on one particular item should not carry too much weight. Rather is it the child's position in regard to a particular developmental sequence that is significant. Moreover, it is the test taken as a whole that will give the truest final result and place the child most accurately; and if the total sequences are truly representative of those aspects of development that it is necessary to measure, they will be sufficiently indicative. Further research alone can show to what extent the new test method will give results that correlate with intelligence test results or with other tests for older subjects.

It is not inconceivable that even clinical tests for older subjects may in the future be differently and more adequately constructed, relying less on a conglomeration of isolated individual test items and more on the recognition of the value of developmental sequences. But that is a question for the future.

Before leaving this question of the possible predictive value of a test and finalising this chapter, the writer cannot forbear to remark that even the hitherto impregnable conception of the constancy of the I.Q. trembles and wavers on its pinnacle, as evidence is accumulated and extended by many workers, of exceptions to the general rule. It is now certain that *no* exact forecast can *ever* be authoritatively made on the basis of tests in any particular individual case.

The conception of the constancy of the I.Q. grew up as a result of large-scale statistical studies, which showed considerable consistency for whole populations on repeated tests. But within such groups were many individual changes of I.Q. from one test to the next. How, then, can anyone still speak of the constancy of the I.Q.? In general, it is probably true to say that whenever a child is already making normal progress in school, is in good health, has a well-adjusted personality and has also a normal home and school background, it is highly probable that his I.Q. on successive tests (if adequately carried out by persons trained in the relevant procedures) will show a high degree of consistency in the results obtained on the same scale. A difference up or down of five per cent. or less is generally regarded as non-significant.

Whenever these conditions are not fulfilled, changes in I.Q. are to be expected whatever age the child may be. Child-guidance cases frequently show a rise of intelligence as measured by tests, after some condition of maladjustment has been corrected by treatment. The I.Q. may change following a salutary change of environment. It may fall or rise following illness or recovery from illness. In psychological diagnosis what is wanted is to give an opinion, based on the best procedures available, suited to the child's age and circumstances, as to his mental condition or status *at the time of test*. There is nothing *necessarily* fixed or permanent about an intelligence quotient as such. It has often puzzled the writer in considering this question why psychologists should for so long have expected that the results of a single test, applied in some one particular hour of a child's life, under particular circumstances, should necessarily carry within it any implication of finality, or suggestion that if repeated the ratio of the child's performance (mental age) to his age at test should remain unchanged. In no other field of diagnostic work is such a condition expected.

Yet the fact remains that in actual practice the I.Q. on well-standardised tests is found to change very little with the great majority of normal healthy subjects. This fact should not mislead when consideration is given to special cases, or to the possible predictive value of a scale based on a study of subjects as young as the children and babies who took part in the present series of studies.

With these comments we must draw this part of the discussion, and also Part I, to a close. Our aims have been to orientate the reader to the novelty of the project, attempt to relate it to other fields of work, and attempt also to show something of the significance of infancy itself and the need for a new approach to the problem of test construction as applied to this early period of life. In Part II we shall turn to the standardisation of the scale and to the frequency distribution and a test-retest study. The preliminary results of the new method of diagnosis will be shown in Chapters VII and VIII.

Part II

STANDARDISATION OF THE SCALE AND DIAGNOSTIC IMPLICATIONS

CHAPTER V

STANDARDISATION OF THE SCALE

Preliminary Investigation and the Building of the Test

As already explained in Chapter II, certain preliminary studies of babies were undertaken before the final sample of infants was tested. The definite testing of babies grew out of these earlier studies. During these preliminary studies a good many notes were taken of observed reactions to various situations, and where the same type of reaction was frequently observed, material for test items emerged which was tried out and either modified, accepted or rejected, before the final testing. Some of the resulting ideas have become new test items. Observations also showed how some items in earlier use might be usefully divided to make two or more stages of difficulty, and so serve to differentiate more exactly one performance from another.

At an early stage a skeleton test was prepared including a proportion of items from existing tests supplemented by these new items. The test itself was under constant scrutiny as results came in. Tables were prepared, and kept constantly revised, for the study of the percentages of children in each month passing each item. Items that were found to be badly placed were moved on an experimental basis to more appropriate positions. Periodically, as the need arose, a full-scale study was made of the findings, and some revisions of the scale resulted.

A great deal of clerical work was involved, including the making of preliminary test sheets or forms for the administering of the tests, and the constant revision of these forms in accordance with changes in the scale. The preliminary forms were eight in number, one for each three months' period up to the end of the second year. Stencils were cut and the forms duplicated, some of this work being done through the kindness of clerical staff at St. George's Hospital. Later, changes in detail were made by hand. On these forms the tentative classification of items was shown in columns, with ample space for comments, descriptions of behaviour, social histories including birth histories and other additional information.

From one to four of these early forms were needed for each test taken.

As soon as the classification of items became more stable it was realised that for any degree of exactness in differential diagnosis (Chapters VII and VIII), these several classes of items must be made as far as possible equal in difficulty, and also equal in the weight they carried at each level of the scale, as well as in the total result. It was also an early decision to aim at a rather larger number of test items than is usual, especially in the first year of life where development is most rapid. At the same time it was important that the final test should not be unduly cumbersome, nor too lengthy to administer. Such practical matters as simplicity of scoring and ease of arriving at a quotient were taken into account from the beginning. This precluded any elaborate method of weighting test items. It was decided that actual numerical equality of the five groups of items was more suitable, provided that on the basis of average scores (see below) the different types of ability tested in what later became separate sub-scales could be shown to be equal, or very nearly equal, in difficulty at each level of development. This was the ideal aimed at and approximately achieved.

In the completed scale five sub-scales emerged, each consisting of 52 items (from birth to two years) giving a total of 260 items in the test. There are three items for each week of life in the first year and two items for each week in the second year. Naturally each child is given only a cross section of the test items appropriate to his age and ability level (Part III). The entire test takes from twenty to forty minutes to administer.

As the material on the provisional forms was collected and the forms themselves from time to time revised, some means of organising the complex data for detailed study was needed. After some experiment a convenient and useful means of organising the data for revision and standardisation was arrived at. The large sheets of ¼-inch squared paper used in statistical work were employed, and as results came in the information was entered in detail on these "charts". One such chart was prepared for the items of each of the five sub-scales appropriate for testing in each *month* of age. The first month locomotor items formed one unit of results for standardisation, the second month another, and so on. Thus there were 120 such sections of the results, each recorded on one such chart. Items likely to be needed in testing children of different ability levels were numbered perpendicularly as far as required on the left of the charts, and the actual names of the children tested in that month of their age across the top. A pass symbol (✓) or minus (—) was placed in each appropriate square. It was thus possible, by counting across, to obtain quickly the percentages of passes, so far, for each item, and these were entered on the charts and also recorded in percentage tables, which were kept constantly revised. Similarly, by adding perpendicularly, individual scores, averages of scores and other information were readily obtained. All this fundamental information resulting from the quite extensive preliminary arithmetic associated with the standardisation and equalising of the five sub-scales was recorded in an easily accessible form on these charts, which have been used throughout and found invaluable. They remain a permanent record from which also information about individual children can readily be obtained, and they supersede the somewhat cumbersome and frequently revised preliminary forms; although these forms also are preserved and filed for reference. This information from the charts can be readily transferred to punched cards when a more detailed statistical analysis of the findings is undertaken.

As soon as the scale became fairly stable, provisional forms for further testing were printed, all the items being arranged on one printed sheet, which saved a great deal of labour. A working alphabetical card index of all children seen was used from the beginning so as to be able to trace a test quickly, note children seen more than once and so on. Social and other information was summarised on these cards. A further card index was made when all the data needed had been collected, and on this the details of test results were summarised in a form convenient for the preliminary statistical analysis of the results. Each child has a General Intelligence Quotient allotted on the total test result, and also a separate score, mental age and quotient for each of the five sub-scales. None of these mental ages or quotients could be worked out until the standardisation was complete.

Measures Taken to Ensure Accuracy

In a study of this kind there are endless possible sources of error, as every research worker will appreciate. To reduce the danger of errors in the procedure, the following precautions were taken:

1. All the tests for the final sample were carried out by one

examiner. To have only one examiner responsible for the testing tends to eliminate error due to differences in interpretation. The detailed nature of the work on this scale and the large number of items leave room for interpretative errors, differences in standards of assessment and other personal sources of error or lack of uniformity in the testing. When a test is in the making, such sources of error are liable to be much greater than after a procedure has been built up and detailed instructions prepared for administering the scale.

2. Mothers of the babies were present throughout the testing whenever this was possible. This eliminated possible sources of error in the data collected, such as in getting exact dates of birth, weights of babies at birth, social information, etc. All information was entered on the forms or otherwise recorded in the presence of the mother *at the time of the test*, and was subsequently transferred to the research records. This information was also supplemented and verified by reference to the records available in the centres and nurseries. This last precaution was essential whenever for any reason the mother herself could not be interviewed. Every item in the testing was scored while the child was still present and under observation. There was no writing up of notes afterwards. No reliance on memory can be tolerated in work of this kind.

3. The working out of ages was done in all cases as a routine with the calendar. Working out the age of a baby in weeks (and thirds of a week), though a simple matter, is one very liable to error. All such processes were done twice by way of a check. The same precautions were taken in working out mental ages, quotients, scores on the scales and other basic data.

4. The work on the charts, counting items passed across the page and totals down the page, the working out of percentages, additions and so on, all these processes were carried out at least twice, checking where helpful on the slide rule. In addition, every possible form of cross checking was used. Page by page the basic information grew on the charts until at last the position was reached where the building of the statistical superstructure could commence. A considerable amount of information likely to be useful in child psychology is here in these records, some time to be extracted and made available in other studies. Therefore, every care taken to ensure accuracy is laying a foundation for further investigations on this same sample of children.

The Sample

To obtain a good representative sample of infants of the ages required for this purpose is no simple matter. Good samples of school-children can be obtained more easily. In fact, at the primary school ages it is possible to get good representative samples of the population without undue difficulty if certain precautions are taken. This is because the vast majority of children of school ages are compulsorily in attendance somewhere at school, and official information is available about them. Many studies of school children, intelligence surveys and surveys for other purposes have been carried out. The writer has taken part in one such large survey (Roberts, Norman and Griffiths, 1935, 1937, 1938), and has also conducted other smaller ones for specific purposes.

With children under school age, the sampling problem is formidable. There are, however, various institutions that babies attend where systematic studies can be carried out. Of these the most useful are the Infant Welfare Centres. Attendance at these is of course voluntary, but most mothers take their young babies there for periodic examination. It is therefore possible by persistent and regular attendance to obtain a good sample of Infant Welfare children. Naturally it is of little use to rely on only one such centre, unless it is the only one in the area selected or is indeed representative of the entire community. Usually several such centres must be used, selected from different localities so as to get as varied a sample as possible. There is, however, no guarantee that children of the ages required will necessarily be in attendance when the examiner visits the centre!

The Welfare Centre population must be supplemented by other groups of children. In London there are in some areas Day Nurseries for the young children of mothers who are in employment. Here the children are usually in attendance all day, and it may therefore be possible to find and test several babies of the required ages in an afternoon. Four or more babies can be conveniently tested in one session. Of course the examiner must in all cases be ready to fit in with the programme of the nursery, allowing for meal-times, sleeping-times, medical inspection and so on, recognising also that staffs are normally extremely busy and ideal arrangements cannot be expected for conducting a psychological test. The matrons of nurseries and their assistants were found most kind and helpful and ready to make facilities available whenever possible.

From the point of view of building up a representative sample, care must be taken in regard to the proportion of Day Nursery children included. This should not be large, because, of course, the Day Nursery population is highly selected; in a considerable proportion of the cases the mother is the sole breadwinner. These comments apply even more definitely to babies in residential homes and nurseries.

The ideal method of building up a sample might be to start by obtaining official lists of all babies born in a certain area within a certain period of time and then attempt to test a complete cross-section of them. In London certain sections of the community form a floating population. The housing problem, the unsettled lives that many families live, the frequent need for both parents to be employed, all these and other factors would militate against getting large or reasonably complete samples. Many of the children originally ascertained would have left the district before it was possible to test them.

A further point that might be useful to others in planning work with children of these ages is the difference to be found between obtaining a good sample of babies in their first year and obtaining a good sample in their second year. If all the Infant Welfare Centres in an area are visited, a sufficient number of young babies can usually be found in attendance, but the second year presents difficulties. It appears that fewer children in their second year are in practice taken to the centres, probably owing to a variety of circumstances. In the first few months of a child's life, the young mother is anxious to learn all she can about the care of her baby, and probably also feels reassured by taking the child regularly to the centre. Later on, if the baby is doing well, she may not come so often. This means that it is more difficult to build up adequate numbers of older babies. There is also the complicating factor that many mothers are eager to find employment. Such a mother brings her baby when he is young to the centre but, as soon as he is old enough to be left, she finds a vacancy in a Day Nursery or leaves him with a relative or other person during the day, and is unable, because of her employment, to bring him regularly to the centre. Day Nurseries do not usually take babies under six or eight months of age; most of the babies enter the nursery at about ten or twelve months and remain until old enough to go to school. So the visiting examiner finds populations in the Welfare Centres becoming more difficult from the sampling point of view as the babies get older, and in the second year it is very difficult indeed. There is a temptation to compensate for this by testing the more adequate numbers to be found in the Day Nurseries, but, as explained above, this would lead to bias in the sample. The solution seems to be to supplement the numbers by testing other children outside these institutions by every means available, although finding and testing these extra children is frequently very time-consuming. In any case, the second year is probably the most difficult throughout the child's entire career from this point of view. Our own sample in the second year we know to be somewhat less satisfactory than the first-year sample; but much of the difficulty was overcome through the kindness of the staff at one large Welfare Centre. The Health Visitors from this centre visited the homes of babies of the needed ages and made definite appointments for them to be brought to the centre for the examinations. The total sample, when the two years are taken together, is a reasonably good one, as will be seen when we study the frequency distribution.

How, then, was the sample built up? When this work was commenced, because of a very full programme of other clinical work, only a small proportion of the investigator's time was available each week for this work and no systematic sampling of the population was possible. A beginning was therefore made by testing babies whenever they were met with. This preliminary sample included: (*a*) a group of babies seen in residential homes; (*b*) children seen in clinics and outpatient departments of hospitals, the younger brothers and sisters of patients but themselves normal healthy infants; (*c*) the children of friends and colleagues; and (*d*) children met with anywhere, or children whose parents had heard of the work and were willing to "lend" their babies for a test. This preliminary sample, although rather haphazard, was actually very varied and not too unrepresentative of the community.

Later in the work, when more time became available, the investigation was limited to the Borough of Kensington, and most of the final sample are babies born in this area between 1947 and 1951. Kensington was found to be a good area for the purpose. Most valuable of all was the ready co-operation that was met with everywhere. The Medical Officers of Health and their staffs, Matrons of Nurseries, Health Visitors and their staffs, and above all the parents of the children, were without exception helpful and interested. Having telephoned for an appointment and explained what facilities would be helpful, the investigator found herself able to go freely into the various institutions and select (on the basis of age) the children required for testing. More will be said about the circumstances of the test, the test environment and so on, in a later chapter.

The total area chosen was found convenient in every respect. Some 3,000 babies are born here each year. It is from the sampling point of view a varied area, so-called "good residential" sections alternating and intermixing with poorer ones. There is a large business community, with many large firms, establishments and workshops, as well as many more small retail businesses. There is a professional element also, including doctors, teachers, artists, actors, social workers of various groups and all types of students. There are large blocks of flats, also many large houses, some of them divided up into flats, others into single rooms, suites of rooms and so on. There are hotels, hostels and boarding establishments of every variety. There are also some of the poorest residential areas of London to be found within the Borough. Stretching southwards from Kensal Rise, it includes the whole of North Kensington to the borders of Fulham, Chelsea and Knightsbridge. It also includes South Kensington and Earl's Court. In this area probably every facet of London life is to be found.

Whether the Borough has been successfully sampled it is impossible to say, but every effort to do so has been made. The vast majority of the children were seen in Infant Welfare Centres. Centres were visited (1) in a large varied but on the whole good area; (2) in a more consistently average area; and (3) in a markedly poor area.

A somewhat smaller group was obtained by sampling all Day Nursery populations in the Borough. Small groups in two residential nurseries were included, although these were outside the area. A considerable number of children resident in the area were seen privately in their own homes or by appointment elsewhere. A number were found in the waiting-rooms at outpatient departments. Some of the tests in the preliminary sample already described, where they were sufficiently complete, were also included.

All these children were selected and tested on the basis of age alone, effort being made to test at least twenty babies in each month of life. Naturally they varied to a very great extent in ability, and a few were found to be suitably classified as very backward, physically handicapped and so on. These were all included in the total sample unless "*referred*" as in any way presenting a probem. No hospital cases were included and no private patients.

The Final Sample

The final sample, excluding the incomplete early tests and preliminary studies, contains 571 cases, that is 571 first tests. A number of these children have been seen more than once, a few a number of times, as will be described later; for the moment we are concerned with the 571 first tests only. These tests were carried out in institutions and elsewhere, as shown in Table I below.

TABLE I

THE SAMPLE

Infant Welfare Centres	370
Day Nurseries	113
Residential Nurseries	14
In their own homes or seen privately	44
Seen in outpatient departments of hospitals (not patients)	30
Total	571
This sample contains:	
Boys	292
Girls	279
Total	571

(During the period of the testing, rather more boys than girls were born in the area.)

The sample contains six pairs of twins and one set of quads.

Parental Occupations

Perhaps the best way to test the representative nature of the sample is to make an analysis of the occupation groups to which the parents of the children belong. This has been done. It may become possible to do this more exactly for an urban population such as London when detailed results of the recent British Census are available. Meanwhile, the best alternative seemed to be to take, as a basis for comparison, the classification of occupations of employed males in the U.S.A., as shown by the results of the 1940 Census there, revised on the basis of that presented earlier by Goodenough. (See Goodenough and Anderson, 1931.) Their classification of the occupations is as follows, showing the percentages of men in each employment group. (See Carmichael, 1946, p. 25.)

Classification of Occupations of Employed Males in U.S.A. (1940 *Census*). *After Florence Goodenough* (*Minnesota Scale of Paternal Occupation.*)

		per cent.
I.	Professional	2·71
II.	Semi-professional	7·16
III.	Clerical, Skilled Trades, Retail Business	14·13
IV.	Farmers	15·26
V.	Semi-skilled Occupations, Minor Clerical, Minor Business	23·89
VI.	Slightly skilled Trades and Occupations requiring little training	14·56
VII.	Day Labourers of all Classes, including Agricultural	22·29

How does the present sample compare with this when analysis is made of the occupations of the parents? The fathers belong to all these groups in so far as this could be expected in what is essentially an urban sample. Thus it includes no farmers and few agricultural labourers, so that the number of fathers in group VII is very few. The relationship between the remaining classes is found to be surprisingly similar to those in Goodenough's classification. In order to make the results comparable, as this is an urban sample, we have added in the table below the expected percentage of farmers and of agricultural labourers that would be needed to make this sample more completely representative of the country as a whole, should this be desired. This would require a total sample of 837 children and, accepting Goodenough's percentages, the close approximation of our figures to hers for the groups tested is shown in the table below. For 19 children tested no information was available concerning parental occupation. These are omitted from the percentages in Table II.

It will be seen from this table (Table II) that the relationship between the groups I, II, III, V and VI in the present sample, when shown in this way, is very closely comparable with the relevant groups in the American study. We may, then, safely regard the present sample as a good one, recognising its limitation as a purely urban sample; and recognising that, to complete this study and make the sample representative of the total community, some attempt should be made to include an equivalent number (128) of children whose fathers are farmers (group IV) and an equivalent number also of other agricultural workers and labourers, namely about 186 less 29, or 157 for group VII.

TABLE II

PATERNAL OCCUPATION

(*Comparison with Minnesota Scale (Goodenough)*)

Groups	*Actual No. of Children Tested*	*Adding Rural Groups*	*Percentages of 837*	*Percentages (Goodenough)*
I . .	28	28	3·34	2·71
II . .	66	66	7·89	7·16
III . .	117	117	13·97	14·13
IV . .	0	(128)	(15·26)	15·26
V . .	188	188	22·44	23·89
VI . .	124	124	14·81	14·56
VII . .	29	(186)	(22·29)	22·29
Totals .	552	837	100·00	100·00
No information	(19)			

TABLE III

OCCUPATIONAL ANALYSIS OF AN URBAN SAMPLE

Groups	*No. Tested*	*Percentage*
I. Professional	28	5·07
II. Semi-professional	66	11·96
III. Clerical, Skilled Trades, etc. .	117	21·20
IV. Farmers	0	0
V. Semi-skilled, Minor Clerical, etc. .	188	34·06
VI. Slightly skilled Trades, etc. .	124	22·46
VII. Labourers	29	5·25
Totals	552	100·00
No information	(19)	

Nonetheless, the sample as at present constituted may form a basis for comparison with other urban samples, if the actual percentages of children in each group are given as they stand.

Keeping the same classification therefore, this information is shown in Table III on page 57.

Standardisation of the Scale and Equalising of the Sub-scales.

The Standardisation Material.—As the work proceeded, it was decided to test if possible a minimum of twenty babies in each month of life. The youngest child seen was just two weeks or fourteen days old. The first-month babies, twenty-four in number, were therefore all in their third or fourth week or at the beginning of their fifth week. Care was taken in the matter of the month to which the child belonged; thus for example, if born on the 6th May, the child commenced his sixth month on the 6th October and, although just five months old if tested on that day, his result was placed with the six months' data. No child is included in this study if he was over twenty-four months of age (even one day over) at the date of the test. Thus, if tested on his second birthday, he could not be included, as he strictly belonged to the twenty-fifth month.

As has been explained, there was greater difficulty in getting adequate samples of children in the second year of life, and to some extent at the end of the first year, and so, for the purposes of standardisation only, a few second tests of children, first tested when a few months old and seen again later, were included. This served to increase the data and make percentages, averages, etc., more representative in the second year. Care was taken to include as few as possible of these second tests and also to ensure that an adequate time interval existed between the two tests in each individual case, such that there was no overlapping whatever in any of the test items taken on the two occasions. A period of six months between the tests was taken as a minimum for this purpose. Taking into consideration the rapid development of babies in the earliest stages (see Chapter II), this is a satisfactory interval, being relatively much wider than a similar interval would be at any later age. Forty-seven such retests were included, for the purposes of the month-by-month standardisation only.

In the sample of 571 babies, fourteen were found on test to be very backward generally, defective or near defective, or handicapped in some specific direction, sufficiently to upset the delicate month-by-month standardisation (percentages and scale averages). Especially was this so where more than one of these cases occurred in a particular month—for example, a pair of very backward twins. The monthly samples were naturally small. (See Table V.) These fourteen were therefore excluded from this part of the standardisation work only. They were, of course, reincluded in the work presented in Chapter VI. After these changes were made, the total number of tests included in the standardisation work described here was 604 (571 + 47 − 14).

The study of the percentages of children passing each item in each of the sub-scales, month by month, was carried out parallel with the equalising of the scales. Percentage graphs for the first four months have already been presented in Chapter II to illustrate the rapidity of development at that level. Later it was found useful to build these tables and graphs after combining the results into two-monthly groupings, which helped to smooth the curves particularly in the second year, where already development begins to proceed rather less rapidly. This can be clearly seen from the accompanying table (Table IV) and diagram (Fig. 6).

This graph and table illustrate the development of speech from the first month to the twenty-fourth month. These test items will be found described in Chapter XIII (Speech Scale) and listed in Appendix II.

Percentage tables and graphs were similarly prepared for each of the other sub-scales, namely Locomotor Development, Personal-Social Progress, Hand and Eye Development and Performance. These are all very similar in shape.

Equalising the Sub-scales.—The equalising of the sub-scales of the new test was the most difficult and laborious part of the standardisation work, before it resulted in the derivation of the final test from the data. Terman and Merrill (1937) worked to obtain two sets of tests of similar difficulty, at each age level, for the two forms of their revision of the Binet-Simon Scale, Form L and Form M. They discuss the complexities of this problem in Chapter II of that work. Like them, we have found it necessary to work empirically, manipulating the scales stage by stage, until the desired result, or a close approximation to it, was obtained. In the present case the work was particularly delicate, because there were no less than five sub-scales. It was important that all of these should be as equal as possible in difficulty at each age level; that

TABLE IV
HEARING AND SPEECH (SCALE C)
Actual percentages (N = 604) (Two-monthly Groupings)

(See also Fig. 6)

	Months											
First Year Items	1 *and* 2	3 *and* 4	5 *and* 6	7 *and* 8	9 *and* 10	11 *and* 12	13 *and* 14	15 *and* 16	17 *and* 18	19 *and* 20	21 *and* 22	23 *and* 24
1	81	100	100									
2	75	100	100									
3	68	100	100									
4	40	92	100									
5	13	90	100									
6	19	88	100									
7	6	57	94	100								
8	19	51	86	100								
9	4	41	90	100								
10		35	98	100								
11		2	65	96	98	100						
12		14	67	89	97	100						
13		12	52	91	98	100						
14		4	46	83	100	100						
15		0	12	80	97	100						
16		24	40	63	100	100						
17		0	12	67	95	100						
18		14	23	56	98	100						
19			4	37	84	94	98	100				
20			4	32	75	100	100	100				
21			4	32	70	83	98	100				
22			10	32	70	96	100	100				
23			6	28	57	90	94	98	100			
24				15	54	77	94	100	100			
25				11	44	77	90	100	100			
26				11	33	77	86	98	100			
27				2	26	69	81	100	100			
28				4	34	60	90	98	100			
29				.2	34	58	77	94	96	100		
30				2	9	50	71	90	100	100		
31				2	26	40	69	86	98	100		
Second Year Items												
32					8	29	60	76	89	92	98	100
33					5	21	52	76	92	100	100	100
34					2	17	48	82	96	98	100	100
35					2	12	37	62	75	82	98	100
36						8	34	62	81	90	98	100
37						2	12	30	66	84	98	100
38						4	15	32	58	72	91	97
39						0	8	38	57	74	93	100
40						0	6	18	47	70	81	97
41						2	6	14	34	62	84	92
42							0	16	41	56	79	85
43							0	2	17	42	70	82
44							0	6	23	40	63	75
45							2	6	26	36	67	80
46								10	19	34	58	75
47								2	13	26	40	62
48								0	2	12	26	52
49								2	8	24	44	50
50									6	18	30	55
51									2	18	37	45
52									2	14	28	42
No.	54	51	52	46	61	52	52	50	53	50	43	40

Total N = 604

is, at each *month* of age. Fortunately rather more test items than were actually needed were taken with the vast majority of the children, thus enabling the least useful or reliable items to be dropped. Testing was carried well below and well above the limits now necessary with the completed scale. Some tests were so framed that they could if necessary be divided into two items. In only a very few cases, where classification problems did not conflict, it was possible to retain a useful item by moving it from one scale to another, but in this work the classification problem was paramount, and the scales had to retain their separateness of character whilst aiming at equality of difficulty, a somewhat different problem.

Work was begun by working out the average number of items expected at each month of age in each sub-scale; that is, the expected average score. (See explanatory note to Table V.) Then, proceeding from the first month, as soon as the testing for that month was ready and details entered on the charts, each scale was examined on the basis of actual average scores obtained in each month. The aim was to get these within one whole number of the average expected and with the first six months a closer degree of equality was aimed at. It will be seen from the averages given below in Table V that this aim has been very largely attained, although in one or two places, notably at the seventeenth month, the nature of the sample (which was a difficult one) produced somewhat lower results.

Thus, beginning at the first month and proceeding month by month, the scales were gradually made more equal, changes being indicated on the charts already described. The effects of such changes were studied with the help of the data already entered on the charts, with the percentage tables also, and the provisional quotients of the tests available. It was necessary in each individual instance to weigh the effects, for example, of omitting a particular item where a sub-scale appeared too easy at that point, and study the effects that this change would have at successive months also, and whether it would seriously upset the months already traversed. Every decision had to be made on an experimental and provisional basis and left provisional until the work had proceeded some distance in each case beyond that point. Where a sub-scale was too difficult at a particular level in relation to the other four scales, some interchange of items, or division of a suitable item into two parts, was indicated. The first few months' results were fairly easy to straighten out in this way, but everything was left on an experi-

HEARING AND SPEECH (SCALE C)

PERCENTAGES OF BABIES PASSING EACH ITEM FRO

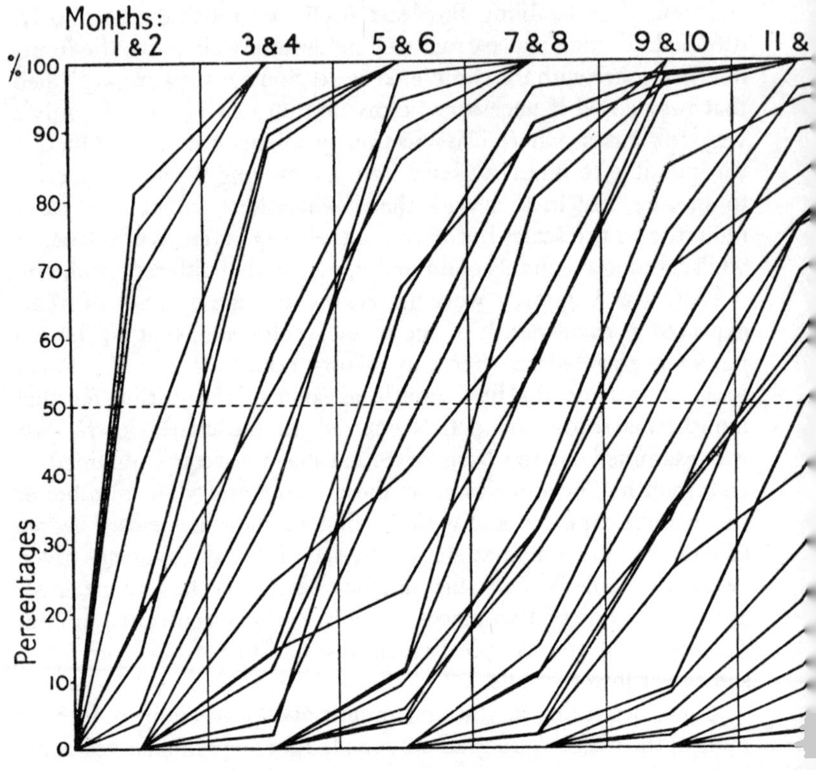

FIG. 6.—Showing rapid early development gradually slowing down in second y

mental basis, with notes made of alternative possibilities as the work proceeded. No changes could be made (such as accepting additional items) that would invalidate any of the test results of the final sample, as that would have involved much further testing. Frequently after covering this work on the scales for some distance satisfactorily it was found that a scale suddenly became too difficult or too easy in relation to the others and to the expected average score. Then it was necessary to retrace our steps, revise once more, studying percentages in relation to the effects of possible further changes, not only on the months still to be standardised, but on work already completed at earlier levels. It is not surprising that this phase of the work occupied many months and involved much arithmetic, but finally the scale

H TO TWO YEARS (TWO-MONTHLY GROUPINGS)

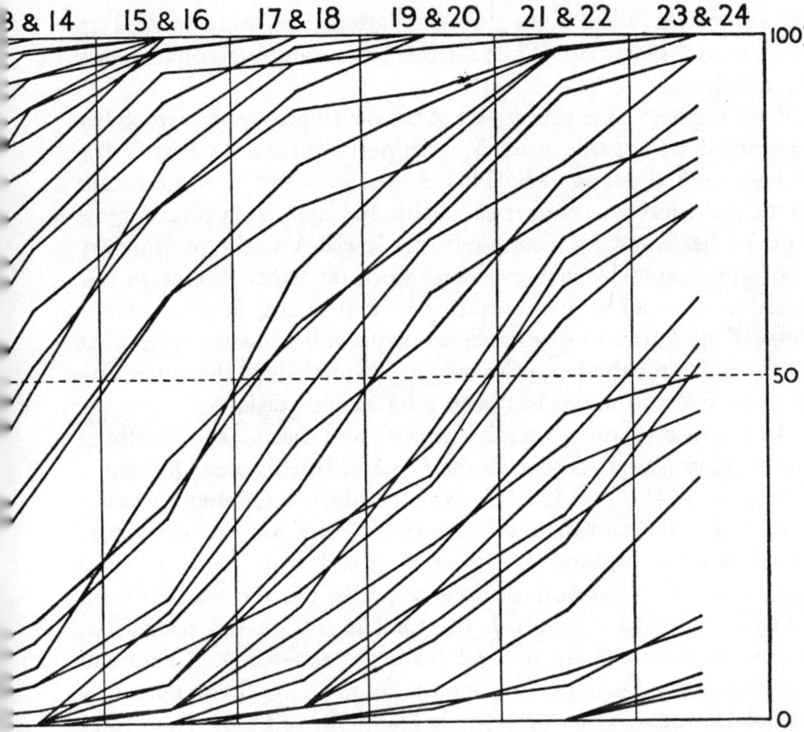

details of Test-items, see Chapter XIII and also Appendix II—Speech, Column C.)

emerged, if not perfect at least very close, as will be seen, to the degree of equality of difficulty aimed at for the sub-scales. In every case it was felt that the dropping of a particular item had been an improvement, the least valuable or reliable items being in every case the ones that were discarded. Moreover, the finer discrimination in the scores that resulted from the division of certain items was also felt to be an improvement.

Finally, all the changes made—and they were considerable, especially in the second year—had to be carefully registered on the 120 charts on which all this work was done. Items omitted, divided or transferred were so treated on the charts, and final scores, averages, etc., worked up. Not until the scale had reached its final form and every item was firm in its place (with a new identifying number allotted to it) could any accurate intelligence quotients be assessed. These were next arrived at and entered with each child's result, and at a later stage mental ages and quotients on each of the sub-scales (some 4,000 quotients altogether) were worked up and entered here also. Thus all the basic data was conveniently summarised.

Looking back over this aspect of the developing scale, which has resembled an organic growth, it appears surprising that it has indeed worked out so well. This is due no doubt to some extent to the inclusion of a number of reliable and adequately placed items from earlier work, for example from Gesell. Also the preliminary and quite extensive observational work on which the scale was based was found to have been time well spent, because of the detailed background of experience it provided concerning what to expect from babies of different ages. Nonetheless, the equalising of these five sub-scales has been a formidable task.

In the next chapter we shall present and discuss the results of the standardisation as seen in the General Intelligence Quotients. These we shall call G.Q.s (*General* Intelligence Quotients) rather than I.Q.s, so as to distinguish a result based on this new scale, which is rather differently constructed and more broadly based than is usual, from results of other tests that use the familiar term I.Q.; and also to distinguish the total result on the scale from quotients that may be derived from the sub-scales. These will be known as: Q.A. or Locomotor Quotient, Q.B. or Personal-Social Quotient, Q.C. or Speech Quotient, Q.D. or Hand and Eye Quotient, and Q.E. or Performance Quotient. However, in general it will be sufficient to know the separate scores on the sub-scales in order to study a child's result; only in special cases where some specific handicap or disability is being investigated would it appear necessary to arrive at the quotients on the sub-scales. Instructions for obtaining the quotients will be given in Part III and in Appendix I. Q.A., Q.B., etc., are used instead of the more usual A.Q., B.Q., etc., as A.Q. and also E.Q. already have other meanings.

Explanatory Note to Table V

Arriving at the Expected Average Monthly Scores

The total number of items = 156 in the First Year and 104 in the Second Year. The average number of items in each sub-scale in the *First Year* is $\frac{156}{5} = 31{\cdot}2$, there being 3 items on the total scale for each *week* of life. If we divide 31·2 by 12, this gives 2·6 as the expected average score at the *end* of the first month and also the monthly increment throughout the first year. Now the average age of the babies in the first month is 3 weeks or 21 days, as no child was tested under 14 days old. The expected average in each scale for the first month is therefore $\frac{21}{30}$ or ·70 of 2·6 = 1·8. (See the first figure in the third row in Table V.) In the second month, the expected average is 1½ times 2·6 (the average age of the babies being taken as half-way through the second month) = 3·9. The averages for the other months from 3 to 12 are found by adding the expected increment of 2·6 to each month in succession (Table V, third line down), to the end of the first year (29·9).

In the *Second Year*, the total number of items is 104, or 2 for each week of life, and therefore $\frac{104}{5} = 20{\cdot}8$ items is the average for each scale. Dividing by 12, we get 1·75 as the monthly increment for the second year. The total to the end of the first year is 31·2 items; adding *half* the expected increment to obtain the mid-point of the 13th month, $31{\cdot}2 + \frac{1{\cdot}75}{2} = 32{\cdot}07$ or 32·1. (See Table V, 13th month.) We now continue to add the expected monthly increment of 1·75 to obtain the expected averages for the 14th and successive months to the 24th month, and use these figures corrected to the first place of decimals as shown in the table overleaf.

Table V

TABLE OF AVERAGES

Showing the Results of Standardising and Equalising the Five Scales on the Basis of Average Scores

Months	1	2	3	4	5	6	7	8	9	10	11	12	13	14	15	16	17	18	19	20	21	22	23	24	
No. of Babies Tested in each month	24	30	27	24	26	26	25	21	30	31	25	27	30	22	29	21	22	31	22	28	21	22	16	24	Total 604
Expected Average Scores in each Scale	1·8	3·9	6·5	9·1	11·7	14·3	16·9	19·5	22·1	24·7	27·3	29·9	32·1	33·8	35·5	37·3	39·0	40·7	42·5	44·2	45·9	47·6	49·4	51·2	See explanatory note on page 64
Average Scores—Scale A	1·9	4·0	6·6	9·9	11·9	14·0	17·0	19·8	22·5	24·9	26·7	30·7	32·6	34·5	35·8	38·1	39·0	41·6	42·2	44·9	46·4	47·5	50·0	50·5	Locomotor
Average Scores—Scale B	1·6	3·8	6·9	9·0	12·4	14·3	16·9	20·1	22·2	25·0	27·0	30·1	31·7	33·8	35·4	36·5	37·5	40·9	41·6	44·6	46·6	47·5	48·8	51·3	Personal-Social
Average Scores—Scale C	2·0	4·2	7·0	9·6	11·9	14·3	16·8	20·3	22·7	25·7	27·4	29·8	31·5	33·4	35·2	37·1	37·8	41·2	41·0	44·6	46·5	47·8	49·7	51·9	Hearing and Speech
Average Scores—Scale D	1·7	3·7	5·8	9·2	11·5	13·8	17·0	19·5	22·1	24·5	26·5	30·0	31·7	34·0	36·3	38·0	38·7	41·4	42·0	44·6	45·6	47·4	49·7	50·7	Hand and Eye
Average Scores—Scale E	2·2	3·6	5·9	9·0	11·8	14·2	17·8	20·5	22·5	24·8	26·4	29·3	31·7	33·9	36·0	37·2	38·4	42·0	43·3	44·7	46·8	47·7	50·2	51·8	Performance
Total Average Scores	1·89	3·87	6·43	9·35	11·90	14·12	17·10	20·06	22·40	24·96	26·78	29·97	31·83	33·90	35·74	37·40	38·26	41·46	42·04	44·67	46·38	47·57	49·67	51·24	

CHAPTER VI

THE FREQUENCY DISTRIBUTION AND GENERAL VALIDITY OF THE SCALE

HAVING described in some detail the building and standardising of the scale, we now approach a study of the General Intelligence Quotients of the children, and the frequency distribution, using the entire sample of 571 first tests.

In order to study the consistency of the scale throughout its extent, it is necessary to eliminate the effects of the age factor, and as quotients are widely used and understood, to turn the scores on this test also into quotients seemed the most suitable method. Scores were therefore translated into mental ages and then into quotients as follows. The total score of each child in the first year of life was divided by three, as there are three items in the total scale for each week of life. This gave the mental age of the child in weeks. One item over was counted as ·3, two items over as ·7. In the same way the actual or chronological ages of the children were worked out by the calendar in weeks and thirds of a week. Thus, where there was one day over the completed weeks, it was ignored, two or three days extra counted as one-third or more exactly ·3 of a week, four or five days over as ·7 and six days over as a complete additional week.

$$\text{Thus Mental Age (M.A.)} = \frac{\text{items passed}}{3}$$

$$\text{General Quotient (G.Q.)} = \frac{\text{M.A. (mental age)} \times 100}{\text{C.A. (chronological age)}}$$

To give an example of this: Let us suppose that a baby aged 16 weeks and 2 days passes altogether 56 items, then C.A. is 16·3 weeks, mental age is $\frac{56}{3} = 18{\cdot}7$ weeks, and the general intelligence quotient is $\frac{18{\cdot}7 \times 100}{16{\cdot}3} = 114{\cdot}7$, or 115 G.Q.

There is an additional correction to be applied in the case of those babies who are tested at age 8 months or younger. This is described below.

In the second year of the tests there are two items for each week. Thus the chronological ages of babies in the second year are worked out in weeks and half-weeks and the total scores are divided by 2 instead of by 3 to obtain the mental age. Then the quotient is readily obtainable by dividing the mental age by the chronological age and multiplying by 100 as before. (See also Appendix I.)

There are, however, certain difficulties inherent in the application of the quotient method to the youngest babies which other workers have also met with. In fact, the quotient method as applied in the earliest months of life has aroused some scepticism, and it has even been assumed that intelligence quotients cannot be accurately assessed in children under about 6 months of age.

The difficulties would appear to be due to a complex set of circumstances, which cannot be fully unravelled here, but to which reference must be made. In the first place there are undoubted individual differences as between one child and another from the beginning of post-natal life. These differences appear at least as great as at any later stage of development. When scores are first turned into quotients this factor of individual differences appears strikingly evident at once, as will be seen from the table of monthly Standard Deviations given below. But this effect of a very wide dispersion in the results is somewhat exaggerated by certain statistical effects of the quotient method at this early age level, and for this a correction has been devised. It is also complicated by certain other factors to be now considered.

1. There is first the undoubted factor of real and measurable individual differences in inborn capacity present from the beginning. Babies are by no means all alike. They differ very widely from one another in every measurable direction.

2. There is the further complication of the *maturity* of the child at birth. It is obvious that a premature baby is a "younger" baby than others of the same chronological age. The handicap of prematurity, for such it is, is greatest at the beginning of life, and tends to become less important as the child grows older. But this factor may be of great importance if a quotient is taken during the first few months of such a child's life. Even a small degree of prematurity, say 3 or 4 weeks, may place the baby temporarily at a serious disadvantage in relation to full-term babies. This is at once seen in certain other more obvious directions, such as his smaller size, lower birth weight and so on, and is liable to affect

the quotient to an extent that has not, so far as we are aware, as yet been fully investigated.

3. Some babies have had difficult or even traumatic birth experiences, and therefore are handicapped to some extent during the earliest weeks or months afterwards.

4. Factors of post-natal illness, emotional disturbance, environmental changes and so on, any of these may tend to complicate the situation and may possibly affect a test result. (See Chapter II.)

In this work and in regard to this question, a definite point of view must be established to enable a course to be steered through the many controversies that are liable to arise. Before any consideration can be given to the several problems involved in measuring the possible effects of 2, 3 or 4 above, on a test result, an authentic method of measuring the intelligence or ability level of babies in general must be established. For the time being, the fact of individual differences as such should be accepted without too much enquiry into its causation, or into adjacent problems, until other studies, future research, have thrown further light on the effects of special conditions, some of which may be shown in due course to be transitory and others to be more permanent.

In this study, therefore, the scores on test results were turned into mental ages as described above, and the general quotients assessed in the first place on the findings as they stood. Monthly Standard Deviations were then found in order to study the consistency of the method. All the test results included in the sample were here treated on an equal footing, even although there were factors such as those described under 2, 3 and 4 above operating in some cases. Having done this, it was soon clear that a factor purely statistical, larger and therefore more important than any of those mentioned, was operating to distort the results in these early months. This effect was greatest with the youngest babies, and diminished as the chronological ages increased. This effect appears to be a function of the age factor, and is due to taking any particular arbitrary point in a child's life, or in a group of children, as the starting-point for a test, which then has no further background or perspective as it were "in time". It is the opposite of what statisticians call a ceiling effect, and one which might be called a "floor" effect. It can be clearly seen in the tables given below. (Tables VI and VII.)

In the first month these first raw or uncorrected quotients

showed results ranging from 50 to 185 and a Standard Deviation of 41·31. This wide range became gradually narrower, and the dispersion less, month by month until after the eighth month, when a more consistent dispersion was established, with a Standard Deviation in the neighbourhood of 12·0. It was found that this deviation of approximately 12·0 also applied fairly consistently throughout the second year, and appears in fact characteristic of this new scale. Some correction was obviously needed for the early months.

This effect does not appear in testing older children because credits are given in calculating mental age for the years below the point at which the actual testing of a particular child begins. When, however, a scale provides for testing babies almost from birth, some adjustment of both C.A. and M.A. is indicated. The ages of these youngest babies need to be calculated from some date prior to the point where the test begins, and therefore, as this scale begins in the first month, we must calculate from some point prior to the actual date of birth. After all, birth, though a convenient date from which to measure a child's age, is but an incident or single event in the course of a continuous existence that began some time before. The problem is, how far back in time to go? Proceeding empirically and after some experiment, the convenient method was arrived at of adding eight weeks to both actual age and mental age as measured by the tests, for all babies below eight months of age, before working out the General Quotients. The baby whose result was G.Q. 185 in her first month now has the more accurate quotient of 117; the baby who was 50 is now 83 and so on. Thus if a child of age 3 weeks passed all items to 5 weeks, his uncorrected quotient would be 166, and this although he was actually only 2 weeks advanced! Similarly, if at 5 weeks a child passed tests to only 3 weeks, his uncorrected quotient would be as low as 60, a result suggestive of defective level, a very serious matter. After the correction is made, the first of these two children has a quotient of 118, a good result on this test, and the 2 weeks retarded child has a quotient of 85, a low but not seriously low result.

The validity of this method will be found in retest studies, which will show how the earliest test made in a particular case compares with the same child's results later on. One or two such cases will be shown at the end of this chapter.

To illustrate this point, we now present a study of the Standard

TABLE VI

Standard Deviations of the First Year, before and after adding Eight Weeks to Mental Ages and Actual Ages for Tests below Eight Months

Month	*No. of Cases*	*Average Quotient (uncorrected)*	*Standard Deviation (uncorrected)*	*Average Quotient, Final*	*Standard Deviation, Final*
I .	24	104·63	41·31	100·66	11·12
II .	30	104·60	32·99	101·83	13·88
III .	27	98·48	21·28	99·04	12·19
IV .	25	100·96	19·23	100·52	12·31
V .	27	100·37	17·31	100·26	12·42
VI .	27	96·04	16·54	97·15	12·41
VII .	22	99·82	14·95	99·86	11·56
VIII .	22	102·55	13·97	102·00	11·35
IX .	27	—	9·06	98·85	9·06
X .	29	—	13·70	101·79	13·70
XI .	23	—	9·90	99·83	9·90
XII .	25	—	10·23	101·80	10·23

Note.—The correction of adding eight weeks to both actual age and mental age before working out quotients applies only to babies below eight months of age.

TABLE VII

General Intelligence Quotients and Standard Deviations for the First Two Years (three-monthly groupings)

Months	*No. of Cases*	*General Quotient*	*Standard Deviation*
I to III . .	81	100·59	12·74
IV to VI . . .	79	99·39	12·59
VII to IX . . .	71	100·17	10·67
X to XII . .	77	101·13	11·64
XIII to XV . .	73	99·59	11·01
XVI to XVIII . .	72	98·58	12·69
XIX to XXI . .	66	98·68	12·65
XXII to XXIV . .	52	98·90	12·62
Total . . .	571	—	—

Deviations as a measure of the dispersion of the results in monthly groupings for the first year of the tests, together with the final estimate of these same dispersions after the correction just referred to above has been applied, adjusting all the quotients of babies below eight months of age. It will also be seen that, as the deviation is modified, so do the quotients approximate closer to 100.

It will be seen that the uncorrected Standard Deviations show a steady drop from the first month to the eighth month. After this correction, the Standard Deviations are seen on the average to be close to 12·0 throughout. This is seen more clearly when the results are shown in three-monthly groupings and continued to the end of the second year. (See Table VII.)

The Frequency Distribution

Let us now examine the frequency distribution of the whole group (N = 571), after this correction has been applied.

The distribution is shown in Fig. 7. The curve is normal. The average General Intelligence Quotient of the total sample of 571 babies between 2 weeks and 104 weeks of age is seen to be very close to 100, being 99·69. The Standard Deviation which we have just studied in some detail is seen to be 12·1209 for the total group. Thus 12·0 may be taken as the approximate Standard Deviation of the new scale.

The relationship of this scale to other scales will be investigated in further research. Already a number of children tested as babies on the new scale are being tested, as they reach their third year, on the Stanford Revision of the Binet Scale, and the Terman-Merrill Test. The new scale is also being extended beyond the second year, so that detailed studies will be possible on the relationships between these several tests. The reason for the somewhat narrower Deviation of this scale, as compared with the other scales mentioned, is its different character, for it measures the child's abilities on a broader front. More stress is laid on manipulative skills and on locomotor development than is the case with the Binet Tests. These do not of course cover the period when these matters of acquiring the fundamental motor skills are so significant, and they are in consequence more narrowly intellectual. The broader the test and the more varied the abilities measured, the narrower the Deviation on the total test. When we come to a further analysis of the dispersion of results on the sub-scales, the reverse will be found, as these sub-scales are limited in range to tests of a particular type and the dispersion is wider. But these further studies must be left for publication later.

It should be noted that in view of the differences between the Standard Deviations of different scales, differences of interpretation of the results are of great importance. The Standard

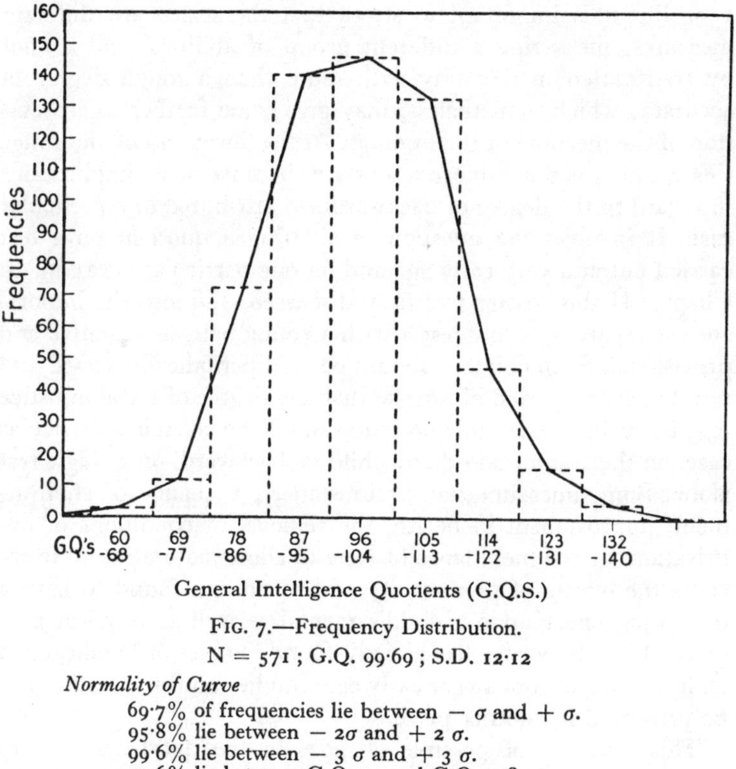

General Intelligence Quotients (G.Q.S.)

FIG. 7.—Frequency Distribution.

N = 571 ; G.Q. 99·69 ; S.D. 12·12

Normality of Curve

69·7% of frequencies lie between $-\sigma$ and $+\sigma$.
95·8% lie between -2σ and $+2\sigma$.
99·6% lie between -3σ and $+3\sigma$.
50·6% lie between G.Q. 92 and G.Q. 108.

Deviation of the Stanford Revision is approximately 15, and that of the Terman-Merrill Revision about 17 to 18, for the youngest children. This means that higher quotients can be obtained on these tests at the upper end of the distribution than are possible on the new scale, and much lower results at the lower end of the distribution.

The question of the point at which a result may be suggestive of mental defect must be considered with care. As will be seen, the entire range on the new scale will probably be between a little over 60 and a little below 140. The sample includes at the lower end several very handicapped children. The lowest result was *G.Q.* = 66 and the highest *G.Q.* = 137. Only five children are above 130. A result of 132 on the new scale might be regarded, in consideration of differences of dispersion, as roughly equivalent to I.Q. (Stanford) of 140 and to I.Q. (Terman-Merrill) of roughly 150. But it is important to stress that the scales are different measures, measuring a different group of abilities, and cannot by transmuted in this way with more than a rough degree of accuracy, which, nonetheless, may give some further interpretation of the meaning of the findings. At the lower end of the range this warning is much more important, because of its implications in regard to the degree of backwardness attributed in a particular case. It involves the question of allotting a quotient on a test carried out at a very early age and on one particular occasion. In Chapter II this matter was fully discussed, and also the importance of regarding a low result with a young baby as tentative and provisional. Such children should be seen periodically, tested and retested over a period of time so that any degree of social injustice may be avoided. Certainly no action should be taken in a particular case, on the assumption that a child be backward, on a single test alone. Sometimes unusual circumstances, a change of environment, improvement in health, the removal of conditions of deprivation, or the mere lapse of time to allow maturation to overcome the effects of prematurity and so on, are found to have a mitigating effect upon a child's mental as well as physical progress. This the writer has already found in cases of handicapped children tested from a very early age. Studies on this question will be presented in another place.

This question of possible changes in the quotients of very young children raises other questions, among the most important of which in this connection is that of the reliability of the scale. Below will be found what evidence has so far been collected during this research on the general validity of the test.

General Validity of the Scale

No systematic programme of retesting selected samples or unselected samples of the population has so far been undertaken, although this is contemplated. It happened, however, that a number of children were seen more than once in the course of the testing, and a few were seen several times. A total of 60 children belonging to the main sample of 571 were seen twice, and it may be useful first to see how the second test on these children compared with the first. In many cases the two results were very close—in some cases identical. No second test was more than 12 points above or below the first test in any case. The group of 60 retests includes eight children who from the retest point of view may be regarded as special cases. In these eight cases severe illness or other special circumstances were found to have been followed by a change in the quotient when compared with the first test. It is probable that these conditions had a deleterious effect on one or other of the tests according to the circumstances; for it was found that where such special circumstances preceded the first test only there was a rise in the quotient seen in the second test; conversely, where the special conditions arose between the two tests, a drop in the second result was measured. In a few cases where further tests again were taken, a rise in the result was found from the third test onwards. For the moment, the figures include all children without exception who were seen twice, remembering that at these very tender ages subtle changes readily take place in a baby's reactions, and that these may be reflected in a test result. In fact, this particular test appears to be a very delicate measuring instrument, especially in the first year of life, responsive to subtle changes in a child's psychological state.

Differences in Age at First and Second Test

The distance in time between the two tests varied from 7 weeks to 70 weeks. As mentioned earlier, development is very much more rapid in the early weeks and months of life than later on. The short 7 weeks interval between tests was in the case of a baby seen at 2 weeks of age and afterwards at 9 weeks. At the latter level a child is quite different from what he was at 2 weeks, and in this case there was no overlapping of tests taken. This is true in all cases retested, that there was no overlapping of tests taken. The average interval between tests was 30 weeks.

Time Intervals between First and Second Test

Range: 7 weeks to 70 weeks.
Average interval between tests: 30 weeks.
In no case any overlapping in tests taken.

Test-Retest Correlation. (See Scatter Diagram, Table VIII.) The two sets of tests were correlated with the result: $r = \cdot 87$.

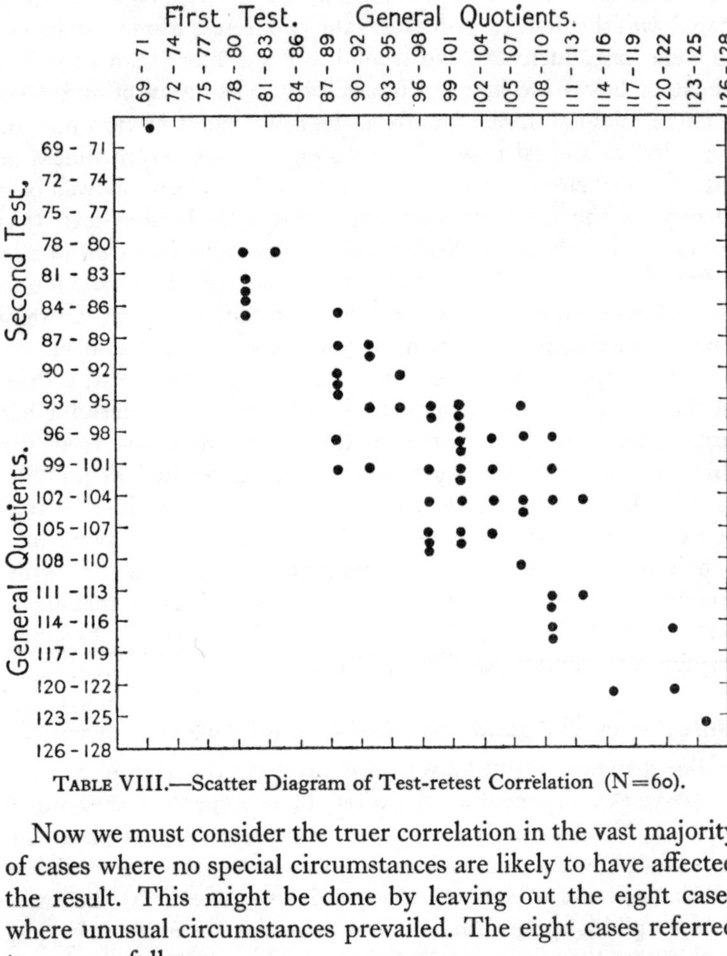

TABLE VIII.—Scatter Diagram of Test-retest Correlation (N=60).

Now we must consider the truer correlation in the vast majority of cases where no special circumstances are likely to have affected the result. This might be done by leaving out the eight cases where unusual circumstances prevailed. The eight cases referred to were as follows:

(1) First Test, 112 Second Test, 103
A drop of 9 points.
Details: (*a*) C.A. 12 weeks, G.Q. 112
(*b*) C.A. 80 weeks, G.Q. 103
Interval, 68 weeks.

This child had a difficult birth experience, an emergency cæsarian was necessary. The child was jaundiced and delicate, but improved rapidly and was doing well at 12 weeks. Later she developed nervous symptoms, and was slow at crawling and fearful of any attempt to walk. There was little locomotor activity at 80 weeks and a low score on this sub-scale. This caused a drop in the quotient. She still was quite good in other directions. The problem appeared psychological.

(2) First Test, 90 Second Test, 100
A rise of 10 points.
Details: (*a*) C.A. 12 weeks, G.Q. 90
(*b*) C.A. 20 weeks, G.Q. 100
Interval, 8 weeks.

This baby was four weeks premature, was delicate and had feeding difficulties. When first seen he was improving, but was very much under weight, as was to be expected. Eight weeks later he was making great strides, and the effects of prematurity and post-natal illness were being left behind, with an accompanying rise in the quotient. This rise in quotient after an interval has been noted in other premature babies, seen when very young, and also in under-weight children, such as full-term but very tiny twins.

(3) First Test, 91 Second Test, 103
A rise of 12 points.
Details: (*a*) C.A. 13 weeks, G.Q. 91
(*b*) C.A. 50 weeks, G.Q. 103
Interval, 37 weeks.

This case had a bad birth history (the child scarcely survived), followed by post-natal malnutrition. By twelve months he had become a healthy baby of normal weight. His generally improved condition was accompanied by an improved G.Q.

(4 and 5). Slightly premature twins.
First twin: First Test, 103. Second Test, 109.
Details: (*a*) C.A. 32 weeks, G.Q. 103
(*b*) C.A. 62 weeks, G.Q. 109
Interval, 30 weeks.
Second twin: First Test, 100. Second Test, 109.
Details: (*a*) C.A. 32 weeks, G.Q. 100
(*b*) C.A. 62 weeks, G.Q. 109
Interval, 30 weeks.

These babies were very small at first and the second twin was very delicate. They tested at 100 and 103 during their eighth month and both at 109 in their fifteenth month. Excellent progress in all directions was made between the tests.

(6) First Test, 109. Second Test, 97.
Details: (*a*) C.A. 25 weeks, G.Q. 109
(*b*) C.A. 71 weeks, G.Q. 97.
Interval, 46 weeks.

This little girl made excellent progress at first and appeared a normal healthy baby. However, she was later found to be slightly spastic, and was making no attempt either to crawl or walk when seen at 71 weeks, although she was doing well in other directions on the tests. This was sufficient to depress the quotient.

(7) First Test, 111 Second Test, 119.
Details: (*a*) C.A. 88 weeks, G.Q. 111
(*b*) C.A. 99 weeks, G.Q. 119
Interval, 11 weeks.

This child, who was enjoying the first test and about half-way through, saw his mother who was holding her younger baby slip and almost fall. Nobody was hurt and with an older child the slight incident would have passed unnoticed. But the child under test cried out and showed symptoms of fear, and although the test was afterwards completed, the effects of this little fright are apparent in the result. This is shown by the second test taken 11 weeks afterwards, which gives a fair assessment of his ability level. These circumstances are mentioned to exemplify the comments on this subject made in Chapter II, for with a young child even a small upset can put him off the test and make further concentration on the tasks involved difficult. The sudden slamming of a door, barking of a dog, overturning of a chair or box of toys, such incidents as these can, if the child is nervous, cause tears and a breakdown in the test, due to the momentarily aroused insecurity. If the test is continued the result is likely to be affected, as in the case described. Of course, here other emotional factors were no doubt also operating.

(8) First Test, 101. Second Test, 92.
Details: (*a*) C.A. 50 weeks, G.Q. 101
(*b*) C.A. 95 weeks, G.Q. 92
Interval, 45 weeks.

This boy, a Day Nursery baby, reacted quite differently at the second test from his bright outgoing responses when seen at the nursery on the first occasion. At the second test he was silent, almost morose, and scored very low on the speech column. It was found on enquiry that he had had a particularly prolonged and unhappy period of hospitalisation between the two tests and had barely settled down again at the nursery.

Further studies of detailed results on the scale and individual results on the sub-scales will be found in Chapters VII and VIII, where profiles of test results will be presented.

It may be revealing to omit the 8 cases just described—which are the only ones among the 60 retests in which such conditions pertained—from the correlation and see what effect this has on the result. This has been done, and the correlation of the results of the two tests on the remaining 52 children, whose histories showed no such disturbing or unusual conditions, arrived at, with the result: $r = \cdot 92$.

We may therefore regard a correlation (test-retest) of about ·9 as typical of this scale.

A Further Retest Study

1. Several children were seen more than twice in the course of this work, and one little boy was followed through with repeated tests from 5 weeks old to 52 weeks. He was seen seven times during his first year. The results of these seven tests are given below.

Tests	*C.A. at Test*	*General Intelligence Quotient*
I	$5\frac{1}{3}$ weeks	126
II	$9\frac{1}{3}$ "	125
III	$15\frac{1}{3}$ "	127
IV	$20\frac{1}{3}$ "	127
V	$35\frac{1}{3}$ "	128
VI	45 "	129
VII	52 "	126

The consistent way in which the scale is capable of working in the case of a healthy, normally progressing child is clearly exemplified here. The correction for age of babies under 8 months was applied here in the first four tests. This boy was intelligent. We now therefore show a backward one.

2. Here is a child seriously retarded who was tested five times between the ages of 8 months and 40 months. The first four tests were done on the new scale, and the fifth also, but here it was possible to go on into the beginning of the third-year tests of the Stanford Revision, and the relevant credits were added.

Tests	*C.A. at Test*	*General Intelligence Quotient*
I	33 weeks	67
II	44 ,,	69
III	60½ ,,	63
IV	74½ ,,	66
V	3 years 4 months	69

3. Here is a premature baby tested five times. He is a fundamentally intelligent child, gradually overcoming the effects of the handicap of prematurity.

Tests	*C.A. at Test*	*General Intelligence Quotient*
I	4 weeks	111
II	7⅔ ,,	113
III	24⅔ ,,	118
IV	35⅔ ,,	123
V	86½ ,,	123

Perhaps sufficient has been said at this stage of the research to illustrate the consistency of this new method of assessing the general intelligence of these very young subjects and its general reliability. In the next chapter the general thesis will be further illustrated by profile studies.

CHAPTER VII

PROFILE STUDIES OF NORMAL INFANTS

In the present chapter we come to the first part of a study of the Developmental Profiles of the children tested in the main sample. Developmental Profiles provide a further method of studying the abilities of individual children, and provide also a means of comparing one child with another in a new and different way. Without any attempt to subscribe to or formulate any theory of psychological or ability types, or even to claim or suggest any permanence for the shape of the profile in any particular case, we shall nonetheless show profiles in groups, to illustrate what appear to be tendencies in certain children or groups of children, and to illustrate the great variety of reaction over the total field.

Developmental profiles, which may be illustrated by graphs or histograms, show the relations between the results on different kinds of test in individual cases. These have been used by other workers in their studies of infants, notably by Charlotte Bühler (1935), who drew profiles in the form of graphs of her cases. She did not present separate quotients, but based the profile on the developmental levels of the items passed. This can of course be done on our data, the profile being drawn on the mental ages or on the scores alone; indeed, this will often in practice be more convenient (though somewhat less accurate beyond the end of the first year). But if it is desired to compare one child with another of a different chronological age, or to compare one child's result with his own result taken at some other time, quotients, in so far as they eliminate the age factor, give a more suitable basis for comparison.

To express a child's result in the form of a profile is to provide a personal picture or record, such as a photograph might be, to show the shape presented by the varying ability levels, the qualitative rather than the quantitative nature of the mental picture.

From the diagnostic point of view, the profile would appear to be rich in possibilities, showing at a glance where a weakness or mental disability lies, or in what direction exceptional progress may be expected. Characteristic profiles indicate the specific effects of disabilities both mental and physical upon the several levels of the sub-scales, and therefore upon the total mental level or status of a child. Therefore, from the diagnostic point of view, which is the main theme of this work, the profile becomes the sequel towards which we have been working, the culmination of the various aspects of these studies of infants. It gives the final hint or clue to the questions: "What is the cause of this particular child's difficulties?"; "Is his disability due to a general retardation or to some specific handicap?" The profile method appears to help us in answering these questions, and is therefore justified in spite of the additional work involved in the somewhat detailed assessment. (See Appendix I.)

The profile method would, however, be of little value if the several scores on the tests did not rest back upon some degree of statistical equality in the separate scales. A score of, say, 20 must have the same meaning in terms of mental level in one scale as it would have in any of the other four scales, otherwise the profile would be merely misleading and valueless. As we have shown in Chapter V, the five sub-scales in this new scale are all very nearly equal in difficulty, to achieve that having been the main task of the standardisation (Chapter V); and so it is now possible with some confidence, and for the first time, to build profiles on the results of testing babies, that show with some degree of accuracy the total mental picture in any individual case at the time of test. (See Table V.)

Whether the profile has any permanence—that is, whether it maintains its shape on successive tests in the course of the individual history of a child, or indicates any fundamental characteristic or shape in his inborn abilities—can only be determined by further research. But the grouping of cases of normal children of varying ability to be shown below should throw light upon these urgent questions and possibly give some indications for further investigation.

As a preliminary approach, let us first look at some typical profiles of children who display a certain evenness of development on each of the several scales. These are the all-round babies. They are not very numerous. Their progress on the five scales appears to be going forward equally or nearly equally in all directions. The several ability scores march ahead abreast of each other. The result is a profile closely resembling a straight line if shown graphically.

DEVELOPMENTAL PROFILES

Cases 1–4

SHOWING EVENNESS OF DEVELOPMENT

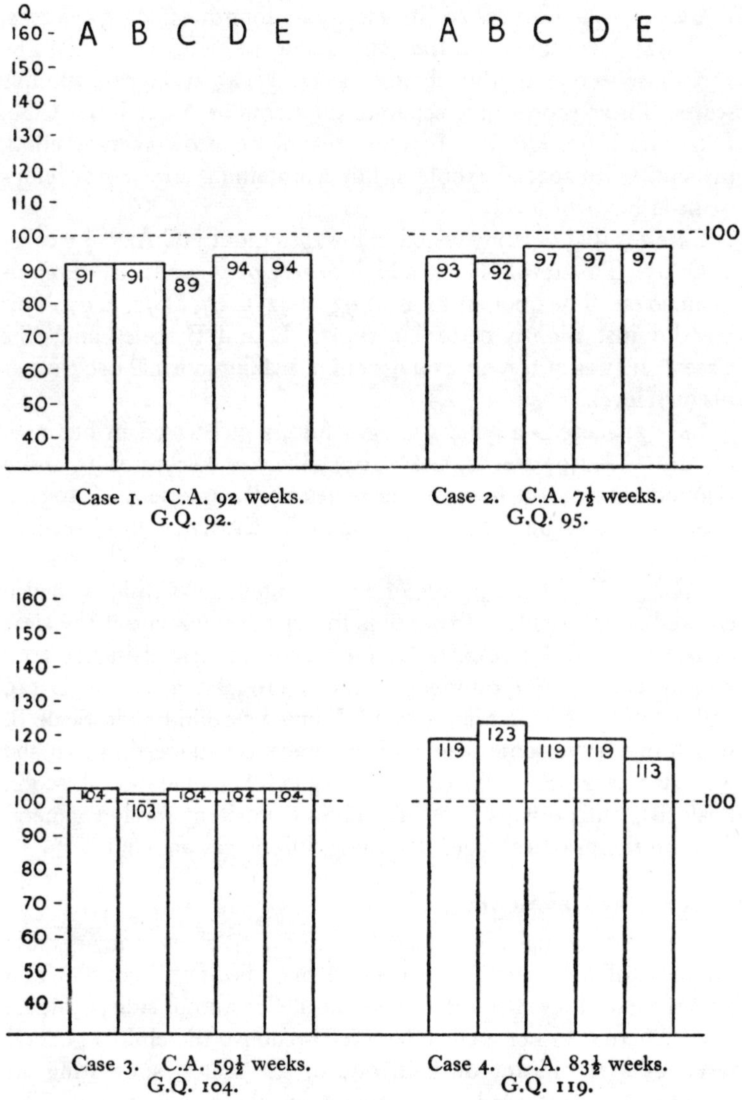

FIG. 8.

In the accompanying diagram (Fig. 8) are shown the histograms of four such cases (Cases 1 to 4). The method of arriving at the separate quotients for the five sub-scales will be found fully described in Appendix I.

Case 1 is a boy tested in his 22nd month (C.A. 92 weeks, G.Q. 92). His scores and the consequent quotients are seen to be very close to one another, being 44, 44, 43, 45 and 45 on the five scales. These scores give separate quotients of A 91, B 91, C 89, D 94 and E 94. He was therefore testing as a low-average child, presenting no special problem, but maintaining an even development at his own level.

Case 2 is that of a boy tested in his 17th month (C.A. 71½ weeks, G.Q. 95). This result shows a high degree of evenness in development so far. The quotients are: A 93, B 92, C 97, D 97, E 97. This boy did just slightly better on the C, D and E scales and, like Case 1, he was at test an average child, making normal progress at his own level.

Case 3: Here is a good average child, a girl tested in her 14th month (C.A. 59½ weeks, G.Q. 104). She has a score of 35 and a quotient of 104 on four of the scales and a quotient of 103 on Scale B. Such a high degree of equality in the five scales is exceptional.

Case 4: Here is the profile of a more intellectual child who also showed a high degree of evenness in her development at the time of test (C.A. 83½ weeks, G.Q. 119). She was tested in her 20th month, her separate quotients being A 119, B 123, C 119, D 119 and E 113. A drop is seen in Scale E and a certain rise in Scale B, which may have some diagnostic significance, suggesting that she was at test a well-adjusted child (good Personal-Social score, Scale B), but perhaps may prove less competent for her general level on the practical side. But these differences are slight.

Locomotor Development

The next group of profiles (see Fig. 9) show considerable evenness of development, except in one specific direction. The first of these show such differences on the locomotor side (Scale A) only. There is either a considerable rise above the child's general level, or a significant drop in one of the scales, suggesting an accelerated or retarded development in that one direction. The number of such cases is considerable, and they raise certain theoretical questions (see below). Of course, where such differences are

DEVELOPMENTAL PROFILES

Cases 5–8

Showing Rapid Locomotor Development (A)

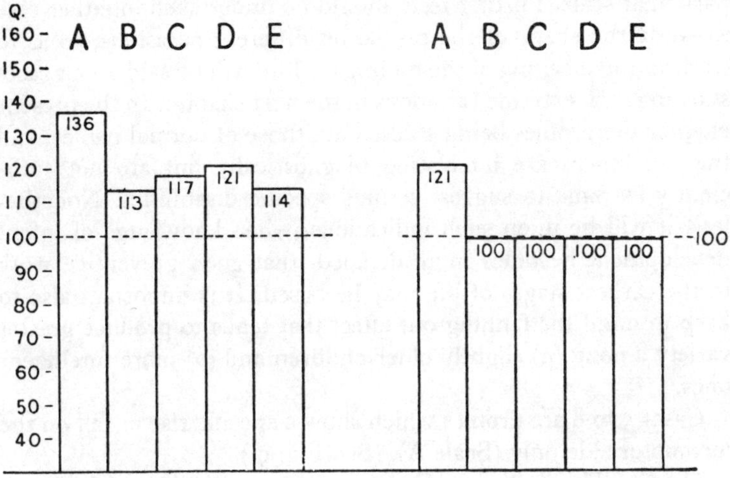

Case 5. C.A. 67½ weeks.
G.Q. 120.

Case 6. C.A. 84 weeks.
G.Q. 104.

Showing Slow Locomotor Development (A)

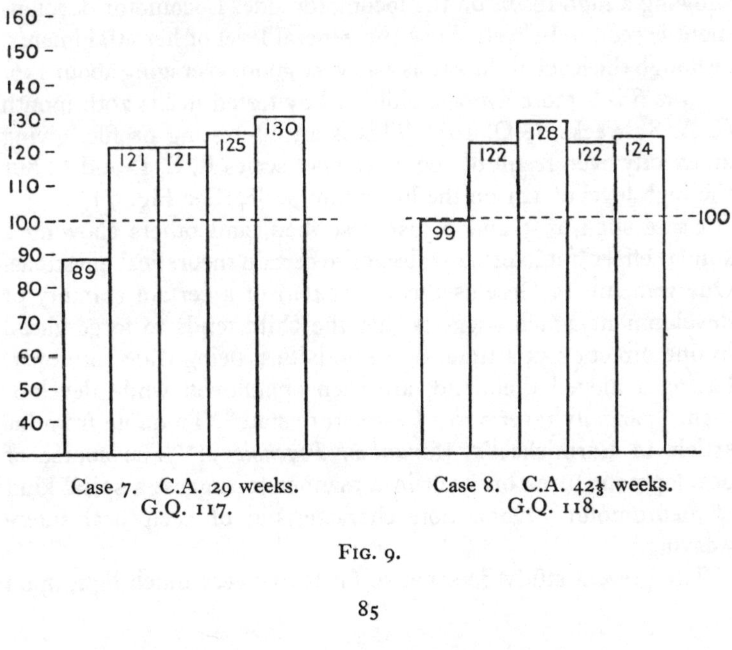

Case 7. C.A. 29 weeks.
G.Q. 117.

Case 8. C.A. 42⅓ weeks.
G.Q. 118.

Fig. 9.

extreme they suggest either some outstanding ability in one direction, over and above the child's general level, or, if it is a drop, some disability may be operating to reduce the score on that particular scale. Further tests should be undertaken in either case to study the shape of the profile on different occasions, so as to confirm the meaning of the findings. More will be said about cases showing such extreme variations in the next chapter. In the present chapter the profiles being studied are those of normal babies, and the differences are interesting diagnostically but are not sufficiently extreme to suggest serious specific disabilities. Nonetheless, it will be upon such indications, when knowledge of infant development becomes more detailed, that good preventive work in the earliest stages of life may be based. It is important also to keep in mind the fanning-out effect that tends to produce greater variety among (*a*) slightly older children and (*b*) more intelligent ones.

Cases 5 to 8 are profiles which show a specific rise or fall on the locomotor side only (Scale A). (See Fig. 9.)

Case 5: This is the profile of a girl tested in her 16th month (C.A. 67½ weeks, G.Q. 120). The separate quotients are A 136, B 113, C 117, D 121 and E 114. She was at test a healthy, active child of superior ability, running and climbing everywhere and showing a high result on the locomotor side. Locomotor development is seen to be well above the general level of her attainments, although the level of the rest is also very good, averaging about 116.

Case 6 is a more average child, a boy tested in his 20th month (C.A. 84 weeks, G.Q. 104). This is an interesting profile, giving an exactly even result of 100 on each of scales B, C, D and E, but the high level of 121 on the locomotor scale. (See Fig. 9.)

Cases such as 5 and 6 just described, and others showing a similar effect but in other scales, raise certain theoretical questions. One remembers Gesell's theory (1946a) of a certain spirality of development which suggests that the child tends to forge ahead in one direction at a time. Some activities, being transitory only, having achieved their end, are then abandoned while development "partially reverts to a less mature state". To quote from his article in Carmichael's *Manual of Psychology*: "The course of development turns on itself in a manner to suggest a spiral kind of neuromotor organisation characteristic of reciprocal interweaving."

The present study does not so far throw very much light upon this matter. The differences as observed might be readily explained by reference to the well-known doctrine of "span of attention". This doctrine, when applied to the observed facts, may indicate that the child's general mental energy being limited at these stages of development, he is obliged to be selective in regard to those aspects of developing interest that are fundamental to his progress.

This is particularly relevant to the problem of mental development in the second year, where the field of possible activity becomes wider and the claims on the child's attention more complex. His energy becomes insufficient to maintain evenness of development at a level indicated by his total quotient, in *all* the possible measurable directions at once, and the general restlessness of this period is no doubt associated with these circumstances. The child is therefore forced to interest himself mainly in one set of activities at a time, and develops crazes or fashions, now for running and climbing everywhere, now for special or particular toys or kinds of play activity, or again for listening to and trying to imitate everything that is said around him as well as the noises of animals, motor-cars, trains, etc. The parents often report this kind of thing by such comments as: "He doesn't play with toys much now, he's just climbing everywhere"; or, "He has a perfect craze for bricks, and even cries when I want to take him out and he has to leave his toys"; or again, "She is chattering all the time now, stands at the window talking about everything that goes by; ought I to make her *play* with her toys?" They report these temporary crazes, which die out after a few weeks and give place to some other trend of development as the child's main interest.

The indications are complex. On the one hand the undoubted fact underlies this controversy that children do at all times as individuals differ from one another in every measurable direction, and this in spite of certain limitations within the framework of which normal progress must proceed. Some children will be found to do better than others, not only in the general level of their achievement but in regard to specific abilities. In infancy the seeds of these future trends are present, and these early indications are therefore likely to be reflected in the results of tests framed to measure such potential differences. But these circumstances may also be overlaid and complicated, in any attempt to interpret results, by the fluctuations of the child's developing interests from time to time. There is a stage early in the second year when most children are learning to walk, when the locomotor aspects of development are uppermost in interest and the child wants to explore his physical environment to his fullest capacity. He therefore spends a large part of his waking life creeping, pulling himself up by furniture, climbing into chairs, climbing steps, rolling over on the floor and so on, according to his stage of locomotor progress. His interest in manipulation of toys may at this time flag a little; he may also become more silent than previously, less anxious to be taken up and played with. He becomes altogether for the time being a physically active person. Farther on in the second year there is a return to locomotor interests which again become all-absorbing, the child wanting to run, to climb everywhere, to explore the garden and, if allowed, the street also and the world beyond the home. During this period the child's progress in other directions may appear to slow up, but the slowing up is relative only, the child returning his attention in due course to earlier activities or phases of his total mental growth, when the absorbing interest in the one particular type of activity abates. What effect these fluctuations of interest may have on actual profiles of children has not so far been determined.

In the present state of knowledge and in view of the great variety to be found in the profiles of children of different ages within this early period, it is impossible to formulate consistent theories. We must therefore be content at this stage merely to describe and analyse from this point of view the data available.

Case 7 is the profile of a somewhat younger child than those already mentioned, who appears highly intelligent but definitely slow for her level on the locomotor side. She was tested in her 7th month (C.A. 29 weeks, G.Q. 117). The separate quotients were A 89, B 121, C 121, D 125 and E 130. The low score on A is explained to some extent by the fact that she was earlier a delicate baby physically.

Case 8 (C.A. 42⅓ weeks, G.Q. 118): This boy is also a highly intelligent child, somewhat slow for his own general level on the locomotor side, although the result here is normal for his age.

Personal-Social Development

Differences in Personal-Social development are interesting because of their possible relationship to factors of maladjustment on the one hand and to speech development on the other. These

DEVELOPMENTAL PROFILES

Cases 9–12

High and Low Personal–Social Progress (B)

High on Scale B | Low on Scale B

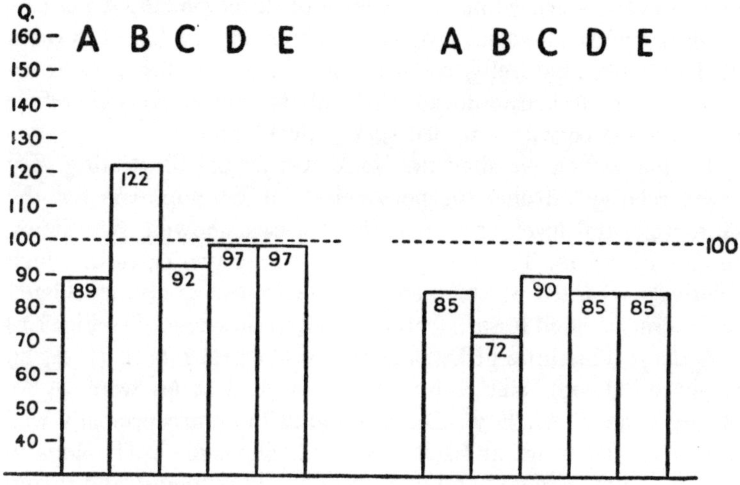

Case 9. C.A. 89 weeks.
G.Q. 99.

Case 10. C.A. $28\frac{2}{3}$ weeks.
G.Q. 84.

Low B Results associated with Poor Speech (C)

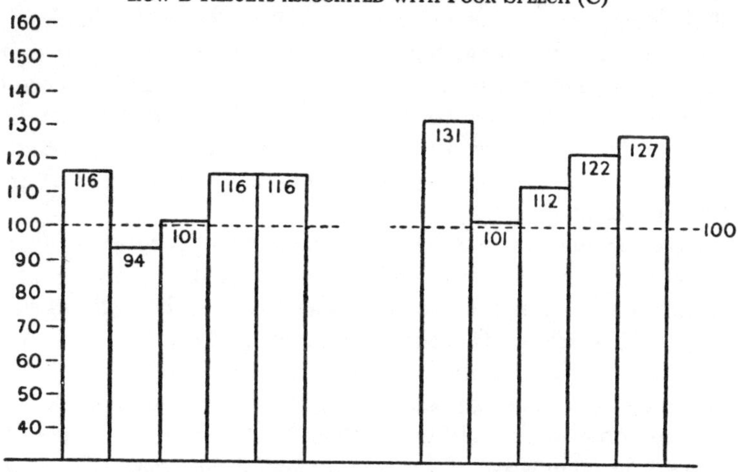

Case 11. C.A. $14\frac{2}{3}$ weeks.
G.Q. 109.

Case 12. C.A. $60\frac{1}{2}$ weeks.
G.Q. 119.

Fig. 10.

two are not altogether separate problems. A good personal-social development involves an outgoing attitude to others which normally results in a conative trend towards speech, this being one of the functions of speech or pre-speech, an attempt to convey ideas to others according to the level of development. A poor or inhibited personal-social progress, such as may be found in cases of deprivation, naturally tends to result in an unwillingness or inability to try to communicate with others, and is likely therefore to be associated with retarded speech development.

In this section we shall first look at a profile illustrating very great relative advance in personal-social development for the child's general level, and secondly at a case showing retardation in this direction. These will be followed by two cases in which relatively retarded personal-social development is also associated with some, though lesser, degree of speech slowness. (See Fig. 10.)

Case 9: This little girl was tested in her 21st month (C.A. 89 weeks, G.Q. 99). Her results on the several scales were: A 89, B 122, C 92, D 97, E 97. She was found to be exceptionally well adjusted for her age and self-possessed. She came easily alone to the examination room, and was friendly and outgoing, and this in spite of having a very mediocre result on all the other tests.

Case 10: This is the profile of a young baby, a boy tested in his 7th month (C.A. 28⅔ weeks, G.Q. 84). He showed a level on three of the scales of 85, was even doing well at speech for his level, vocalising and babbling, but was not yet taking much notice of people or passing items of the personal-social scale at his general level. It is probable that this would be readily corrected when he came to the stage of realising the social significance of his sounds and began to imitate speech more deliberately. (Quotients: A 85, B 72, C 90, D 85, E 85.)

Cases 11 and 12 present very similar pictures to each other, but at different G.Q. levels and very different ages. (See Fig. 10.)

Case 11: This is the profile of a girl seen in her 4th month (C.A. 14⅔ weeks, G.Q. 109). The other quotients were: A 116, B 94, C 101, D 116 and E 116. She was therefore down on the personal-social scale (B) below her general level, and speech was also to some extent affected, although she actually reached an average level in view of her chronological age. She was when tested neither noticing people nor responding to speech at the level she achieved on scales A, D and E.

Case 12: Here is a boy tested in his 14th month (C.A. 60½

DEVELOPMENTAL PROFILES

Cases 13–16

Studies of Speech Development

Relatively High Speech Development

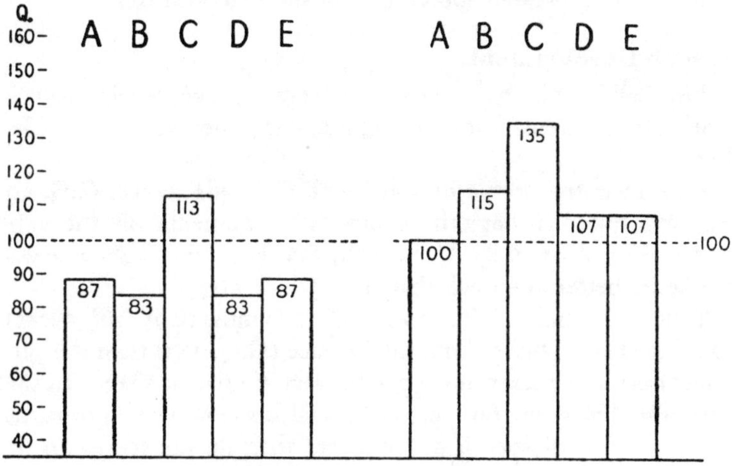

Case 13. C.A. 38⅓ weeks. G.Q. 90.

Case 14. C.A. 76½ weeks. G.Q. 113

Relatively Low Speech Development

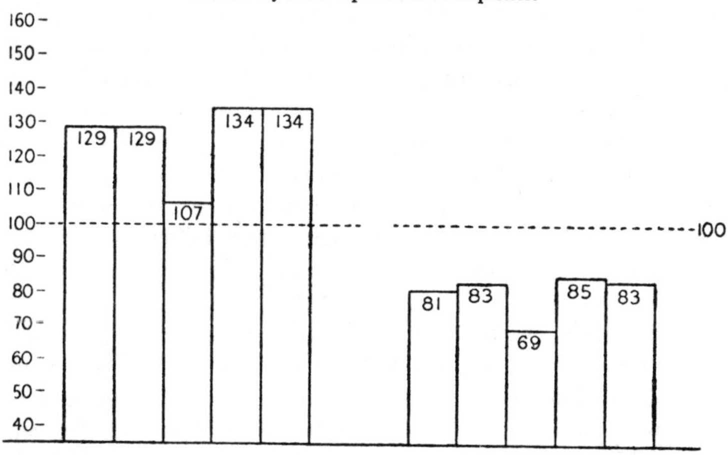

Case 15. C.A. 22⅓ weeks. G.Q. 127.

Case 16. C.A. 60½ weeks. G.Q. 80.

FIG. 11.

weeks, G.Q. 119). Other quotients were: A 131, B 101, C 112, D 122 and E 127. He is therefore seen to have been well above average level in general development and in three of the scales, but, like Case 11, he had a poor personal-social development and a somewhat depressed speech level associated with this.

Speech Development

We shall now look at a few cases where speech development is markedly different from development in other directions. (See Fig. 11.)

Case 13 is the profile of a girl with C.A. 38⅓ weeks, G.Q. 90. She was tested in her 9th month. The quotients on the sub-scales were: A 87, B 83, C (Speech) 113, D 83 and E 87. She was markedly better at speech than at anything else.

Case 14 is similar. This is a girl of 18 months (C.A. 76½ weeks), of somewhat higher general intelligence (G.Q. 113) than the previous case, but presenting a profile very similar in shape. In this case also the score for personal-social development approaches nearer to that of speech development than do the scores on the other scales. Other quotients: A 100, B 115, C 135, D 107, E 107.

Case 15: This little girl was tested in her 6th month (C.A. 22⅔ weeks), and found to be a highly intelligent baby (G.Q. 127), normally outgoing and active. Other quotients: A 129, B 129, C 107, D 134, E 134. She did exceptionally well on scales A, B, D and E, but her level dropped on Scale C. She had so far made only a little above average progress in the direction of speech, and was an unusually quiet although happy baby. There was no question of observed maladjustment in this case, nor any suspicion of deafness. Her speech progress was actually above the average for her chronological age, but nonetheless well below her level in other directions. These details are seen reflected in the profile (Fig. 11).

Case 16: Here is the profile of a boy seen in his 15th month (C.A. 60½ weeks, G.Q. 80). Other quotients: A 81, B 83, C 69, D 85, E 83. This is therefore a case of slow general development. The profile shows quite serious retardation at speech development, although personal-social progress is consistent with the general level. He is therefore to be regarded as a non-intellectual child, showing serious backwardness at speech. This slower speech development in children of generally low G.Q. is character-

DEVELOPMENTAL PROFILES

Cases 17–20

Studies of Manipulative Skill

Relatively High Manipulative Skill

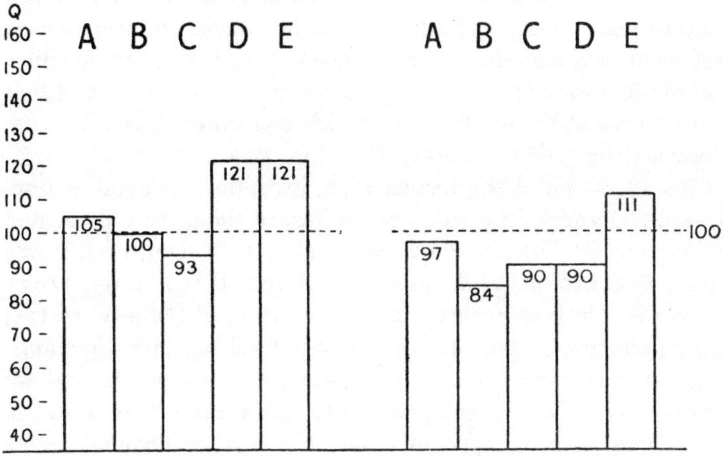

Case 17. C.A. 63½ weeks.
G.Q. 108.

Case 18. C.A. 96½ weeks.
G.Q. 94.

Relatively Low Manipulative Skill

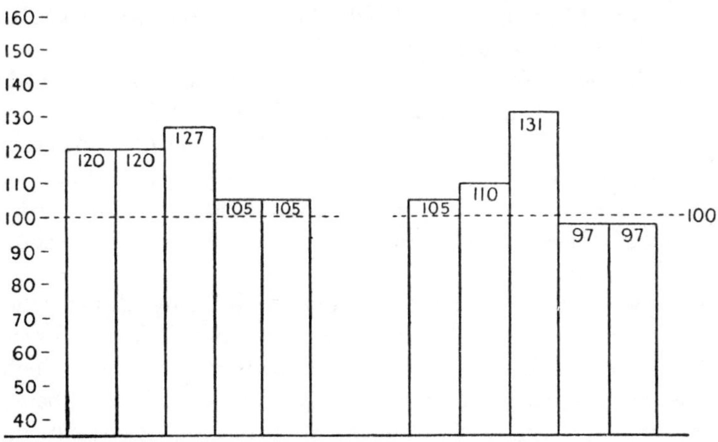

Case 19. C.A. 14 weeks.
G.Q. 115.

Case 20. C.A. 92 weeks.
G.Q. 108.

Fig. 12.

istic, and found in many cases at the lower end of the frequency distribution. (See Chapter VIII, Cases 25 to 28.)

Manipulative Skills (Scales D and E)

Turning now to some cases that show anomaly on the practical or performance side, we find here, too, occasional children, whose profiles in each case show a higher level in the histogram on either Scale D or E or both of these; and there are also other children who are slow at manipulating materials or incompetent with toys. These are the unhandy babies. (See Fig. 12.)

Case 17 is one of the former type, exceptionally good at tests of scales D and E in relation to the rest of the picture presented by her results. This child was seen in her 15th month (C.A. 63½ weeks, G.Q. 108). Other quotients: A 105, B 100, C 93, D 121 and E 121. On both scales D and E she reached the level of 121, doing performance tests far beyond her level in other directions. This was also associated with a lower result at speech, and we appear to have here, even at this early age, a case of a practical as opposed to a verbal type of child; but further detailed retest studies of the profiles of such children as this are needed before such conclusions can be safely drawn.

Case 18: This is the unusual profile of an average child in his 23rd month (C.A. 96½ weeks, G.Q. 94). Other quotients: A 97, B 84, C 90, D 90 and E 111. He shows a somewhat irregular development with a definite rise on Scale E.

Cases 19 and 20 show the reverse picture of those just studied.

Case 19: This is a boy tested in his 4th month (C.A. 14 weeks, G.Q. 115). Other quotients: A 120, B 120, C 127, D 105 and E 105. This case therefore shows superior levels on scales A, B and C, suggesting good progress on the locomotor side and also socially and at early speech, but showing results of only average level on scales D and E.

Case 20: This is a much older child, a girl tested in her 22nd month (C.A. 92 weeks, G.Q. 108). Other quotients: A 105, B 110, C 131, D 97 and E 97. This child's profile therefore shows a high degree of irregularity, the range or "scatter" of her results being from 97 to 131. She does brilliantly at speech, but her results on scales D and E are of only average level. Here again one may ask: "Is this a verbal child, likely to do well verbally in the future and less well on the practical side of the curriculum? Or is this merely one of the fluctuations of development to which reference has

DEVELOPMENTAL PROFILES

Cases 21–22

Closely Similar Profiles in a Pair of Twins

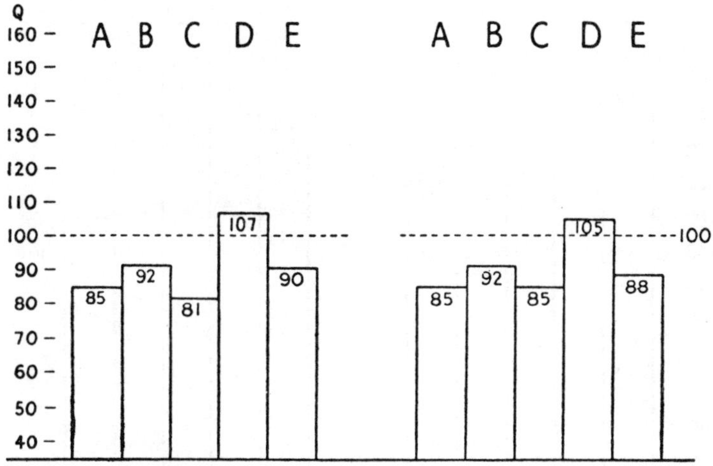

Case 21. C.A. 45⅓ weeks. G.Q. 91.

Case 22. C.A. 45⅓ weeks. G.Q. 91.

Fig. 13.

already been made?" At this stage, nearly two years of age, where the child is approaching a level at which she will soon be able to tackle ordinary verbal tests, such as those in the Binet Scale, the results are more likely to be predictive than is the case with younger babies. But some slight degree of maladjustment may also be suspected where such a wide "scatter" in the results exists. (See Fig. 12.)

Profiles of Twins

How do the profiles of twins tested at the same time look in relation to one another? (Fig. 13.)

Cases 21 and 22 are non-identical twin boys tested in their 11th month (C.A. 45⅓ weeks. Both boys had G.Q.s of 91).

Case 21, the older twin, had quotients as follows: A 85, B 92, C 81, D 107, E 90.

Case 22, the younger twin, had quotients of A 85, B 92, C 85, D 105, E 88. The profiles (Fig. 13) show the striking likeness in the shape of these two sets of results.

DEVELOPMENTAL PROFILES
Cases 23–24
Two Highly Intelligent Babies

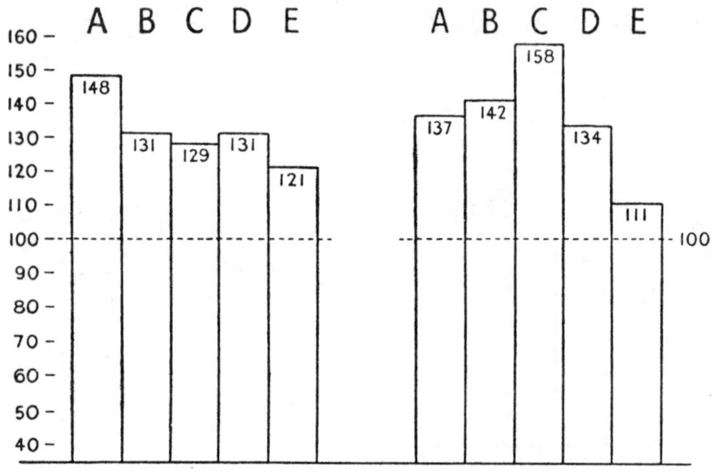

Case 23. C.A. 40 weeks.
G.Q. 133.

Case 24. C.A. 76 weeks.
G.Q. 137.

Fig. 14.

Another set of twins, girls seen at 27 weeks, had quotients as follows:

(*a*) A 80, B 94, C 80, D 80, E 75. G.Q. 82.
(*b*) A 80, B 89, C 80, D 80, E 80. G.Q. 82.

To conclude this chapter, it may be of interest to look at the profiles of two of the cleverest children in the sample, one in the first year and one in the second.

Profiles of Superior Children (See Fig. 14)

Case 23: This is the profile of a boy seen in his 10th month (C.A. 40 weeks, G.Q. 133). The other quotients were: A 148, B 131, C 129, D 131, E 121. Here the results are seen to be a little varied, but all are high. At under 10 months this boy was pulling himself up by the furniture and had learnt to stand alone. He was climbing into chairs and almost walking. He was babbling freely, using long sentences of jargon, and was also using two words clearly and in their right context. He could sing a little in response to music and enjoyed rhymes sung to him. He showed interest in mechanical toys and already looked at pictures with interest. He could manipulate a pencil a little, and could open the first set of the test boxes, taking off the lid and removing the cubes without help. He was well adjusted socially and learning self-help nicely, putting his arm ready for his coat, etc. In all directions this child at 10 months showed quite definitely a high level of ability. (See Fig. 14.)

Case 24: This is the profile of a bright little girl seen in her 18th month (C.A. 76 weeks, G.Q. 137). Other quotients: A 137, B 142, C 158, D 134 and E 111.

At 17½ months this little girl could *walk* up and down stairs without climbing but in an almost adult manner, and could be trusted on the stairs alone. She could climb up to stand on a chair, could seat herself at table, could jump off a step and kick a ball. She had exceptionally good body balance for her age. She helped to dress herself, taking off some of her garments unaided, including shoes and socks. She put away toys, with encouragement, and could be trusted with breakables. At the time of the test she was talking freely and clearly in short sentences; she named all the toys in her box, and also the Binet objects in the "naming objects" test at three years. She named ten pictures in the vocabulary test, knew and gave her first name but not her second name. On the performance scale she assembled the three test boxes correctly, played constructively and built a high tower. She scribbled freely with a pencil, made strokes and attempted the circle, but without full success, reaching "circular scribble" stage. She did not enjoy the form boards, and did these to only 18 months' level, but this, we must remember, is her actual age! The test gave approximately an all-round 2 years' result at just under 18 months of age. Her level on the speech scale was higher than this, as will be seen from the quotients and from the profile; the M.A. for C column was 120½ weeks or about 2 years 4 months. (See Fig. 14.)

Perhaps sufficient has been said and shown in this chapter to illustrate the possible use of profiles for studying individual differences in children. The babies studied in this chapter, although of varying ability, were normal infants, presenting no special individual problems for investigation; yet the indications are of great variety of reaction, even between children of similar developmental levels, to tests of different types. The method gives the examiner or research worker opportunity to study in greater detail the mental make-up of a child than is possible if we allot and therefore take into consideration a single quotient only. Moreover, it makes more exact measurement of individual differences in both the educational and diagnostic fields possible, these taking the place of mere impressions or hunches, upon which most examiners of infants and young children have at times been obliged to depend.

In the next chapter we shall see these individual differences in the developmental profile in a more exaggerated way in special cases of mental retardation or specific handicap; and the usefulness of differential diagnosis in getting a more detailed and also exact assessment may become more apparent.

CHAPTER VIII

DIFFERENTIAL DIAGNOSIS OF MENTAL HANDICAP IN SPECIAL CASES

IN Chapter VII we studied very briefly some of the varied profiles of children most of whom were well within the normal range of ability. None of them presented any serious special problem, although a few were somewhat backward.

In the present chapter we shall illustrate our thesis with studies of several groups of backward and otherwise handicapped children, and tiy to show how the study of the shape or pattern of a child's results can assist psychological diagnosis.

Profiles of Backward Children

The first profiles to be shown are fairly straightforward cases of uncomplicated backwardness. In Fig. 15 are shown four profiles of backward babies from the group which comprises the lower end of the frequency distribution. They are all included in the main sample of 571 children, and are very typical of the most backward section.

Before examining these profiles it is pertinent at this stage to enquire at what point, or below what point, in the General Quotient range a child should be regarded as so seriously backward that he is classifiable as mentally defective. As has been pleaded in several places, great care should be taken in any particular case before a child is finally regarded as of defective level because of the extremely young ages of these subjects under consideration, and also because of those factors or special circumstances discussed in Part I that may cause fluctuations in results. It was there urged that several tests of a young baby should be made at intervals before a final diagnosis was arrived at if the result on the first test was low. This cannot be stressed too often. Having devised, standardised and made available a method for assessing the mental level of such young children, there is a responsibility to these same children, and to others like them, in insisting that the test be applied with discretion, and with reservations in particular cases.

Having again reiterated this warning and assuming that fair safeguards will prevail, we must now determine below what point in the new scale a child must be regarded as defective if he should continue to test at that level. This may be determined by the Standard Deviation of the test. On the Binet Scale (Stanford Revision) an Intelligence Quotient of 70 (that is, twice the Standard Deviation of 15 below 100) was usually taken as the borderline between the normal and the sub-normal, taking of course other factors into consideration and allowing for a borderline group between about 67 and 73. The Terman-Merrill Test has a wider Standard Deviation, especially among the youngest children tested in that study, and a determining figure for these young ones at about 66 with a borderline between 63 and 69 would appear appropriate. In the new (Griffiths) scale the Deviation is smaller, being approximately 12·0, so that strictly the determining figure would be about 76 with a borderline between 73 and 79. Certainly children who persistently test as low as this on the new scale are very backward children; those below 73 must be regarded as probably sub-normal. They should be retested at intervals.

Another method of arriving at the determining figure for the borderline between mental defect and normality is to study the lower end of the Frequency Distribution and the numbers of results falling within the lowest two per cent., for this figure of two per cent. is approximately the percentage of mentally handicapped persons usually found in any representative section of the population of this country. Two per cent. of our sample would provide an expectation of about eleven children of the sub-normal group, and the lowest eleven General Quotients are actually 75 or lower. So that 76 appears to be a suitable figure and, allowing for borderline cases, about 73 may be taken as the lower end of the normal range.

Turning now to a study of the profiles of four of these backward children (see Fig. 15), their G.Q.s are: 74, 74, 77 and 78; so that all of these may be regarded as backward or borderline cases on the criteria just stated.

The profile method, however, displays certain interesting characteristics of the relative ability levels of these children. It will be seen at once that these four profiles—and they are very typical at this mental level—are all strikingly similar in shape.

DEVELOPMENTAL PROFILES

Cases 25–28

CHARACTERISTIC PROFILES OF BACKWARD CHILDREN

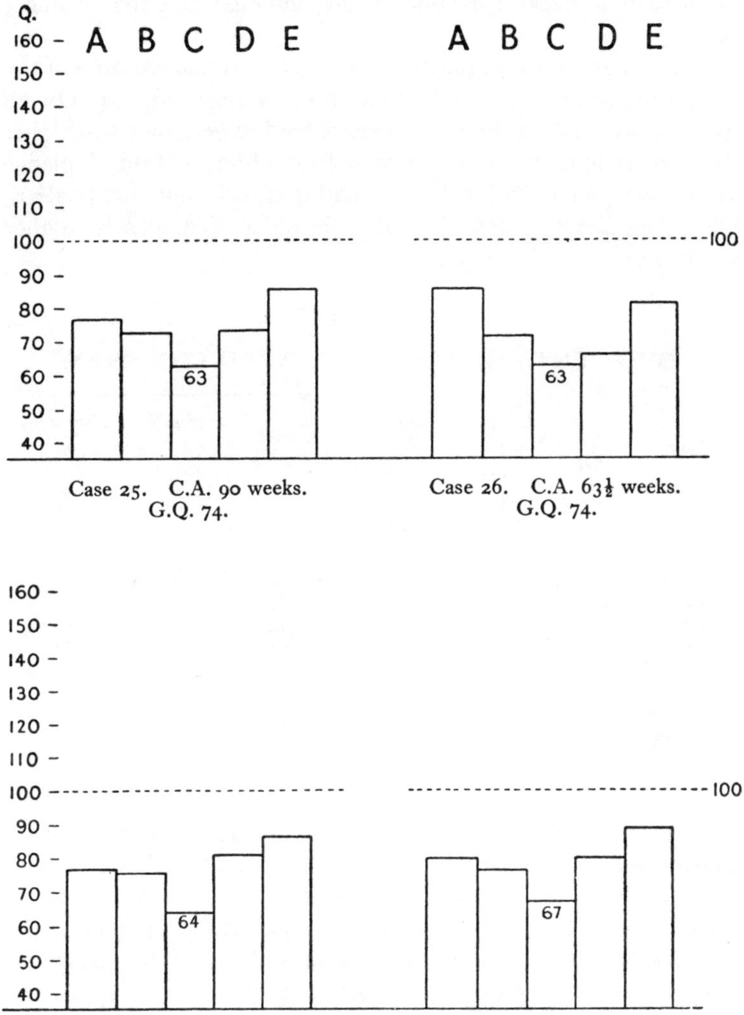

Case 25. C.A. 90 weeks.
G.Q. 74.

Case 26. C.A. 63½ weeks.
G.Q. 74.

Case 27. C.A. 80 weeks.
G.Q. 77.

Case 28. C.A. 39⅔ weeks.
G.Q. 78.

FIG. 15.

They all show a trough in the histogram at Scale C, the verbal scale. The score on C is the lowest in each case, as will be seen also from the figures in the table below. Here the several results of these four backward children are summed and the averages taken.

These therefore are non-intellectual, slow verbal children of the borderline group. On the C scale, they average only 64. On all the four other scales, however, results tend to be somewhat higher than on Scale C, though they vary from child to child. A glance at the average results for the four children will show that Scale E, which measures practical skills, shows a significantly higher result, i.e. 85 on the average.

TABLE IX

QUOTIENTS OF FOUR BACKWARD CHILDREN

Case No.	*G.Q.*	*Loco-motor Scale A*	*Personal-Social Scale B*	*Speech Scale C*	*Hand and Eye Scale D*	*Perform-ance Scale E*
25	74	77	73	63	74	85
26	74	85	72	63	66	81
27	77	77	76	64	81	86
28	78	80	76	67	80	88
Averages:	76	80	74	64	75	85

The indications, then, are that such children as these are likely to continue rather slowly on the verbal side and, if they also continue at this general level, will require a concrete and practical type of tuition later on. They will form that part of the population that needs a type of education specially designed for backward children. The somewhat more encouraging figure of 85 on the average in Scale E (Performance) should be noted.

However, something more vital is here at stake. As these children get older, and assuming that they keep this General Quotient level and this general mental picture, they will inevitably be examined in due course from the point of view of school or other placement. They will almost certainly be given the usual tests, which are mainly verbal in type. If so, the results will not be as shown here, with General Quotients averaging 76, but will inevitably approximate to results on the verbal scale, Scale C (about 64), and will therefore appear to be suggestive of a degree of mental defect. These children will thus be in danger of being so regarded because of a slow development in this one direction, whereas, as the profiles amply show, *each one* of these children is capable of doing somewhat better on *every one* of the other four scales, all of which measure activities important to development. Moreover, they are capable of an average quotient of 85 on Scale E.

It would perhaps be going too far to suggest that the low speech scores, seen so clearly in these profiles, should be regarded as representing a specific verbal disability in every one of such cases, but certainly to throw the results into relief in this way does show in what directions a somewhat better development can be expected and what kind of education might be planned and from what age, to help this problem. Stepping beyond the province of this work for a moment and trespassing upon the educational field, the writer would like to put forward a plea for more definite speech training for young children of this group in Day Nurseries and Nursery Schools, and would suggest that their subjective monologue be encouraged to be expressed aloud, as in play therapy practice, whilst they are occupied with toys and materials; and, above all, that mothers of babies, no matter how young, remember to *talk* and *sing* frequently to their children and encourage the ready verbal response. Other factors are of course relevant here: the general happiness of little children, the avoidance of any kind of deprivation, the extension of knowledge of infant psychology and of the mental hygiene of the very young. For it is apparent that even these near-defective babies have some mental assets that might be developed, and that the placement of babies in institutions for defectives should indeed be only a last resource and delayed as long as possible, lest social injustice be incurred.

Profiles of Spastic Babies

Leaving this problem, the implications of which are too far-reaching to be dealt with adequately here, let us now turn to a study of the profiles of babies suffering from varying degrees of cerebral diplegia, with resulting spasticity. Those selected from the records are cases 29 to 32, shown in Fig. 16. In each of the four cases there is a history of difficult birth. In these cases and for the rest of this chapter graphs are being superimposed upon the histograms to make even more definite the characteristic shapes of the profiles of children suffering from different disabilities.

It will be seen at once that the score in Column A (Fig. 16), which measures locomotor development, is low in each of these four cases, showing the serious effect of this physical disability upon the locomotor side of their progress. But the several states of these four children differed considerably from one another and these differences are also reflected in the mental picture.

In *Case* 29 the condition was most extensive, both arms and both lower limbs being affected to some extent. Tested in her 21st month, this child was making no attempt to walk. If lifted to her feet, she could balance holding on to furniture, but she could not pull herself to the standing position. She moved about the floor a little in the sitting position. She was reported as being "lazy about walking". The examination also showed a weakness on the manipulative side, where she was generally awkward and unhandy and failed all performance tests for her age level. On verbal tests she had a quotient of 85, but because of these disabilities the total result is seriously depressed.

In *Case* 30 the condition was confined to the legs (paraplegia), and when first seen this child was very backward generally. She had the expected low result on the locomotor side (A.Q. 59); the average of the rest of her results, which were fairly even, would be 78 if the Locomotor Score were omitted. She was therefore an all-round slow child, seriously handicapped in regard to locomotor development. Later on, and after medical care, she was retested. She had by then (in her 21st month) achieved a slow and awkward walk, still preferring to cling to the furniture whenever possible. On this second occasion she was found to be improving in all directions with a General Quotient of 87 at 90 weeks of age. Her results on the second test were: A.Q. 68, B.Q. 84, C.Q. 93, D.Q. 101 and E.Q. 90. This profile will be observed to have the same general shape as the one shown, but giving now average results in all the scales except A (Locomotor), which is still far below her general ability level.

Case 31: This little girl was tested at 14 weeks in connection with the main sample of children. As soon as the baby was placed on the blankets she jerked over to one side, being unable to main-

DEVELOPMENTAL PROFILES

Cases 29–32

PROFILES OF SPASTIC BABIES

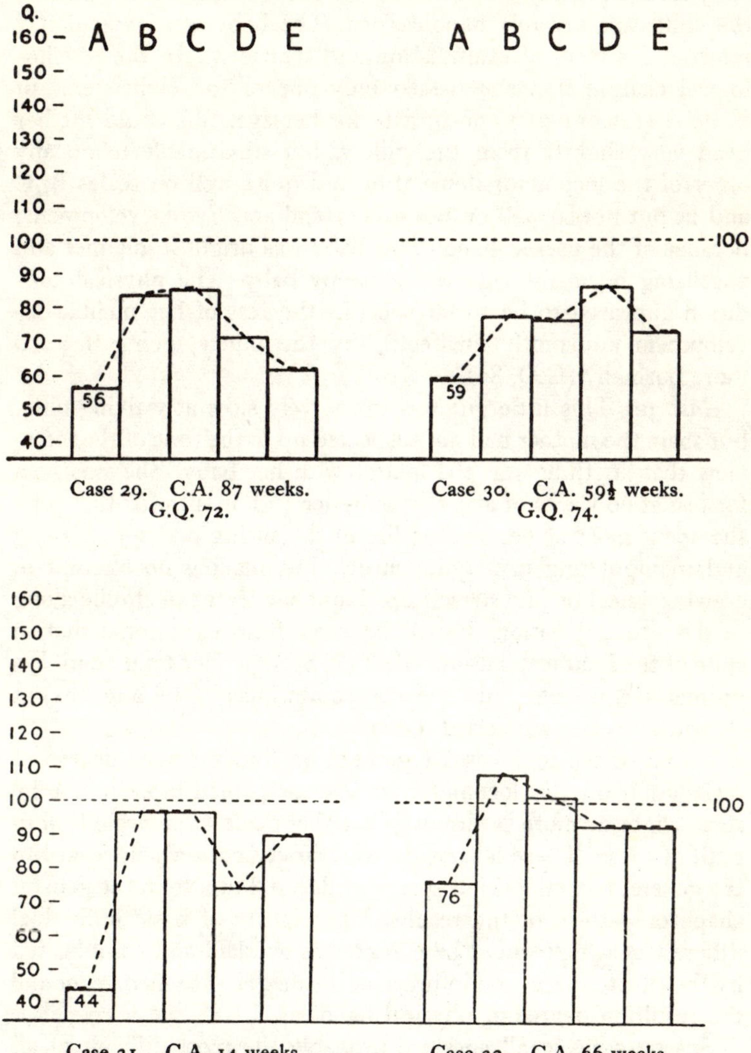

FIG. 16.

tain her balance as placed. One leg appeared stiff and one hand useless. There was a degree of torticollis. The paralysis affected the whole of one side in this case. The mother mentioned that her baby would lie only on one side, but she was quite unaware that the child was severely handicapped. The baby was immediately referred for medical examination and treatment. In the psychological examination she passed only one of the eight items of Scale A (Locomotor) appropriate for her age. She could lift her head very slightly from the pillow, but was unable to do any other of the locomotor items. She did quite well on scales B, C and E, but not so well on Scale D (Hand and Eye Development) because of the useless hand. This baby was bright in manner and vocalising normally. She was a happy baby. The physical condition appeared to be so far specific, the rest of her mental development apparently unaffected by the injury, going forward more normally (G.Q. 80).

Case 32: This little girl was excessively slow at walking only, but again the mother had not suspected up to the time of the interview that anything was the matter with her baby. She was seen for test at 66 weeks of age, that is in her 16th month. At that time she spent most of her waking life in the sitting position, playing and manipulating toys quite nicely, but making no attempt to crawl or kneel or pull herself up. Later she learnt to shuffle along in the sitting position. It will be seen from the profile that in spite of the handicap and its effect on Scale A, her total result is a normal average one, and she does quite nicely (108 and 101) at Personal-Social and Verbal Tests.

Taking these four cases together, we find a severe degree of retardation on the locomotor side, accompanied in each case by some slight or more severe drop in either Scale D or Scale E or in both of these. There is considerable variety not only in regard to the general mental level of spastic children, but also in the general shape or pattern of the results. The picture of basic individual differences which would be expected is overlaid and complicated by the effects, direct and indirect, of the degree of brain damage and the resulting degree of physical handicap.

Spastic cases at all ages are probably the most difficult of all types of handicapped children to assess in regard to general mental development. They also present difficult educational as well as diagnostic problems for the psychologist. (See Dunsdon, 1952.) In many older and more severe cases than these young cases shown here there is frequently mental deficiency and also speech impairment, but among spastic children there are wide individual differences of mental level. There are some of good or superior intelligence whose handicaps appear mainly physical, and others whose sad condition makes them ineducable or nearly so.

The profile method may help to distinguish, by its method of classification and separate assessment of the different fields of development, between the more severely and the less severely mentally handicapped on the one hand and between those who are mainly handicapped in one specific direction. But probably the most valuable service it can render is in its application to these early years, the testing of young babies making it possible to ascertain the effects of physical handicaps, and in particular cerebral palsy, upon the mental organisation almost from the beginning of post-natal life. In this field of the physically handicapped there is scope also for good preventive work as well as diagnostic and educational work for the clinical psychologist in conjunction with the pediatrician in the Infant Welfare Service.

Profile of a Deaf Child

Let us now look at the typical profile of a deaf child, *Case* 33. (See Fig. 17.)

This little boy was seen in connection with the testing of the main sample of babies. He was tested in his 20th month. During the examination he was noticed to watch the examiner's gestures eagerly, and to manipulate materials with some efficiency but in complete silence. He was reported to make a few noises at play, but to have no speech and none of the usual babble of younger hearing children, and was regarded as mentally retarded. He could hear loud noises, including loud voices, but could not hear whispered speech or low tones. He heard the clear note of a bell rung near him, but did not respond to the tuning-fork. He did not understand the speech of others because of a degree of hearing loss, and was in consequence almost completely aphasic.

The profile of this deaf child should be compared with the profiles of backward children shown in Fig. 15. A case of undetected deafness is frequently regarded as mentally backward, but the profile of a deaf child shows a much deeper trough in Scale C.

Following M. M. Lewis (1936) in his work on Infant Speech, we must recognise the complex nature of the normal infant's task in

DEVELOPMENTAL PROFILES

Cases 33 and 34

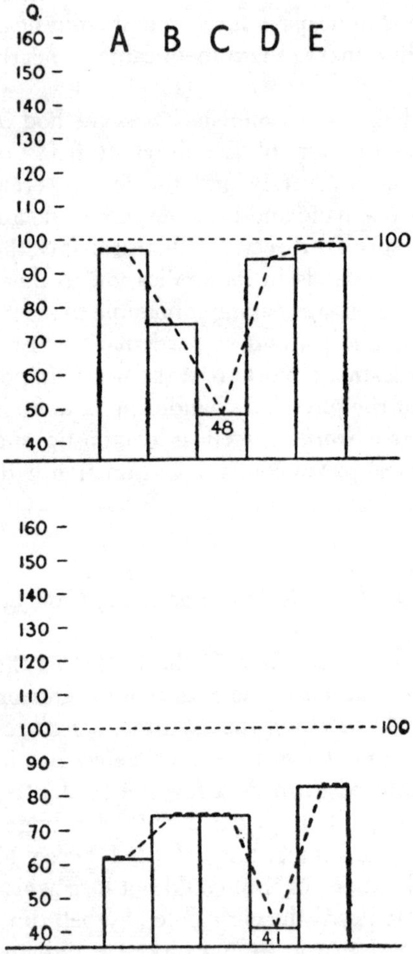

PROFILE OF A DEAF CHILD
Case 33. C.A. 84 weeks.
G.Q. 82.
Speech Development 48.

PROFILE OF A BLIND BABY
Case 34. C.A. 23 weeks.
G.Q. 66.
Hand and Eye Tests 41.

FIG. 17.

learning to imitate speech during the first year of life. For the deaf or partially deaf child, the acquisition of meaningful speech is complicated by the vast complexity of the speech of others, only part of which he hears. Speech is made up of patterns that are both phonetic and intonational; that is, there are varying rhythms, changing and alternating stresses, loudness and softness, and also differences of pitch. (See M. M. Lewis, p. 9.) In all these directions there is meaningful variety and considerable range, much of which is lost upon a child who has any degree at all of hearing loss, and his speech will consequently be affected to a greater or lesser extent.

We must remember also that speech learning depends upon practice, based on the infant's attempts at closer and closer approximation to what is heard. The child with impaired hearing is attempting to copy a defective model, and therefore develops a characteristic type of indistinct and slurred speech. A special type of education is indicated for such children. In this connection the work of I. R. Ewing and A. W. G. Ewing on deafness in young children, and their extensive work on the education of the deaf child, must be mentioned (1930, 1938, 1943, 1944, 1947).

The small boy we are considering shows the typical profile of the deaf child. As a deaf child grows older the trough tends to become deeper in relation to other abilities, unless he is having the special educational treatment that he needs. There is also in this case the lesser drop in the profile in the Personal-Social Scale which we have repeatedly found in such cases, due no doubt to the failure to hear and to comprehend the spoken instructions and urging of the mother in her attempt to train the child. In columns A (Locomotor), B (Hand and Eye) and E (Performance) he achieves a normal result.

Profile of a Blind Baby

Case 34: Here is the profile of a blind baby seen when very young, at 23 weeks (Fig. 17). The lowest result here, as would be expected, is in Scale D (Hand and Eye Development), as of course this child could not follow a moving light or look at objects near her; but when objects (for example, the bell-ring) were placed in or against her hand, she showed a near-average manipulative ability on Scale E. This was, in fact, better than her performance on any other scale. Only a few blind babies have been tested so far by this method. They all tend to show the characteristic drop on Scale D, but vary in regard to their level on the other four scales.

A Case of Inhibited Speech

Case 35: This little girl was tested twice, and we show both profiles in Fig. 18. Although very backward and needing to be given the tests for below two years, she was already just three years of age, and the test was continued in those directions indicated, into the third and fourth years of what will be the extension of the new scale when it is completed. She was at this time quite unable to do verbal tests.

The case was referred to the writer at three years of age because of an almost complete lack of speech. She was regarded as very backward, probably defective, and advice was requested in regard to education or placement. Deafness, although suspected, had been excluded by thorough investigation. As this case is likely to be of some interest to psychotherapists as well as to clinical psychologists, it will be described rather more fully than those that we have dealt with earlier.

As will be seen from the first profile (Fig. 18), the low-speech result was accompanied by slowness on the locomotor side (A), the child being fearful of stairs and not running or climbing normally. There was a history suggestive of emotional disturbance, and the child's psychological condition presented a picture of serious maladjustment. The profile when the child was first seen was a most unusual one. There was the expected trough in Scale C (Speech), the child's performance at speech being barely of the twelve-months' level. She knew two words in their context, but these were reproduced indistinctly. Column A reflects her nervousness and lack of normal adventuring, in climbing, running and general locomotor activity. Column B (Personal-Social) reflects her lack of co-operation in training and general lack of social adjustment in the home. She suffered from temper tantrums and destructiveness. Beyond the home, she was excessively fearful. The general picture so far suggests severe retardation and might also suggest deafness, the profile being similar in shape to that of the deaf child shown earlier. But this child was not deaf. Her high performance, too, on the remaining scales D and E gave some hope that, provided her emotional state could be improved, she might be helped to develop towards a more normal intellectual level.

DEVELOPMENTAL PROFILES
Case 35 (I and II)

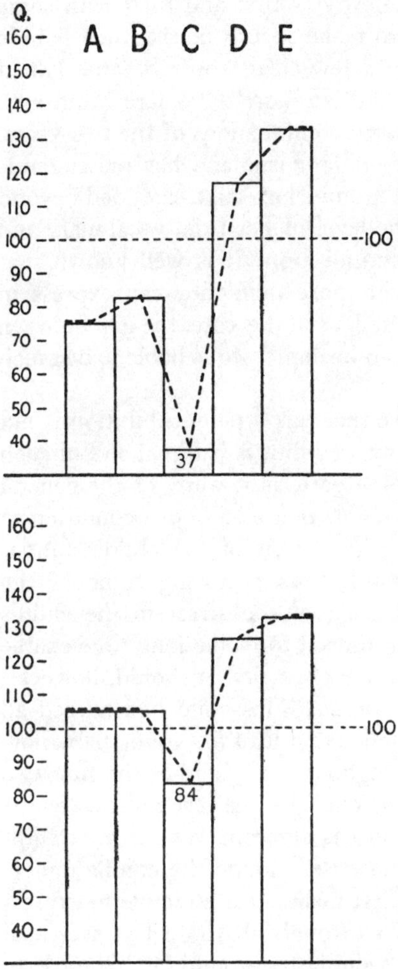

PROFILE OF A CHILD WITH INHIBITED SPEECH DEVELOPMENT (C)
Case 35—I
C.A. 36 months. G.Q. 89.

RETEST
Case 35—II
(after treatment)
C.A. 43 months. G.Q. 111.
Stanford Binet I.Q. 117.

FIG. 18.

Following the first psychological investigation, she was seen regularly for several months for play therapy with speech help. During this time she began, slowly at first and then with some acceleration in her progress, to make speech noises, then babble long strings of it, until at last a few clear words became joined together in brief phrases such as "No more", "Where Mummy", "All gone", etc., the typical word combinations of the two-years' level. But her comprehension of language and her understanding of what was going forward around her, alike extended beyond what would be indicated by the level of her brief vocabulary and slight attempts at verbal communication. It is well known that children usually understand far more than they can express in speech. Where speech is inhibited, as in this case, the gap between what is understood and what can be expressed is liable to be much wider than usual.

It is important also to realise that this type of inhibition is not within the child's control in any way, but is habitual and of such long standing that it has become part, as it were, of the general psychological make-up of the child. It is a stubborn condition to correct. Moreover, should our treatment of the child's fundamental attitude prove successful, thus removing some of the condition that has in the past caused the arrest in the child's speech, this will not quickly or indeed for some long time enable that child to talk, or at least to talk normally. It should, however, enable her to begin to try to do so! This child had missed all those long months of vocal practice that lead the young baby normally from stage to stage throughout the whole of the first two years from birth onwards. This explains the resemblance to the profile of a deaf child, but the cause is different. Where the attempt at speech is inhibited, as in this case, though the child's understanding may grow, when she first makes real attempts to express herself verbally, she has to go through all those lost stages of practising, over and over, what she hears around her. She has to live through what Gesell would call the stages of *maturation*. It takes time for such a child to catch up, setbacks occur with the variations in the degree of emotional improvement, and treatment is likely to be lengthy. When this patient at last began using brief phrases and had also become happier, more active and to some extent better adjusted, a re-examination was undertaken with the result shown in the second profile (Fig. 18). The improved levels on all the scales except E, where she maintained her original high level, reflect her improved confidence in physical activity (A), her better social adjustment (B), her now rapidly developing speech (C), and her response to opportunities for manipulation of toys and materials (D). There is still a deep trough at C in spite of the quite phenomenal degree of progress made in this direction. The indications are now not merely hopeful but good, the general quotient now being 111, and, given further speech progress, this is likely to go still higher.

When first seen, this child, because of her disability on the verbal side, was quite unable to tackle the Binet Simon Test. When retested on the Griffiths Scale six months later, she was also given the Binet Test, being by then able to do some of it, in order that her level thereon could be ascertained and compared with her second G.Q. This result on the Binet Scale was 116. Taking into account the difference in the Standard Deviation of the two scales, this result is very close to the second G.Q. of 111, and is about what would be expected for a child of this G.Q. level. She also did the Goddard Form Board Test at the high level of 5 years, her actual age being then 3½ years! There is, then, no doubt that we have here a fundamentally bright child seriously inhibited in speech, as well as in general development, by severe emotional maladjustment. She still has a long way to go before her condition can be regarded as satisfactory, but the prognosis is good. It would be going beyond the scope of this report to enter into discussion of the emotional problem.

This case has been included here to illustrate the use of the profile method of diagnosis in many puzzling cases of neurotic or maladjusted children; and also the difficulties of distinguishing in certain cases the deaf from the defective, the severely maladjusted from the imbecile, the generally backward from the child with some specific disability. In this case we meet a child at one time regarded as deaf, later accepted as grossly retarded or defective, but who is now seen to belong to neither of these categories but to have been a nervous, unhappy, seriously maladjusted child, capable with help of a more normal development.

Conclusion

With this review of the profiles of special cases, we come to the end of this chapter and also of Part II. The presentation of the results of this research in these four chapters has necessarily been brief and to some extent sketchy. In every direction there is obviously further work to be done, not only on the scale itself with the further statistical analysis of the findings, but in two main directions.

1. In order that the method may be extended to the study of handicapped children between 2 and 7 years of age (and older), of the groups who present, as we have seen, so many diagnostic problems, it is essential to extend this work by carrying the scale up to about the seventh year, by a further standardisation study on a population of normal children of Nursery and Infant School ages.

2. Much further useful work remains to be done on the implications of the scale so far as we have gone, using the present data and extending them where necessary, in the study of normal babies, of speech development in particular, and of those other skills that make up normal development in this early period.

In Part III we shall present the scale in full and describe the method of its application in the testing of babies, with details for administering the several scales.

Part III

ADMINISTERING THE SCALE

CHAPTER IX

ENVIRONMENT FOR THE TESTING AND STANDARDISED APPARATUS

In Part III we shall describe the method used in administering the scale. The detailed instructions for giving the separate items of the five sub-scales will be found in Chapters XI to XV. However, certain preliminary considerations must first be discussed.

The Environment

An important consideration before attempting to test babies is the kind of environment in which the testing is to be carried out. Young children are sensitive to atmospheres, and whereas for them atmosphere is largely created by the personalities about them, the concrete environment also plays a part. Moreover, the effect of an unsuitable environment on the mother can have an indirect effect, through her, upon the child's reactions.

Tests will sometimes have to be carried out under difficult conditions or in unsuitable premises; but if the examiner is resourceful and knows what constitutes a good environment for the testing, he can use a short interval before the test begins to do something to mitigate conditions. When testing large numbers of normal babies for research purposes, the examiner must accept the conditions he finds in the various institutions and elsewhere, as for example in the children's own homes, and, with permission, quickly assemble those objects in the environment that are essential to his work, and get on with the examination with as little delay as possible. When doing special cases in Child Guidance Clinics, however, more consideration can be given beforehand to what constitutes a good environment for this work. We shall therefore begin by describing somewhat ideal conditions that might be aimed at and towards which psychologists specialising in this field of work might strive.

The Room.—Let us therefore proceed to examine a room suitable for testing any child under two years of age. This should ideally be of medium size, neither so small as to be crowded and leave no sense of space or freedom of movement, nor so large as to appear bare and forbidding. It should be a light room, if possible with a southern aspect, such as might be chosen for a child's nursery. It should be clean and bright, the walls, floor (unless covered) and the child's furniture painted in light tones. A few "properties" should be around, such as one or two attractive nursery pictures or a nursery frieze, a large doll, teddy bear or woolly toy, a large coloured ball and a large wooden horse on wheels. No small toys should, however, be available, other than those provided in the test material. The room should have a homely atmosphere, and this is largely created by the properties. The mother, too, is immediately reassured by the presence of toys or pictures.

Furniture and General Equipment.—The ideal room for convenient testing of babies must not be crowded with furniture. It should be planned so as to be easily adapted for testing babies of any stage of development from birth to two years. Different equipment is needed for use with babies of different ages. There should be a divan, not necessarily full size, firm but comfortable. A box-ottoman type of divan is a good idea, but is not essential. There should be a brightly coloured cover (washable) and blankets. The divan is used for taking the locomotor tests with very young babies and also to give the mother some rest by allowing her to put the baby comfortably down during the interview. A few large squares of muslin or sheets of paper, such as are used in Infant Welfare Centres, are essential, a fresh one being used for each young baby to lie on. Beneath the paper or muslin a sheet of mackintosh will protect the blankets. These things—blankets, muslin, mackintosh, etc.—must be kept spotlessly clean and stored away in a cupboard or in the ottoman.

Tables.—Two tables are needed. The one should be of normal table height. If there is a divan, this table need not be very large, about 3 feet by 5 feet being large enough to enable two people to be seated opposite to each other and for apparatus and writing materials. But if there is no divan, the table should be longer and about 3 feet wide, so that half of it may be covered by the blankets to make a testing table for the baby to lie on. It should stand near the middle of the room or, if the long one is used, with one end to the wall. The second table should be a kindergarten table of quite low height, suitable for an 18 months'

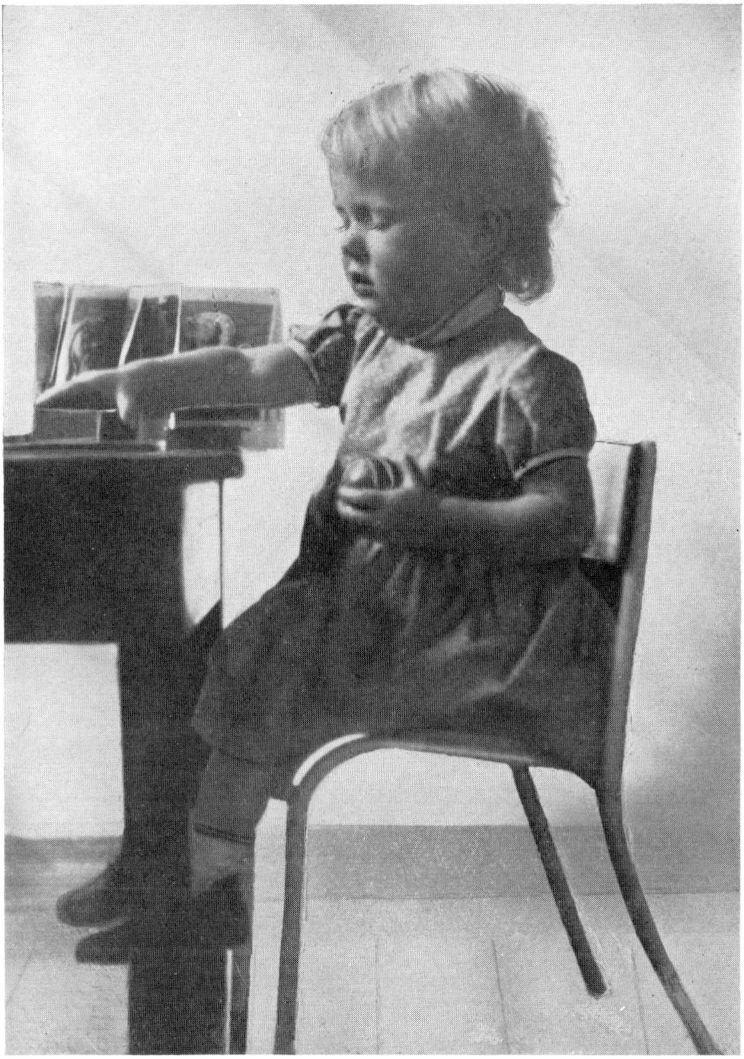

PLATE 10

This little girl is twenty months old. She is placing the insets in the three-hole board. The picture-book is still near her although she has finished that part of the test, and she still hangs on to a little ball that she does not wish to relinquish. Mother is seated near her for reassurance.

PLATE 11 The Apparatus.

child to sit at comfortably (2 feet square and 18 inches high). It can be nested under the large table when not in use. Two ordinary chairs of adult size are needed for the large table, and a kindergarten chair or comfortable low stool (see Plate 1, Frontispiece) for the toddler. A comfortable nursing chair, with cushions, low and without arms, is necessary for the mother to sit comfortably with her baby.

A cupboard is needed, large enough to take the few movable properties and the psychological apparatus, stationery, etc. The floor is best covered with linoleum, as this is smooth and comfortable for the crawling baby or toddler, and is easily kept in a hygienic condition. It should on no account be polished, but washed regularly with soap and water. An open space on the floor might be covered with a soft rug, preferably washable, or, failing this, a dark blanket should be available to be put down for the baby who is at the crawling stage. A folding play-pen is useful but not essential, and the inclusion of this item will depend on the size of the room. A small trolley on wheels, with two shelves, keeps the apparatus handy, and can be moved readily from table to divan or to any part of the room where the crawling child may have deposited himself. (See next chapter.)

The room should be comfortably heated in winter, and a large fire-guard is an essential item. This should protect any power-point, gas tap, etc., as well as the fire itself. There should be a fitted wash-basin with running water, and towels and soap.

Such a room as this would form the background for happy and efficient testing of any baby from birth to two years of age.

The Apparatus

The apparatus has been specially chosen, designed or made, and assembled for this work. It consists of a number of pieces light and easily packed into a small space. The black case with handle and fasteners is an unfitted writing-case, strong, neat and inexpensive, that just takes the apparatus with space in the lid for a file of forms, etc. (See Plate 11 for picture of the entire equipment.)

Full details for administering the test items will be found in Chapters XI to XV. Here we merely list and describe the apparatus, indicating in general its use.

(1) *A small coloured plastic ball that rattles.* This ball is kept for use with the youngest babies. It is useful for attracting the atten-

tion of the young baby before giving the early items in Scale D; because of the soft noise it makes when moved, it almost always arouses interest. When the child's attention has been arrested, the ring or bell-ring items can be more easily taken. It is also useful at a later stage for observing the development of the hand, and noting how the fingers and thumb come round an object.

(2) *A small coloured rubber ball.* This is very useful for getting into rapport with somewhat older babies. At the crawling stage it provides a bright object for the child to crawl after or attempt to crawl after (Scale A). It is also necessary for items in the second year, such as "Plays with ball, rolling" and "Can throw a ball", etc.

(3) *A brightly painted cornice ring with coloured cord.* It is used for such items as "Secures ring by means of string" (D 21) and also D 24, D 25, etc. (See Chapter XIV.)

(4) *The bell-ring.* This is a similar ring to that just mentioned, but without a cord. Instead, two little bells are attached to it. It is used for item C 4 and for early items of the "D" Scale. The sound, being softer even than that of the little hand-bell, is better also for the hearing tests, especially for testing a very young or highly nervous baby. These noise-making instruments must be used very sparingly, any continuous shaking or ringing of bells to attract the child's attention being liable to fatigue or frighten him. The softest tinkle of a little bell will attract the youngest baby without frightening him, and will indeed give pleasure. One tiny boy at $4\frac{1}{2}$ weeks took on an intent expression at the slight sound from the bell-ring, and then, at a repetition of the sound, produced a charming smile, the first smile his mother had observed!

(5) *A pair of red embroidery rings.* These are used for E 21, "manipulates two objects at once", D 19, and elsewhere.

(6) *A handbell.* This is used for item C 4, C 11, C 15 and other items in this scale. (See Chapter XIII.) It is a very small hand-bell, light and easy for a child to manipulate.

(7) *A torch.* Used in item D 1 and elsewhere.

(8) *A tuning-fork.* Used in item C 12.

(9) *A small plastic cup and saucer.* This is necessary for taking a number of items in the Personal-Social Scale (Scale B—see Chapter XII). Being practically unbreakable, it stands up to the somewhat rough usage it sometimes gets.

(10) *A plastic teaspoon.* This is a well-made spoon of teaspoon size, rounded and smooth, as the baby is liable to put it into his mouth during the test.

(11) *A pair of plastic beakers.* These are used for older children. to see if they can manipulate a vessel well enough to pour water from one cup to another (D 45).

(12) *A small wooden toy* on wheels with cord attached. This is used for general observation of locomotor development in the early part of the second year and also for items A 41 and A 42.

(13) *A car* to be pushed along. This is a well-made small tourer that can be pushed about by the child (Tests D 29 and D 36, etc.).

(14) *A car* to be wound up. This is the small "Morris", a well-made little motor-car used with older babies for observing locomotor progress and for several items in Scale D. It is excellent for getting into rapport with both girls and boys in the second year.

(15) *A sleeping doll.* This is also a very useful toy for general rapport purposes with older second-year babies, but its main purpose is for pointing out "eyes, nose and mouth", items B 42, 48, 49, 50. It is a well-made toy, 6 inches high, that will stand alone, with "real" hair, and eyes that open and shut. The doll must not be used as play material to amuse babies not yet ready to be given these items.

(16) *A mirror.* A small practically unbreakable mirror in a frame and with a stand, used for items B 19 and 25, and in other places. A second-year baby who does not yet *say* his own name, but knows it when used by others, will often point to the child in the mirror when asked "Where is Johnny?", etc. One little child of 18 months, previously rather silent, smiled happily at herself in the mirror and said "That's Susie" (her own name) quite clearly, thus passing C 34, and also giving the examiner an immediate indication of her level at speech; for example, "word combinations", item C 46, could straight away be credited.

(17) *A small picture-book.* This is used for items C 32, C 40, and also for B 41. A picture-book is a necessary piece of apparatus for observing children in the second year, as it can give a very good indication of a child's level of maturity in regard to books or pictures. There is a stage when a book or picture is a mere object to manipulate, that rustles when twisted about and makes delightful noises when torn up! Only in the second year, as a rule, does a child gradually learn to become reliable in the use of books. Parallel with this, pictures also, instead of being mere patches of colour with little meaning, gradually become observed more carefully and interpreted. This is rare before the beginning

of the second year. Babies must not be given opportunity to destroy the apparatus.

(18) *A small plastic box* for sweetmeats. This little box should be kept replenished with tiny sweets. It holds about six little sweets. These also are invaluable in getting into rapport with a shy child or keeping the child happy throughout the examination. But their main function is for a study of the way a child picks up small objects, fine prehension, etc. (B 28, D 22, D 23, etc.)

(19) *A tiny plastic doll*, smoothly finished, for one-month baby to hold. (E 6, E 9.)

(20) *Box containing twelve small toys.* This little set of toys is used in the study of language development, in the second year, for items C 37, C 41, C 43, etc. The toys are: chair, doll, ball, horse, dog, cat, cup, spoon, button, car, brick and penny. The manner of administering the tests will be described in Chapter XIII. The toys are packed in the small box. They are *not* glued to a board!

(21) *The form boards.* This is a new set of form boards. There are four boards and four insets. The boards are as follows:

- (i) *The circle board.* This is a square board, with a circular hole into which the large circular inset fits.
- (ii) *The square board.* This is a square board of the same size as the circle board, into which the square inset can be placed.
- (iii) *The two-circle board.* This has two circular holes in it, one larger than the other, to take two round insets.
- (iv) *The three-hole board.* This is a modified version of boards used by Gesell and by Terman and Merrill. It has holes cut to take the large circle, the square and the triangle.

These boards form a graded set which can be used with children from about the eleventh month. Fifty per cent. of babies at 13 to 14 months pass E 33. The apparatus is painted in bright colours with hard Chinese lacquer—the boards orange and the insets blue. These colours are very attractive to children of these ages.

These four boards and four insets provide for a wide range of ability, there being no less than eleven separate stages of difficulty separately measured. In the first stage the child is just able to place the one circle in the circle board. The last stage of doing the three-hole board rotated is reached only in the third year. Ten of these stages are gradually traversed by the baby during his second year. These are items: E 33, E 36, E 38, E 39, E 41, E 43, E 44, E 45, E 46 and E 47. Average babies at two years or less do not pass the three-hole board rotated.

(22) *Four yellow cubes.* These are the four cubes used in the first year for a number of items in Scale E, beginning with E 8: "Looks at box on table", and going on to E 10, E 11, E 14, E 15, etc., until in the second year they are merged into the brick boxes tests in Scale E. They are also used in Scale D for such tests as "Places one lid, box, or brick upon another" (item D 37), "Tower of three" (D 41), etc., "Train of three" (D 49) and other items. These cubes are painted a bright yellow. In items where more than four bricks are needed the two yellow bricks in the yellow test box may be added.

(23) *A packet of paper tissues.* These are used for the various paper tests including: E 2, E 5, E 12, E 18, E 22, E 32, etc.

(24) *The brick-boxes.* This is a new set of three test boxes with lids, each containing two bricks. Each box is virtually a separate piece of apparatus, and for earlier tests *one* box only is used—the red one. (See, for example, E 13, E 16, E 24, E 26, E 28, E 30 and E 31.) After this, *two* of the boxes are used, and later in the second year all *three* boxes are given. The various manipulative and other developmental stages that they measure are described in Chapter IV (Scale E). The idea for this set of boxes came from Froebel's Gift Three. Each set consists of a box, a lid and two cubes. One set is painted red, another set is blue and the third is yellow. The boxes are all the same size and shape, and the lids interchangeable for size. They fit very loosely.

Other workers have recorded ages at which babies first succeed in removing a lid from a box and putting a lid back on. In this new set of apparatus we have been at pains to standardise for size, shape and colour a set of boxes for measuring such skills. This is necessary because of the great variation in the difficulty of the task with the size, shape and material of the box. A child of nine months might manage to get the lid off a cardboard shoe box. At a year or later he might get a round lid off a tin canister, and so on. Some standardisation is necessary if this is to be a useful test. In the new form we have found it remarkably useful. A large number of stages of development can be tested for with this new apparatus. It gives ample opportunity for detailed observation of the development of manipulative skills. This set of apparatus is very popular with the babies; the older children are fascinated by it. It forms an excellent settling-down test and helps rapport.

(25) *A new set of twenty small coloured pictures* mounted on cards.

(26) *A piece of coloured felt* or woollen cloth, about 12 by 20 inches, is needed for test D 39.

(27) *A screw toy.*

(28) *The case.* This has already been described.

A number of containers are provided for the various pieces of apparatus. The examiner will also need a stop-watch, and he should provide himself with those items of apparatus necessary for the third-year tests of the Stanford Revision for those babies, under two years of age, who are capable of passing tests beyond the two-years' level. A few sheets of plain paper and some stumpy coloured pencils are also needed for the babies' scribbled drawings.

Care of the Apparatus

As will be seen, the apparatus contains a number of very small pieces, the loss of any one of which may make a test impossible to give. Great care is therefore necessary in assembling and re-assembling the materials. Small toys are liable to be dropped (or thrown down) by the baby, especially if he is about nine to fourteen months of age. Toys may roll to far corners of the room. These must be retrieved. (The writer can vouch for the possibility of testing 600 infants with scarcely any loss or damage to her first set of apparatus, but this has at times involved much searching in corners and under furniture!) An occasional loss or breakage may, however, happen, and this should be made good straight away. Babies should not be allowed to handle the material longer than is necessary for the required observation to be made.

The apparatus must also be kept carefully stored and in a clean condition. This last is particularly important when testing babies of the youngest ages. The plastic ball and doll, the ring and cord, yellow bricks, etc., used for these young children should be washed after every examination. Also, any piece of apparatus that has been in a child's mouth or has fallen to the floor must likewise be washed before it is used again. A good plan is to have a white enamel bowl or dish handy and, as these contingencies arise, the dirty apparatus should be placed in this receptacle, to be washed later.

The case provided is just the right size to take all the materials required for testing babies from birth to two years. It is a good plan to develop a routine of always repacking the materials into the case in the same way, after checking the contents of each small box. Any article missing is then quickly noted. The piece of felt, folded over the top, keeps the apparatus from rattling, and there is then also just room for a few forms and papers in the lid.

The brightly coloured apparatus is pleasant to use, and gives pleasure to the young subjects under examination.

In the next chapter we shall illustrate the method of approach to the infant and the use of the materials, by detailed studies of babies tested at different ages.

CHAPTER X

THE APPROACH TO THE INFANT IN THE TEST SITUATION

EVERY Educational or Clinical Psychologist who enters the profession from a background of teaching experience finds it necessary to adjust his attitude to the child to fit the new conditions implied in the test situation. The didactic approach gives way to the diagnostic approach. It is not easy to define this difference exactly, it involves a complex of changes; but in general it may be said that the psychologist must forget to teach and remember to observe; he must test for knowledge without betraying knowledge, and at the same time apply a new technique that is largely routine and unambiguous. Thus his function has a dual purpose, for, in testing children of school ages, whether normal children in schools or special cases in clinics, many matters extraneous to the actual test result are being observed and picked up by the psychologist as diagnostician, whilst at one and the same time he is working through a somewhat rigid questionnaire or posing problems in a standardised phraseology and within a standardised general procedure. Yet his manner with the child shows none of this duality; he shows sympathy, kindliness, interest in the child as a person and a desire to understand his difficulties and assess his qualities. He can break off the test to hear an anecdote bursting to be told, or allow a child to draw a picture, if that is likely to help his diagnosis. His assessment of test results forms an exact and scientific core of procedure and yet is overlaid, supplemented, edged as it were, by a fringe of observation and impression that tempers his attitude to the child and makes a more complete and understanding diagnosis possible. This is a skilled technique and implies special training. It also involves in some sense a veiled conflict for the psychologist.

In testing babies and very young children this situation is still further complicated by the immaturity of the subjects under test and by their complete lack of experience of anything approaching an examination. The older child may be aware that he is on his mettle, or is at least capable of understanding and responding to the examiner's suggestion that he should do his best. He accepts reassurance as to the nature of the test. The baby may not even understand the words used and is deaf to exhortations of any kind. He responds positively or negatively to a situation and is quite unaware that any kind of examination is going forward. In one sense the whole situation is in the hands of the examiner to manipulate; in another sense the child is himself master of the situation and, indeed, at times master of ceremonies! Yet the scientific core of exact observation and recording of results must remain unimpaired, while there is at the same time fluidity of procedure, involving a constant adjustment to circumstances on the part of the examiner, while the child apparently leads him where he will.

The duality or conflict of method is therefore even less veiled than before, and the need for some kind of special training even more evident. For on the one hand the child, if he is to be tested at all, must be kept happy and, with all but the youngest, happily occupied throughout the test; the mother's anxiety as she watches the child's varying performance must be allayed and her desire to correct or cajole him sympathetically restrained; the apparatus must be marshalled, protected from the child's inroads and produced at the psychological moments; yet all the while, on the other hand, the examiner quietly observes, records results on the printed form, prepares for the next test and observes again. The child explores, manipulates, adventures in the new environment. All that the examiner wants to know about him is there, flowing by as the child takes up a toy, investigates or discards it, babbles or laughs, crawls or trots about the room, runs to mother for reassurance, sits at the table and builds a high tower, and so on and on. There are two tasks. On the one hand, this freedom of exploratory activity on the part of the child must not be checked but *utilised*. The examiner must observe, select, crystallise and record as much of it as is relevant. On the other hand, he must somehow direct this activity into channels that will answer the questions the test asks. The child must himself have a feeling of unimpeded (indeed encouraged) self-activity, and yet must at the same time through this activity answer these questions. This involves, as it were, tactfully coercing him into doing what is wanted, and for this the attractive apparatus is an ally. It is therefore necessary to build up a very subtle and delicate technique. Moreover, this technique must be capable of almost moment to moment adjustment and modification. Probably no two tests are given in exactly the same manner, although the general procedure is the same. The result should provide exactness of observation without insistence towards the child, precise recording without rigidity in the procedure. But after some practice and considerable tact and patience, coupled with a genuine interest in children of these ages, the test has a way of following more or less clear-cut channels. It takes on a definite orderly shape, that grows up out of the child's natural interest in those activities it is necessary to observe, rather than out of any arbitrarily imposed or artificial procedure. Something of this will be illustrated below.

Order of Tests.—It will already be evident that no rigid order for taking the tests can be imposed on these very young subjects. The general method of taking the tests of the Binet Scale is horizontally, across the series of test items. Thus, the third-year tests are taken first in order of difficulty, irrespective of the type of test, followed by the fourth-year tests and so on.

It would be quite impossible to take the new scale of tests in that manner. The items are classified into five scales, each of which is a major sequence of items or a series of such interwoven sequences, similar in kind but gradually increasing in difficulty. To take all the tests, for example, for the first month, cutting across the scales, and then the items for the second month and so on, going from locomotor items to personal-social, then to speech, would be laborious, time-consuming and extremely irritating to the child. Moreover, as has already been argued, any rigidity in the manner of taking the tests is difficult or impossible to impose. The best that can be done to introduce some order into the procedure is in general to try to complete the sub-scales one by one. The examiner will not often succeed, and must in any case be ready to switch to another scale when this is indicated; but the attempt should be made. The perpendicular method is more natural to this scale than the horizontal testing of the Binet-Simon method. The sub-scales are virtually separate scales, and can be scored separately and separate quotients allotted. They may therefore be so regarded in the test situation itself. Probably the best way to illustrate the method is to describe how the test might be taken with particular babies of different ages, and to indicate some of the varying circumstances that arise and how these should be utilised to further the test.

The child must, for the purposes of the test, be observed rather than directed, coerced rather than commanded, led rather than driven, indulged rather than frustrated. If the examiner wants the child of fourteen months seated at the low table for the performance tests at the very moment that the child wants to show off his prowess at his newly acquired skill of walking alone, it is of little use to insist. It is better to allow him to show off his locomotor accomplishments, for, after all, his locomotor skill has to be measured as well as all the rest. Presently, satisfied with his skill and the examiner's pleasure in it, he will return with renewed interest to the form boards or the little coloured boxes or the small box of toys. Everything will be done in due order, in the child's order and in his own good time; only thus can he give his maximum attention and effort.

In general, the examiner's manner, when beginning a test, will very largely decide the course of events. It is undoubtedly best to approach the situation in a quiet, composed manner, keeping the voice low and well modulated, and moving when necessary quietly from table to divan and back again. The examiner's attention should not at first be directed towards the child but be given almost entirely to the mother while yet the child's behaviour and demeanour are being unobtrusively observed. It is reassuring to the child to note a friendly interchange between his mother and the examiner. This also gives the young child time to get used to the new environment, used to the examiner's voice and manner, and interested in the first piece of apparatus which has been previously placed, as if by accident, handy to the child on the low table. He may prefer to sit on his mother's lap at first, but when reassured will slide down and take his place at the table and begin to manipulate the apparatus.

This settling-down period is no waste of time in itself, but can also be used for getting from the mother the first essential information about the child. His name, address, date of birth, birth weight, brief history and so on can conveniently be taken down at this stage, and whereas the examiner is quietly observing the child, the note-taking makes this observation less obvious. Also, with the form handy (see Appendix II), it is an easy transition to scoring those items that the child quite soon shows evidence of passing. The test has begun.

Let us now in imagination observe a few children under test and see how they react. We will use a room something like the one described in the last chapter. We are in a clinic where normal babies are being tested for research purposes. The following examples are typical of actual children seen and examined by the writer.

Case 1: Let us begin with an eight-weeks' baby. Before the mother comes with her child the environment is prepared. Blankets are spread comfortably on the divan, the low easy chair is placed near the head of the divan for the mother, and the few pieces of apparatus needed are placed on the trolley in an easily accessible position nearby. These are: the plastic ball, the ring, the bell-ring, the handbell, the torch, the tuning-fork, the stop-watch, paper tissues, four yellow bricks, the tiny doll and the red test box. The form, writing materials and examiner's chair are ready at the table. The room is comfortably warm and welcoming.

The mother is shown in with the boy in her arms. The examiner moves forward to greet her and look at the baby, who is asleep in his shawl. The mother is shown to her chair, and it is suggested that she may like to put baby down, as he is asleep. Baby continues to sleep, lying on the divan, with his mother seated quite close to him. She is grateful for this and looks round the room with interest. The examiner explains briefly the purpose of the test, that it is to find out how clever her baby is and if he is progressing satisfactorily. Immediately she asks: "Shall I wake him?" But the examiner does not want the child to awaken suddenly in a strange room and cry. Instead, he proceeds to get the basic information. Presently, to the sound of the voices and before the note-taking is quite finished, the child stirs and wakes. He is left to lie and look up at the wall or light until the note-taking is finished. Then the examiner moves quietly to the baby, saying: "Hullo, hullo," etc., varying the tone a little. Sometimes a child of this age will respond immediately with soft vocalisation, "a—a—a", etc. This child remains silent but has a good look at the examiner. Putting out the light, if it is above the child, or turning him gently from the main window light, the examiner takes the torch and, still talking to him softly, does the first eye test, D 1; then passes on to the bell-ring and takes D 2, 3, 4, 5 and 7 in succession. Rattling the small plastic ball in one hand and still holding the ring in the other, he next takes D 6. The test is going very well, but at this stage the child becomes restless. The mother is asked to loosen the shawl and let him kick. As she bends over him to do this, he smiles up at her and gurgles a little and begins to kick happily. While the mother is tending the child, it is possible to score items D 1 to

D 7, six of which have been passed and one (D 7) failed. The examiner has also observed the baby's recognition of the mother (B 5) and smiling (B 4); also vocalisation (C 3).

The child is now in a favourable mood and position for the locomotor items. Unless the rapport is very good, the examiner avoids moving the child straightway, so takes the tests that can be done in the dorsal position: A 2, A 5 and A 7. He also now takes the paper tests, E 2 and E 5, if the child continues happy. The baby is then gently turned over to the prone position, while items A 1 and A 4 are taken. It is then possible to complete any further locomotor items that the child can do, continuing until it is obvious that he can pass no more. The tests are well graded, and at this age *five or six* items failed in succession bring the particular sub-scale to an end. Of course, when the child is in the prone position and it is found that he lifts his head well up (A 4) but cannot raise his chest (A 10), he also fails A 15 and other prone items. Also, if he is in the dorsal position and fails A 7, there is no need to take A 12 and so on.

All this time the examiner has been listening for vocal sounds. At this point the child is again restless, and so the mother is asked to take him up and hold him in a sitting posture on her knee. She does so, talking to the child meanwhile, and he looks up at her and makes a softly repeated cooing sound: "oo—oo—oo." This is entered in the margin provided. So C 5 can now be scored, as well as C 3 and B 6. With the child happily supported on the mother's knee, the rest of the tests are quickly taken: reactions to the bell-ring and handbell, "grasping an adult's finger", "holding the doll", etc. The examiner then looks carefully over the test sheet to see if further items in any of the scales should be taken. The general impression is of a child progressing very satisfactorily, strong and healthy, active and alert. The examiner tells the mother this and thanks her for bringing the baby to the clinic. As she is shown out, the mother exclaims: "It was all very interesting. I had no idea my baby could do all those things already." She goes away very happy. The examiner returns to the form and scores the test, with the following result: A Scale, 6; B Scale, 5; C Scale, 5; D Scale, 7; E Scale, 5. This gives a total score of 28, so that the mental age is $\frac{28}{3} = 9\frac{1}{3}$ weeks and the child is $1\frac{1}{3}$ weeks above his actual age. As this boy is under eight months old, the correction described in Chapter VI must be applied, as follows. Eight weeks are added to both C.A. and M.A. before the quotient (G.Q.) is worked out.

$$\text{C.A.} = 8 \text{ weeks} + 8 = 16 \text{ weeks}$$
$$\text{M.A.} = 9\tfrac{1}{3} \text{ weeks} + 8 = 17\tfrac{1}{3} \text{ weeks}$$
$$\text{G.Q.} = \frac{17\tfrac{1}{3} \times 100}{16} = 108$$ [1]

The interview has taken twenty minutes.

It will be observed, on reviewing this test, that the child himself even at this young age indicated when a change in the tests to be taken or a change of his position was needed, and that, far from this holding up the test, it facilitated it on every occasion. Of course a child of this age, if he is physically comfortable and does not break down into crying, is comparatively easy to test. We studied a young one first because of this. The next child, a girl of nine months, requires more ingenuity on the part of the examiner.

Case 2: The preparations for testing a child of nine months are similar to those described above, except that more of the apparatus will be needed and part of the examination may possibly be done at the large table. The divan is put ready, though it may not be needed; a rug on the floor may be more acceptable if the child is bright and already crawling. She is not likely to need the low table. The relevant apparatus is ready on the trolley, and the red test box may possibly be the best piece to place on the table. Two chairs are placed opposite each other at the large table.

The mother and child arrive and the mother is invited to sit at the table opposite to the examiner, but she keeps the child on her knee. The examiner sits unobtrusively observing the child, talking to the mother and taking the brief history. After rattling the red test box, he places it near the child. She looks up reproachfully and hides her face against the mother. He proceeds with the history but presently he touches the lid of the box temptingly and asks: "What's inside?", giving it another shake. Again she retreats. He continues writing. When the child looks up again, he takes a red lead pencil and scribbles on paper near her, leaving the pencil lying near by. She ignores this and takes up the red box! She shakes it as the examiner did earlier (delayed imitative reaction (E 24)), and smiles at the sound. He asks again softly: "What's inside?" She struggles to manipulate the lid and manages to get it

[1] See Appendix for details of obtaining G.Q.s and also the quotients for the sub-scales.

off and pokes at the contents with her forefinger, but has no idea of removing them. The examiner takes the box gently and slowly tips out the two bricks and puts them back again, then returns the box to the child, again shaking it. Again she merely pokes at the bricks with her forefinger. He then takes the two cubes and offers them to her. She takes them one in each hand. He next offers a third brick; she immediately drops one of the others for the third. He offers another and again she drops one of those she is holding. The examiner now scores plus for E 15, 16, 17, 20, 24 and 26, but minus for E 28.

The child is now enjoying the test, and the mother, who has twice checked herself of an impulse to help the child, is watching with interest. The examiner produces the little box and pushes a small toy towards the child and, when the little hand comes forward to take it, he slips the box inverted over the toy, asking: "Where is it?" The child immediately lifts the box but has forgotten the toy underneath it. He repeats the test, with the same result, and scores E 23 plus and E 27 minus. He now has her approximate level on Scale E, but the rapport is again wearing thin, so he quickly takes E 25 (minus) and E 18 and 22 (both plus). The child has during this period made various babbling sounds, and these the examiner has written in the margin of the form in the space provided: "Loo-looloo" and "Kicky". Later on she says "ti" several times, which the mother explains is the last syllable of "pretty". The child has no clear words yet.

The child has been on mother's knee at the table more than five minutes and she now begins to squirm and retreat from the examiner. Moreover, she now uses a wide movement of the left arm and sends cup, box and other toys to the floor, looking after them as they go (D 18). The examiner suggests that she may be happier on the floor for a change, and the mother sits the child in the middle of the rug on the floor. Immediately she becomes a sunny smiling baby, reaching after the coloured ball rolled towards her, and struggling unsuccessfully to crawl towards it. She sits alone quite well and turns around when prone on the floor. She does not yet stand when held up by the mother, nor pass any further locomotor items. The examiner brings the rings, little handbell, mirror and other toys nearer and proceeds with the test while the child is happy on the floor; and quite soon he is able to confirm the specialisation of thumb and forefinger noticed earlier, but is now quite sure that she does not yet show fine prehension.

She does not yet pull the ring about by the string, nor understand how to dangle it by the string, but she does manage to pick the string up with a scooping movement of third and fourth fingers and secure the ring by means of it. She therefore passes D 17, 18, 21, 22, but fails items beyond that level.

In this way the test is happily completed while the child is on the floor. If her interest is for the ring, the examiner takes all the items he needs with that piece of apparatus, then gently distracts her with the mirror or the bell and so on. Every now and again her concentration snaps and she hurls things about, but even this occurrence can be utilised if the examiner notes whether she merely "knocks" or "sends" objects to the floor as she did when at the table, or if it is a definite *throw* from the hand, required to pass D 26. Finally mother and child go away quite happily, the child clutching a coloured paper tissue that she has accepted as a "parting gift" and, although she does not yet quite "wave bye-bye", her happy expression is a pleasant farewell.

This child's final scores are: A Scale, 23; B Scale, 22; C Scale, 21; D Scale, 22; E Scale, 24; a fairly even result. At just nine months she is 39 weeks old. Then her M.A. will be $\frac{112}{3} = 37\frac{1}{3}$ weeks. So her G.Q. will be $\frac{37\frac{1}{3} \times 100}{39} = 95{\cdot}6$ or 96. She is therefore a child of rather slow average ability.

Case 3: Let us now in imagination observe a bright boy in his sixteenth month, 66½ weeks old, being tested.

For a child of this age the low table and chair or stool are needed. The examiner therefore places these ready, and also the mother's chair just behind the stool, so that if the child feels insecure during the test he can lean back against her knee to recover his normal emotional tone. On the table are placed two of the test boxes, the red and the yellow. But as soon as they enter, the child upsets all these plans by his strong desire to run all over the room and explore! The situation is accepted good-humouredly and he is left to wander round while again use is made of the quiet and reassuring task of note-taking and conversation with the mother to get him used to the situation. The examiner, however, notes that the child moves rapidly on his feet in a fast trot (A 38). He still sways from one foot to the other and staggers a little, so mother is asked how long he has been walking alone and we learn that he has been doing this for about a month, that is from about

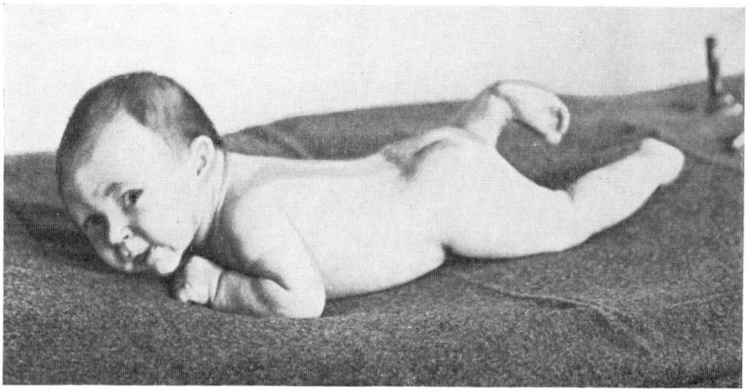

PLATE 12

At six weeks' old this boy, although strong and well grown, has not yet much muscular control, but he can lift his chin well up, and is already thrusting with his hands against the blanket in a vain attempt to push himself up. The stimulus was the gentle shaking of the bell-rattle above him. He turns his head and eyes slightly in the direction of the sound.

PLATE 13

At fourteen months, this boy is walking and climbing stairs. He likes to walk down when helped, as seen in the picture, but is more at home on hands and knees. Note the concentration in his expression. There are several stages in the progress towards learning to manage the stairs, as will be seen by a study of the Locomotor items for the second year. (See Chapter XI.)

Plate 14

At nine months, this boy is unafraid. He sits alone and is crawling, too, though mainly backwards. He goes after and is interested in everything. His balance is good. He likes, however, to hold on to his feet while sitting on the floor.

Plate 15

With several novel objects near him, he tries to secure them all, and while holding the plastic saucer in one hand and a toy lorry in the other, his eyes are on a coloured ball that he will "go for" in a moment. (Same child as above, Plate 14.)

the average age for walking. After dashing aimlessly about the room, he trots over to the divan and struggles up on to it, showing that he can climb on to a chair or couch. The examiner produces the ball and rolls it towards him; the child needs help to get down, but shows he can keep his balance whilst stooping to get the ball (A 39). The child is next coaxed to try to throw the ball, but he holds on to it determinedly. So the examiner gets the little tourer and sends it across the floor to him. The child immediately throws the ball away with a beautiful overhand movement (D 42) and goes for the car. Before sitting down with a bump on the floor, he looks up with a philosophic grin and says: "Dow-ar-doh!" which the examiner writes uncomprehendingly in the margin. Mother laughs and explains: "We play that at home; he means 'Down I go!'" While the child pushes little cars around on the floor, further speech reactions are noted. He says "car" and "key" quite clearly, bringing the latter repeatedly to the examiner for the car to be rewound. He makes car noises. With the child still on the floor, the examiner produces the mirror and asks who is there in the mirror. The baby points, looks up at his mother and smiles comprehendingly. The examiner asks: "Where is Jimmy?" and the child points to the mirror, so he can score C 34, but the baby cannot yet *say* his own name when asked. He looks at the book with interest and soon throws it aside, passing E 33 and E 40, but does not yet name objects in pictures. Now he struggles to his feet, so the rest of the locomotor items are taken. He passes A 41 and A 42, but nothing beyond. Mother reports that he climbs up stairs but is afraid to come down, so a note is made to observe him on the stairs at the end of the test, A 36 is provisionally scored plus but not A 43; thus at last the A Scale is completed.

The child's attention is now drawn to the brick boxes on the table. Mother draws her chair nearer, and the child is now eager to sit at the table. Immediately he has taken the lids off the boxes and is tipping out the bricks, and so the examiner begins to score E 34, E 35, E 37, E 40 and E 42, which are all completed by this child in a play way without any instructions. The examiner now definitely tests for E 49, giving the baby the third box and taking this item as described in Chapter XV, but he cannot quite manage this test. Tipping out the six bricks, the examiner proceeds very slowly and talking in a low voice to the child to build a tower. The child knocks it down in play and all enjoy the joke. Then, placing the first brick ready, the examiner hands a second one to the child, saying: "Now you make it", and he is soon building a tower. He manages as far as four bricks but no further (B 37, D 41 and D 43, but not D 47). The examiner now proceeds to make a bridge of the boxes and also a train of three bricks which goes merrily under the bridge to the accompaniment of train noises! (See Fig. 25.) The baby is charmed with this play, but is quite unable to imitate the making of the train. (The bridge belongs to the third-year tests.) The form boards are next taken, and as the boy has done well with the boxes, the examiner begins with the two-circle board. The child immediately passes E 39 and E 46. So the square board and circle boards are next taken together. E 43 is passed but E 47 is failed. He passes E 45, getting all three insets into the three-hole board, but fails this rotated. All the form board items can now be scored.

The examiner returns to the speech column and produces the box of little toys, putting aside the form boards and boxes on to the handy trolley. He now proceeds to take out the toys one by one and place them very slowly before the child, asking the mother please to be careful not to *name* any of the toys. The exact order is not important, but in general the easiest should appear first, thus the cup (a pause), the spoon (again a pause). The boy takes up the spoon and plays stirring the cup. The examiner then produces pussy, dog, horse, etc. By this time the child is chattering away merrily as these small toys appear. He handles them and looks closely at them, kisses the little doll and sits her on the chair and so on, and the following clear words are recorded: "chair", "key", "wow-wow", "car", said quite distinctly, but no others. The examiner therefore scores C 51 plus and takes the others by the indirect method, asking: "Where's the pussy?" "Give me the horse", or even "Ball, *please*" in a coaxing tone is sufficient. The child identifies a total of nine objects, five by pointing correctly and four by previously naming them, so he passes C 50. The examiner counts up the child's heard vocabulary, and adds other words mentioned by mother, using his discretion and experience of the child's stage of speech development gained throughout the examination. He can credit with certainty a vocabulary of sixteen clear words, and so the child is credited with C 44 but not C 49. He produces masses of babble still, but not any clear or definite word-combinations yet, but these are not far away. He will be producing them soon. With the child happily at play with toys, the examiner glances over the items and takes any further ones necessary, such as D 51 and also the B items. The baby scribbles freely but is not very interested, passes D 38 but not D 46. At last, reluctantly, this boy waves "bye-bye", also says "Bye" and takes his leave with his mother. The examiner does not forget to observe him on the stairs. The examination has taken thirty-five minutes. His final scores are: A Scale, 42; B Scale, 41; C Scale, 46; D Scale, 44; E Scale, 45.

He has therefore done very well, with a high Speech score and very good Hand Work and Performance. In assessing results with children in their second year, items of the first and second years must be dealt with separately because there are three items for each week of the first year and only two items for each week of the second year. This boy is therefore credited with M.A. 52 weeks for the first year, where he passes everything, and the following additional second year items: A Scale, 11; B Scale, 9; C Scale, 15; D Scale, 13; E Scale, 14. Total second year items = 62. Then M.A. = 52 weeks + $\frac{62}{2}$ = 83 weeks. So his G.Q. will be:

$$\frac{\text{M.A.} \times 100}{\text{C.A.}} = \frac{83 \times 100}{66\frac{1}{2}} = 125 \text{ G.Q.}$$

Perhaps sufficient has been said in this chapter to illustrate the general procedure of testing infants. The examiner must go with the child, not pull away from him or try to force either his pace or his direction. Gradually, with practice and developing skill, the testing of babies, far from being a difficult undertaking, becomes a delightful experience, assuming of course that the examiner possesses a "flair" for handling young children and a genuine interest in the very young. After about eighteen months of age the testing begins to approximate nearer to the testing of older children. But throughout the pre-school period a play approach to the test situation appears indicated; more especially will this be so when testing special cases, including retarded or emotionally disturbed children. We hope to take up this theme in another place, when the tests have been more fully applied to children beyond the age of two years.

Summary

1. Go with the child and *use* his restlessness, curiosity and flight of attention to *further* the test.

2. Any test may be taken twice, but no test more than twice,

unless this is specially mentioned in the details for that item.

3. Tests may be taken in any order, but in general some attempt should be made to complete the scales one by one.

4. Begin to test a child at a point equivalent to six items or two months below his actual age, e.g. a three-months' baby from the beginning of the test, a six-months' baby from about item 10, and so on. Then continue up and down the scale until the child has passed at least six items in succession in each sub-scale, and also until he has failed six items in succession in each sub-scale.

5. Full instructions for scoring the test, and further information for testing older babies will be found in Appendix I.

6. For a full inventory of the test items, see Appendix II.

The Gesell Developmental Schedules [1]

It will be obvious to the reader familiar with Dr. Gesell's work that a proportion of the items described in the following pages, especially in the locomotor series, are similar to items in his scale. Certainly the present writer has learned a great deal from the detailed observations made by Gesell in his numerous writings. These items are necessary in any scale that purports to cover the child's development with any degree of completeness and present a reliable diagnostic picture. However, each item, whether original to this scale or used previously by other workers, has been revised and modified in accordance with the needs of this particular research and the purposes of a standardised scale. The items are placed in each sub-scale in strict order of difficulty on a statistical basis (percentages of babies passing each item month by month), and the choice of items has been dictated also to some extent by the standardisation of the scale and the equalising for difficulty of the five sub-scales. (See Chapters V and VI.)

[1] The Gesell behaviour tests and items are organised as an integrated system of developmental diagnosis. The procedures and schedules are described in a basic clinical manual entitled *Developmental Diagnosis: Clinical Methods and Pediatric Applications*, by A. Gesell and C. S. Amatruda, second edition, revised and enlarged, 1947 (New York, Paul B. Hoeber, Inc.), pp. xvi and 496.

CHAPTER XI

ADMINISTERING THE LOCOMOTOR SCALE (SCALE A)

Significance of the Locomotor Sequence

THE locomotor scale measures in some detail all that series of developing skills that result in the achieving of the upright posture by the child and lead on to learning to walk, run, climb and so on. Later the child, having become mobile, learns to adventure far afield and explore his environment. In this study we follow this developmental sequence as far as the end of the second year, but development in this direction continues thereafter throughout childhood.

This sequence of gradually acquired skills is of great significance and importance in the first two years of life, and is therefore appropriately included in any comprehensive study of normal infancy. When, in addition, the possibility of "differential diagnosis" in special cases is accepted (see Chapter VIII), the importance of measuring in detail the locomotor sequence, and including it in a total scale of tests, becomes more evident. In these early phases of life the rate of progress in this direction is most relevant in assessing mental level. Although locomotor skill differs in kind from more narrowly intellectual activities, and although its relevance to the main trend of development may become less as the child grows older, while he is still at the stage of *learning* these skills they draw to a large extent upon his mental energies and ability to concentrate, as do all other acts of learning at this stage. Later on these physical acts, together with the power to maintain posture, balance and rhythm, become part of the child's total habitual reaction and response to his environment at the physical level.

The detailed items of the locomotor sequence as standardised for this scale are given below.

Administering the Scale

In administering the scale any test may be taken twice, if the first result is indecisive or ambiguous.

Care must be taken not to tire the young baby by taking too many locomotor items in succession. The procedure should be varied by interspersing items from other scales if the child becomes restless. There is no need to test deliberately for any item in the scale that can be definitely observed without testing. This would prolong the examination unnecessarily. What we want to ascertain and record is the child's achieved stage of development in regard to this sequence, not his ability to react to any artificial situation.

In the instructions, the month in which the item is appropriate is indicated in brackets after the numbered item. This indicates the stage at which 50 per cent. or thereabouts of babies pass the test.

In scoring the items, the pass symbol (√) or minus sign (—) should be placed in the square provided below the number of the item. (See Figs. 1–3 in Chapter II.)

Scale A

DETAILS OF THE LOCOMOTOR SCALE (SCALE A)

First Year

Items *First Three Months*

The baby:

1. Lifts his chin up slightly when lying in the prone position.
2. Pushes with both feet against the examiner's hands.
3. Holds his head erect for a few seconds.
4. Lifts his head well up when lying prone.
5. Kicks his feet vigorously when put to lie down.
6. Is active in his bath, kicking his feet, etc.
7. Lifts his head up slightly when in the dorsal position.
8. Can roll from side to back.

Second Three Months

9. His back is firm when held in the sitting position.
10. Lifts his head and chest up when lying prone.
11. Holds his head erect continuously.
12. Lifts his head and shoulders when in dorsal position.

13. Can roll from one side right over to the other.
14. Plays with his toes.
15. First crawling reaction: Pushes on hands, draws up knees, etc.
16. Sits with slight support, e.g. can be left sitting among pillows in pram or cot.

Third Three Months

17. Can roll over from back to stomach or from stomach to back.
18. First stepping reaction (*a*): Moves feet alternately as if dancing when held up.
19. Tries vigorously to crawl, using both hands and feet (Crawling II).
20. Sits alone for a short while.
21. Stepping reaction (*b*): Feet now go definitely one in front of the other.
22. Can turn himself around when left lying on the floor (Crawling III).
23. Can be left sitting on the floor.
24. Crawling IV: Makes some progress, forwards or backwards.

Fourth Three Months

25. Stands when held up.
26. Sits well in a chair.
27. Can pull himself up from crawling or sitting, by grasping the furniture.
28. Can stand holding on to furniture.
29. Crawling V: Creeps on hands and knees, or gets about freely by some other method, e.g. bear walk.
30. Side-steps around inside cot or play-pen, holding on to railings, etc.
31. Can walk when led, adult holding one or both hands.

Second Year

First Three Months

The baby:

32. Climbs on to a ledge or step when crawling.
33. Can stand alone.
34. Walks alone, at first unsteadily.
35. Can kneel on floor or chair. Balances in this position.

36. Climbs the stairs, climbing up but not yet down.
37. Likes to walk pushing a pram, or toy horse, or other wheeled toy.

Second Three Months

38. He now trots about well.
39. Can stoop to pick up a toy without over-balancing.
40. Climbs into a low chair.
41. Can walk backwards.
42. Likes to walk pulling a toy on a string.

Third Three Months

43. Can climb stairs, up and down.
44. Can jump. Child gives a little jump when standing if pleased, etc., with both feet off floor together.
45. Runs. This is not a trot now, but a definite running.
46. Can now *walk* upstairs, no longer on hands and knees, but holding adult's hand, etc.
47. Climbs and stands up on a chair.

Fourth Three Months

48. Can jump off a step, both feet off the ground together.
49. Can seat himself at table, placing chair first.
50. Walks up and down stairs; has abandoned climbing, but still holds adult's hand or banisters.
51. Can kick a ball.
52. Can be trusted on stairs alone.

A 1. *Lifts chin when prone.* (*First month.*)

The young baby should be placed comfortably on a folded blanket in the prone position. If the child is in the mother's arms, the examiner should ask her to place him on the blanket and stay quite near to him. Most babies from birth will immediately lift the chin up slightly. This is sufficient for a pass in this test at this stage. If the child does not lift the chin, the examiner should speak gently to him or call softly, or ask the mother to do so. The bell or bell-ring may be used, but care must be taken not to startle the child. If the child lifts the head well up at an angle of 25 to 40 degrees, he passes A 4 also.

A 2. *Pushes with both feet against examiner's hands.* (*First month.*)

The child should be lying in the dorsal position. The examiner places his hands, without using any force, in such a position that the child's knees are slightly flexed. The baby pushes either with alternate feet or both together to remove the obstruction. A definite push of the baby scores plus. Sometimes he does this quite strongly, even moving himself backwards a little on the table. The experiment must be carried out gently and the child enjoys this.

A 3. *Holds head erect for a few seconds.* (*Second month.*)

Any baby who has passed A 1 or A 2 may be given A 3. The examiner should take the child gently on to his knee, holding him in the sitting position, and observe whether the child can support his head a little. (The examiner's hand must be in position to support the young baby's head if necessary.) If the child can do this, the examiner should move his knee slightly from side to side to see if the balance is maintained (see A 11), but if the child can hold his head erect, unsupported, for a few seconds only, he passes A 3. If the child is likely to be fretful, the mother should hold him for this test, while the examiner observes and enters the result.

A 4. *Lifts head up when prone.* (*End of second month.*)

This is taken as for A 1, but now the child lifts the head well up, at an angle of 25 to 40 degrees from the table. (See Plate 12, boy of six weeks lifting head.)

A 5. *Kicks vigorously.* (*End of second month.*)

Most healthy babies kick a little almost from birth, when garments allow sufficient freedom. By this stage, quite vigorous alternating movements of the limbs can be observed. Unless the kicking is definite and quite strong, the child does not pass A 5.

A 6. *Active in bath—kicks.* (*End of second month.*)

Mother or nurse will report about item A 6. By the second month baby should be enjoying his bath (see B 3), and kicking feet and sometimes splashing with hands also. Any type of vigorous activity in the bath passes this test.

A. 7. *Lifts head when in dorsal position.* (*Third month.*)

This is a much more difficult test than A 1 and A 4. The baby is placed lying on his back on the blankets. The examiner should call to the child, or talk to him to get him in a happy mood, or ask mother to do so. Then, taking the child's hands—the baby's fingers usually clasp the examiner's thumb—he should pull gently and, still talking to the child, encourage him to try to lift his head from the pillow in preparation for pulling to the sitting position (A 12). Care must be taken not to pull the child up; the baby himself makes the effort, and lifts his head from the blanket but not his shoulders at this stage. Lifting head ever so slightly from the pillow passes A 7.

A 8. *Rolls from side to back.* (*Third month.*)

Place the baby on his side with his face turned away from the mother or from the examiner. (The examiner's hand must be in position to support the child or prevent him from rolling too far.) Then, the examiner again speaking or calling or softly ringing the bell, the child should be encouraged to turn over on to his back towards the sound or towards his mother's voice. The child must achieve this himself to pass A 8; a very slight movement of legs or hips suffices for this change of position.

A 9. *Back firm in sitting position.* (*Beginning of fourth month.*)

The child may be seated on the examiner's knee or on the blankets. The young baby's back is curved in this position, but by about the fourth month the back is straight and firm.

A 10. *Lifts head and chest when prone.* (*Fourth month.*)

When the baby (at about four months old) is placed in the prone position, he can lift head, shoulders and chest, and will push with his hands against the table in an effort to raise himself higher. The method is the same as for A 4.

A 11. *Holds head erect continuously.* (*Fourth month.*)

The child of this age needs little support for either back or head. He holds his head erect continuously. This can be readily observed when the child is seated on mother's knee. He will also be turning his head around as he looks about in a new environment. In cases of any doubt, this should be tested for as in A 3.

A 12. *Lifts head and shoulders—dorsal.* (*Fifth month.*)

(See A 7.) When the examiner now takes the baby's hands, the child can pull himself up a little, lifting both head and shoulders, but does not yet pull himself to the sitting position.

A 13. *Rolls from side to side.* (*Fifth month.*)

The child can now roll right over from one side to the other. Test should be taken as described in A 8.

A 14. *Plays with own toes.* (*Sixth month.*)

The examiner may have to refer to the mother for information concerning this item; but it can frequently be observed when the child is in the dorsal position, particularly when he has been manipulating the ring or other toy and has abandoned it. He will then find his toes. It can also be readily observed in babies who are just sitting; a baby may hang on to his toes to help him to balance in the sitting position. (See Plate 14.)

A 15. *Crawling Reaction I: Draws up knees, etc.* (*Sixth month.*)

Item A 15 is a definite stage in the crawling sequence. In testing for this item we do not touch the child, but encourage him by some bright object or toy placed just slightly beyond his reach (or we may get the mother to call to him). The child will then struggle to move in the direction of the rattle or rattling ball. He makes no progress, but draws up one knee or both alternately or moves his hands, pushing against the blankets in an attempt to go forwards. Any of these slight crawling reactions constitutes a pass at this stage.

A 16. *Sits with slight support.* (*End of sixth month.*)

By about six months the average baby can sit with only slight support. He can sit in pram or cot, supported by pillows, or in a low chair (suitable precautions having been taken). To test for this stage of locomotor development the child may be seated in the arm-chair with cushions placed at his back, to see if he can balance in that position. The examiner's hands must be ready to support him lest he should overbalance.

A 17. *Can roll from back to stomach and stomach to back.* (*Seventh month.*)

By his seventh month the average child is quite adept at rolling over in any direction whatsoever, and it is seldom necessary to test for A 17. The child should be placed in the prone position. Then the examiner catches the child's eye with the coloured rattling ball or other attractive toy and, calling to the child encouragingly, moves it upwards and sideways beyond the child's field of vision. The child rolls over to keep the attractive object in view, or in order to clutch at it.

A 18. *Stepping Reaction* (a)*: Dancing movements.* (*Seventh month.*)

This is the first of several stages towards taking a step in learning to walk. When the child is held up in the standing position and the mother asked to call to him or hold out her hands to him, he jumps about a little with pleasure and lifts his feet alternately, often putting one foot on top of the other and then lifting up the lower foot, etc. We have called this a "dancing" movement, for it is more like a stationary dancing of the feet than an attempt to make progress.

A 19. *Tries vigorously to crawl* (*II*). (*Eighth month.*)

This is the second crawling reaction. Placed in the prone

position and with the attractive object just beyond reach, the child makes no actual progress forwards but his whole body is in vigorous movement as he struggles to reach the object. The knees are drawn up and pressed against the blankets, arms are stretched forwards towards the toy in an effort to move towards it. This stage is quite definitely an attempt to crawl and must be carefully distinguished from A 15.

A 20. *Sits alone for a short time.* (*Eighth month.*)

A 20 is self-explanatory. The mother cannot yet leave the child sitting alone on the floor, but he is quite capable for a short time of sitting unsupported. This can be tested for by seating the child on floor or table (with blankets or cushions near to save him if he over-balances). This item is usually passed without actual testing, on the basis of observation.

A 21. *Stepping Reaction* (b)*: One foot in front of the other.* (*Ninth month.*)

See A 18. This item is tested for in the same way as A 18, but is passed only if the feet are definitely placed one in front of the other, alternately.

A 22. *Can turn around when left on floor. Crawling Reaction III.* (*Ninth month.*)

This is a definite stage in crawling, noted by many workers and found also in this study. To test for it, the examiner should seek a convenient moment when the child is prone on the floor. Then he should roll a ball or set the little car going and allow it to move across the child's field of vision, first towards the right and then to the left; the child will pivot around in the attempt to keep the toy in sight, or to try to reach it. This item is frequently observed without testing for it.

A 23. *Can be left sitting on floor.* (*End of ninth month.*)

By about nine or ten months of age the average baby can be left sitting on the floor with toys to play with and can maintain his balance in this position. The mother can leave him for short periods on blankets in the play-pen to amuse himself with toys, etc. This item also is readily observed during the examination. The mother may be questioned as to the child's habits in this regard at home. (See Plate 14.)

A 24. *Crawling IV: Makes some progress forwards or backwards.* (*End of ninth month.*)

A 24 is passed when the child actually moves about the floor a little, quite irrespective of his direction or method. He may move only a few feet from the position in which he was placed; this is sufficient to pass this item. (See also A 29.) Some babies creep backwards before they learn to go forwards; others get around in a series of pivoting movements and others by rolling. Any of these methods scores plus at this level. (See Plate 15.)

A 25. *Stands when held up.* (*Tenth month.*)

The examiner should stand baby up and support him on his feet, and see if the child can take his weight on his feet and place both feet firmly on the floor or table. He is not expected to stand alone at this stage, being unable as yet to balance in this position, but he can stand on his two feet when supported.

A 26. *Sits well in a chair.* (*End of tenth month.*)

The child now uses a chair. It may not yet be safe to leave him unprotected in a chair, but he can sit in a suitable high chair at the table.

A 27. *Pulls self up by furniture.* (*Eleventh month.*)

A 27 is passed when a baby can pull himself up by the furniture, although he may not be able to maintain this position and may immediately sit down again. It involves changing from the creeping position by grasping the chair or table leg and getting up, first on one foot, then on the other and balancing his body until he has pulled himself erect. A child who can pull himself up by the furniture passes A 27. If he can also stand holding on to the furniture afterwards, he passes A 28.

A 28. *Can stand holding on to furniture.* (*Eleventh month.*)

This item is passed if the child can balance standing and holding on to a piece of furniture. It usually follows A 27 and is the sequel to it, but some babies learn to stand holding furniture or even learn to cruise from one chair to the next without passing A 27 or being able to pull themselves up. Hence the separation into two items.

A 29. *Creeps on hands and knees. Crawling V.* (*Eleventh month.*)

As observed in connection with A 24, there is much variety in the methods used by different babies in getting about the room. To pass A 29 the child must be able to get up on his hands and knees and creep around, or do a bear walk. All four limbs should be used. Some handicapped children never learn to creep, and some very bright children walk so soon after they have pulled themselves up to the standing position that they by-pass the creeping stage. These latter, however, can creep, and should be credited with this. To test for this, the child may be placed in the prone position, and the car set going or the coloured ball rolled as before. If he is able to do so, he will creep after the toy, but this item is frequently and readily observed without deliberately testing for it.

A 30. *Side-steps around inside cot or play-pen.* (*Twelfth month.*)

To pass item A 30 the child must be capable of walking round inside his play-pen or cot holding on to the rails; or he may demonstrate by walking from one piece of furniture to the next, holding on.

A 31. *Can walk when led.* (*Twelfth month.*)

Take the child by the hand when in the standing position or by two hands if necessary, and see if he can balance walking with this amount of help. It is usually best to ask the mother to do this, or to have her hold out her arms to the child who can then, with the examiner's help, take a few steps towards her, but not yet alone.

A 32. *Climbs on a low ledge or step.* (*Thirteenth month.*)

Some babies can climb up a step (for example, between two rooms) when actually still at the crawling stage. Others walk before attempting to climb up a step. The item is passed if by any method the child gets up one step quite unaided.

A 33. *Stands alone.* (*Thirteenth month.*)

The examiner should stand the child on his feet, and then gradually remove the support of his hands to see if the child can stand alone, taking care not to let the child fall. But it is seldom necessary to test for this item; the child who can stand alone will quickly demonstrate this fact to the examiner in the course of the interview.

A 34. *Walks alone.* (*End of fourteenth month.*)

To pass A 34, it is not necessary for the child to be walking well. If he gives evidence of being able to toddle a few steps from one support to another, he passes.

A 35. *Kneels on floor or chair.* (*End of fourteenth month.*)

This item requires some care in assessment. The child has now passed the stage when, whilst hanging on to a chair, he got first on to his knees and then pulled himself to the standing position. In that respect he has been able to kneel for some time. He must now, to pass A 35, be able to kneel up without support from his hands, to *balance* kneeling. At about fourteen or fifteen months old the walking child learns to kneel up on a chair at the table, or on the floor to play with toys on the seat of a tall chair. At ten months a baby can kneel up in his pram so long as his hands hold tight to the sides of the carriage, but now he can kneel without holding on to anything, and on the hard floor.

A 36. *Climbs stairs* (*up*). (*Fifteenth month.*)

To pass A 36 the child must be able to climb up stairs on hands and knees. This is the second stage of a long and complicated sequence of stages whereby the young child learns to manage the dangerous staircases of modern homes. At this stage (A 36) the child may not be able to descend the stairs at all (see A 43); he can, however, mount the stairs or some of them, though not quite alone; to have the mother following him is frequently a condition for his success, giving him the necessary confidence.

A 37. *Likes pushing pram, toy horse, etc.* (*Fifteenth month.*)

Some children enjoy pushing a pram, even on the street, and sometimes even before they can quite walk alone. This is a definite stage in locomotor development, pushing a wheeled toy or even a large pram, and toddling along with it. This gives tremendous pleasure and no doubt a great sense of achievement. Mother can be questioned about this. If the test is being done in a nursery or clinic, there is almost always a horse on wheels or other wheeled toy that a child can push around to demonstrate his ability to pass A 37.

A 38. *Trots about well.* (*Sixteenth month.*)

The child is now confident on his feet and trots about everywhere.

A 39. *Stoops.* (*Seventeenth month.*)

To pass A 39 the child must be able to stoop and pick up a toy without holding on to furniture and without over-balancing. The examiner should again roll the ball across the floor and encourage the child to go after it, and then observe how the walking child retrieves the ball. To pass this item he must be able to stoop to the floor for the ball, pick it up and straighten up again. Some babies sit down first near the ball and then get up; others put one hand on the floor in the bear walk attitude; others hang on to a support. It is passed only if the child stoops naturally and picks up the ball, a considerable balancing feat.

A 40. *Climbs on to a low chair.* (*Seventeenth month.*)

To pass A 40, the child must be able to climb into a low chair to sit in it without help. A low arm-chair is suitable. The child should be encouraged to get up into the chair; he may be persuaded to do so by putting a toy, ball, car or sweetmeat in a situation such that he must climb into the chair to get it. But this is a natural situation readily observed in any environment likely to be used for testing. (See Case 3 in Chapter X.)

A 41. *Can walk backwards.* (*Eighteenth month.*)

Items A 41 and A 42 can often be taken together. The examiner should produce the toy on a string, and himself demonstrate whilst walking backwards how to pull the toy along. The child passes both items if he also takes the string and pulls the toy along, walking backwards. He may however, refuse to do this, but demonstrate in some other connection his ability to walk backwards. If so, he passes test A 41.

A 42. *Walks pulling toy on string.* (*Eighteenth month.*)

(See A 41.) If the baby walks along pulling the toy on the string, he passes this item even though he takes only a few steps with it.

A 43. *Climbs stairs* (*up and down*). (*Nineteenth month.*)

At this stage in the stairs-climbing sequence, the child is still "climbing", not yet "walking", up the staircase, but he can also climb down now. The method of doing this last may be scored generously. Some babies come down backwards on hands and knees, some sit on each step and feel for the next step below with their feet, and so on. If the child comes down (as well as up) unaided, he passes test A 43. (See Plate 13.)

A 44. *Jumps.* (*Nineteenth month.*)

This item is passed if the child gives a little jump on the floor. Both feet must leave the floor together. This item is almost always observed during the floor work in doing the locomotor assessment. If, however, this has not been observed, the examiner should give a little jump on the floor and say, "Look, this is jumping—can you jump?" The child will usually enter into this game and demonstrate his ability to succeed at this. If he has already passed A 48, he also scores plus for A 44.

A 45. *Runs.* (*Twentieth month.*)

The child is now in his twentieth month or thereabouts. It is important to distinguish between a "trot" and a "run" in this connection. The child who earlier passed A 38 could get about quite quickly, but he was not yet running; he moved along with his feet rather wide apart, swaying from one foot to the other (see Case 3, Chapter X.) By running we mean the definite leggy run used by older children, each foot being lifted well up and behind as the other goes definitely forward. This involves much finer body balance, and to pass A 45 the child's performance must approximate to a definite run. This item can usually be scored as the result of observation, but if necessary can be readily elicited by getting the child to run after the ball and kick it.

A 46. *"Walks" upstairs.* (*Twentieth month.*)

In his management of the stairs the child now walks upstairs, having left behind the creeping-climbing method of even a few weeks ago. He may still, however, prefer hands and knees or some other method when he is descending the staircase.

A 47. *Climbs to stand on chair.* (*Twenty-first month.*)

(See also A 40.) At this age children frequently climb up to look out of the window, or reach something from a shelf and become adept at climbing on chairs for these purposes. An ordinary kitchen or dining chair is intended. This might be placed near the window and the child's attention drawn to something outside; or placed near a shelf and a toy or sweetmeat placed on the shelf. Some such natural situation will usually demonstrate whether or not the child is mature enough to pass this item.

A 48. *Can jump off a step.* (*Twenty-second month.*)

In testing the stair climbing, or even more naturally when seeing the child and his mother out of the clinic, opportunity readily arises for getting a response to A 48. The child should jump off the lowest step of a flight, or from a low stool or box of similar height, quite without help. Care must be taken to see that the child does not merely step down. Both feet should be off the floor together.

A 49. *Can seat himself at table.* (*Twenty-second month.*)

Circumstances lend themselves readily to observing if the child can pass A 49. The examiner needs only to place attractive apparatus ready on the table and say, "Can you bring that little chair (or stool) and sit yourself here by the table? We are going to see more toys." The exact wording is not important. The examiner should encourage the child until it becomes clear whether or not he can seat himself unaided at a low table.

A 50. *"Walks up and down" stairs.* (*Twenty-third month.*)

If the child can now *walk* up and down stairs, having abandoned climbing either up or down, he passes A 50. Most active children reach this stage by the end of the second year. The child may still need to have an adult hold his hand while he also holds on to banisters, but he now goes in the upright position both up and down the staircase.

A 51. *Can kick a ball.* (*Twenty-fourth month.*)

To pass A 51 the child must be able to kick a ball without over-balancing. He should be able to run towards the ball and give it a good kick. Some babies, however, are a little nervous of this, and yet can be found quite able to kick a ball; they dribble it little by little across the floor, without lifting the foot very high. This ingenious method may be accepted as a pass, if the child also passes A 45.

A 52. *Trusted on stairs alone.* (*Twenty-fourth month.*)

This item explains itself, for the child can now manage without the helping hand of the adult and manipulate the stairs alone. He may, however, temporarily retreat into climbing on the way down again. If so, he still passes A 52 (but not A 50) if he can go *alone* up and down stairs by any method.

CHAPTER XII

ADMINISTERING THE PERSONAL-SOCIAL SCALE (SCALE B)

In an earlier chapter (Chapter II) we have perhaps sufficiently stressed the importance of the child's social background and his adjustment to it; and have also discussed the significance of the mother-child relationship for normal progress in all directions from the beginning of life.

We now come to an inventory of the somewhat narrower trend of developing abilities which are the expression of this social development, the items being points at which it is possible through detailed observation and experiment or enquiry to determine the child's stage of progress in this process of social adaptation. The presence and help of the mother or mother-substitute is essential for a complete assessment on this scale. In the nature of the case, certain items can only be assessed from the mother's report of the child's behaviour in the home and elsewhere. But those items for which we depend on the mother's report must be kept as few as possible, and every effort must be made to observe and test for as many as possible of these items of the Personal-Social Scale.

Below is the list of the 52 items of this scale as standardised. It will be noticed that there are 32 items in the first year and 20 in the second. The 32nd item in this scale is the least difficult of the 5 items numbered as 32 in the five scales and, as one additional item was needed in the first year to complete the required number ($5 \times 31 = 155$) of 156, No. 32 of this scale became automatically a first-year item. This also corrected the total number needed for the second year, which is 104 (two for each week).

As before, the items should be scored beneath the numbers on the form.

Any test may be taken twice, not necessarily immediately after failure, but no test more than twice.

Scale B

DETAILS OF THE PERSONAL-SOCIAL SCALE (SCALE B)

First Year

Items *First Three Months*

The baby:

1. Regards persons—momentarily.
2. Is quieted if crying by being picked up.
3. Enjoys his bath.
4. Smiles.
5. Recognises mother visually.
6. Vocalises when talked to.
7. Follows moving persons, especially the mother, with his eyes.
8. Returns the examiner's glance with smiling back or cooing.

Second Three Months

9. He is friendly to strangers.
10. He resists when the examiner tries playfully to take the ring or toy; he tries to hold on to it.
11. He frolics happily when played with.
12. He stops crying when talked to.
13. He now turns his head deliberately to a person talking or calling to him.
14. Makes anticipatory movements when mother goes to lift him up.
15. Holds on to a spoon.
16. Stretches his arms to be taken up.

Third Three Months

17. Drinks from a cup.
18. Manipulates spoon or cup in play.
19. Reacts to his own mirror image (I): Looks at it thoughtfully.
20. Knows strangers from familiar friends.
21. Shows prompt reaction to situations, e.g. at table.
22. Shows displeasure if toy is taken away.
23. Helps to hold cup for drinking (hands go round cup).
24. Pulls off his hat.

Fourth Three Months

25. Reacts to his own mirror image (II): smiles at or plays with it.
26. Waves bye-bye.
27. Shows affection. That is, gives back a show of affection.
28. Finger feeds, using fine prehension. Picks up small pieces of food.
29. Plays with cup, spoon and saucer in a way consistent with some understanding of function.
30. Obeys simple requests: "Give me the cup (toy, etc.)."
31. Plays "Pat-a-cake" (clapping).
32. Puts small objects in and out of cup or box in play.

Second Year

First Three Months

The baby:

33. Tries to help dressing, puts arm ready for coat, etc.
34. Can now hold cup for drinking (but is liable to spill a little).
35. Uses a spoon himself, but is not yet very efficient.
36. Shows shoes on request.

Second Three Months

37. Tries to turn a door-knob.
38. Cleanliness—asks when he needs attention.
39. Manages cup well—half full.
40. Can take off shoes and socks (if unfastened for him).
41. Likes adult to sit and show picture-book.

Third Three Months

42. Parts of body (I): Can indicate eyes, or nose, or hands, etc.
43. Cleanliness—bowel control complete.
44. Uses a spoon well, feeds himself.
45. Has complete bladder control by day, but not yet at night.
46. Tries to tell experiences.

Fourth Three Months

47. Asks for things at table in words—at least two articles.
48. Knows two parts of body by name.
49. Knows three parts of body by name.
50. Knows four parts of body by name.

51. Can open a door.
52. Helps to dress or undress.

B 1. *Regards person—momentarily.* (*First month.*)

This item is relevant in testing babies under a month old. The examiner should talk to the baby to attract his attention and note if the child looks at him in response. A momentary glance is all that can be expected below two weeks, but thereafter the child should be fixating for gradually increasing periods. In this personal-social column it is the glance at the examiner in response to speech that is required.

B 2. *Quieted when picked up.* (*First month.*)

This is easily tested for during the examination, for, should the child whimper at all, the mother may be asked to take him up and the child usually quietens down at once. If this opportunity does not arise, the mother should be asked about this item. Most happy, normally developing babies cry very little and are readily quieted when taken up, unless very hungry.

B 3. *Enjoys bath.* (*Second month.*)

It should be noted that this is quite a different item from A 6. There it was the activity of the child that was indicated. This item is credited if the baby enjoys being bathed. Bathing the baby is something of a social occasion and is normally enjoyed by babies from a very early age. Mother should be asked about this item.

B 4. *Smiling.* (*Second month.*)

The average baby smiles at about six weeks old. (See Plate 2, Chapter II.) The examiner should observe this himself, and a smile can usually be elicited, if the child is capable of it, by talking to the child or getting the mother to do so.

The earliest true smile recorded in this study was at $3\frac{2}{3}$ weeks. There is, however, an earlier stage before true smiling that must not be mistaken for smiling or credited as such. This is a softening and curving of the facial muscles but without a true smile of the lips. We have called this "the happy look". It can be observed in some babies from a very early age, about fourteen days. It precedes true smiling.

B 5. *Visually recognises mother.* (*Second month.*)

There is no doubt about this item when it is present. A glance at Plates 2 and 3 (Chapter II) will show an intelligent child recognising the mother, first with a lovely smile and afterwards with an intent expression attending to what she is saying. After the examiner has been holding the baby's attention, he should step aside and ask the mother to bend over the child. He will at once observe the change of expression if the child has reached this level of maturity.

(A further item, "recognises father", was included in an earlier version of the test. It was found, however, very difficult to assess, as many babies in the early weeks scarcely see their fathers except at week-ends. A few did not see their fathers at all. The results were ambiguous and this item was dropped.)

B 6. *Vocalises (coos) when talked to.* (*Third month.*)

This is an important item, demonstrating that the child is utilising the social situation at this early stage in relation to speech, and is preparing an attitude essential to "imitation of sounds" which must lay the foundation, later on, of true speech development. It is a positive response to the social situation. Any sound in the way of a social response (other than crying), that the child makes during the test period, scores plus.

B 7. *Follows moving persons with eyes.* (*Third month.*)

Moving a little way (about two yards) from the child, after holding his attention in some other test, the examiner should walk slowly about the room, still talking to the child. The test is passed if the child follows him with the eyes for a few seconds. The test may be tried a second time during the test period if the child does not succeed the first time. The child should be on the mother's lap in a comfortable sitting position.

B 8. *Returns examiner's glance with smiling or cooing.* (*End of third month.*)

This item explains itself. By this age (about three months) the baby is capable of very definite social response to friendly persons. A smile, or a definite cooing sound, in response to the examiner's overtures is sufficient to pass this item. Smiling at mother or other familiar person (B 4) is *not* a pass in this item.

B 9. *Friendly to strangers.* (*Beginning of fourth month.*)

In a few further weeks or months the baby will be more conscious of differences between people and less immediately responsive to the overtures of strangers. Still later he may evince some negativism. At this early age (about 3 to 4 months) the normal baby is friendly to every stranger who takes notice of him, especially if the mother is present. It is the child's attitude in general that is tested here, and mother may be asked about this. The examiner must then judge of the child's stage of development from his experience of the child during the test, e.g. his allowing the examiner to take him up, etc.

B 10. *Resists adult who tries playfully to take ring or toy.* (*End of fourth month.*)

After giving the child the ring in connection with testing for the ability to grasp an object (item D 9), the examiner makes sure that the child is holding it firmly and then gently tries to take it from him, asking playfully, "May I have it?" or "Give that to me", etc. If the baby tries to hold on to the ring, he scores plus. A less mature child would relinquish it at once.

B 11. *Frolics when played with.* (*Fifth month.*)

Mother should be asked to play with the baby in her accustomed way, and the examiner should note the child's response. This should involve physical movement as well as laughter or smiling, and general signs of enjoyment at being played with.

B 12. *Stops crying when talked to.* (*Fifth month.*)

This item involves a five-months stage of maturity. Most younger babies require to be taken up when in distress before they will stop crying, but at this stage the child should be capable of being reassured by the mother's approaching voice and will stop crying on hearing her. Opportunity to observe this may occur during the test. If not, the mother must be carefully questioned about this. If the baby is not capable of this, the mother will say at once ruefully: "Oh no! I always have to pick him up." (*Note*: A child of this age is not likely to stop crying if he is very hungry.)

B 13. *Turns head to person talking.* (*Fifth month.*)

Quite tiny babies may be observed, when in the company of several adults, turning the head towards each person speaking in turn, even although they probably do not yet understand anything of the conversation. The sound of a strange voice will often elicit this response. The writer has frequently observed this reaction in the waiting-room at Infant Welfare Centres, or when noticing a child outside in a pram, the little head coming curiously round on the pillow to look at the person talking. If the child has reached this stage of maturity, the reaction can be readily observed during the test, especially at the beginning, when the examiner's voice is new to him, during conversation with the mother. It is seldom necessary to test for this item.

B 14. *Anticipatory movements when about to be lifted.* (*End of fifth month.*)

The mother should be asked to talk to the baby and to pretend to take him up when he is down in the dorsal position. At this stage the child does not deliberately stretch his arms or try to lift himself towards the mother, as he will do later (B 16), but there is a generalised overflowing of physical activity and indications of excitement in anticipation of being lifted. This is sufficient for a pass at this stage.

B 15. *Holds a spoon.* (*Sixth month.*)

By some time in the sixth month a baby can usually hold on to a spoon if allowed to do so. A plastic spoon is used for this test. This should be *offered* to the child for him to hold. It must not be put into his hand. If the child takes and holds the spoon firmly by the handle, he passes this item. If, however, he takes it up from the table himself, a much more difficult performance, it does not matter which way round he secures it, he is credited with passing this item.

B 16. *Stretches to be taken up.* (*End of sixth month.*)

(See also item B 14.) To pass this item the baby must respond to the mother's overtures by deliberately stretching up his hands towards her or trying to lift himself up.

B 17. *Drinks from a cup.* (*Seventh month.*)

A child of this age (seventh month) cannot yet manage a cup or even help to hold it, unless he is very advanced. He can, however, drink from the cup if it is held to his lips. Mothers frequently give a small drink of water, fruit juice, etc., from a cup, even if the baby is still on the bottle. The mother should be asked about this, and if the child is in the habit of taking even a small quantity direct from the cup he can be credited with B 17.

B 18. *Manipulates cup or spoon in play.* (*Seventh month.*)

The child, seated on his mother's knee, should be held near the table, on which are placed near to him the plastic cup and spoon. The child should now be able to pick these up and manipulate them. It is not necessary that he should show in his play with these objects that he understands them yet as utensils. His movements may be awkward and he may send them to the floor, but if he is able to pick up each in turn (not together yet) and manipulate them a little, he passes B 18.

B 19. *Reacts to mirror image—I: Looks at.* (*Seventh month.*)

Seated on his mother's knee or on the floor, the child should be shown the mirror held up in front of him, and asked: "Who is this?" or "Where is the baby?", etc. At this stage most babies stare at their reflection with interest and rather solemnly. If they play with the image, "talk" to it or smile at it, they also pass B 25. They pass this item B 19 if they just *look* at the reflection.

B 20. *Knows strangers from familiar friends.* (*Eighth month.*)

The baby has now passed beyond the stage of being usually friendly to any stranger who takes notice of him. He now knows the various members of his own family and a few other friends, neighbours, etc., and is beginning to be less easy with strangers. This stage of development expresses itself by shyness (retreat) or resistance or even crying if a strange person is too attentive. The experienced examiner soon knows when a child has reached this stage in his social awareness by the child's first few reactions to himself. Insecurity is liable to be very operative at this stage and the child should be left on the mother's knee as much as possible, or the mother should be seated near him. The mother should be asked about the child's attitude to strangers, to confirm this stage of development. The child passes the item if he shows by his manner, especially at the beginning of the test, that the examiner is somebody new or strange. (See Case 2, Chapter X.)

B 21. *Prompt reaction to situations, e.g. at table.* (*Eighth month.*)

Happily seated on the mother's knee or with mother supporting him up at the table, the baby of about eight months old reacts as if in a familiar situation. His hands begin to explore or reach for objects placed near him on the table. He accepts the situation promptly and without fuss, indeed with enthusiasm. If there is crying or resistance, or if the child shows a lack of interest, he does not pass this test.

B 22. *Displeased if toy is taken away.* (*Ninth month.*)

The object of this item is to see if the child has reached a stage such that he can express himself negatively in his own interest. He can, for example, make a fuss if a toy is taken from him. When the child is happily manipulating objects and holding on, for example, to the cup, the examiner holds out his hand and says: "Give me the cup", etc. When the child still hangs on, he gently but deliberately takes the cup away. The child passes this test if he shows displeasure, anger or annoyance. It should be immediately handed back to him and the child reassured. We do not like giving this item, as it is somewhat unkind or is liable to spoil the rapport in a sensitive child. There is usually, however, little danger of this if the attractive object is promptly restored to the child. It is sufficient to see that he is about to make a fuss, and the incident should not be allowed to develop to the point of tears.

B 23. *Helps to hold cup for drinking.* (*Ninth month.*)

This is the second stage of learning to manage a cup for drinking. After the child has been manipulating the cup in play, the examiner (or mother) should hold the cup to the child's lips as if to give him a drink. (A little water may be in the cup, if desired.) The examiner should then observe whether the little hands begin to come round the cup to try to help in holding it. Both hands should make contact with the cup to pass this test, but they are not expected to be very efficient or appropriately placed; the adult *manages* the cup.

B 24. *Pulls off hat.* (*Tenth month.*)

The child's own cap, bonnet, etc., should be placed on his head, and the child, being indoors, will almost certainly want to pull it off. If he does so, he has passed this test. If he does not do so, the examiner begins a little game, pulling the hat gently down over the baby's face and then putting it on again. This should be sufficient to give the child the idea of what is wanted.

B 25. *Reacts to mirror image—II: Smiles at or plays with.* (*Tenth month.*)

To pass B 25 the baby must not only *look* at his reflection in the mirror but must also either smile at the baby in the glass or play with it, kiss it, turn the mirror over in search of it, etc. Any additional reaction that shows an intelligent awareness of something in the mirror is sufficient to pass this item. (See B 19.)

B 26. *Waves bye-bye.* (*Eleventh month.*)

This item can be left to the very last. As the mother carries baby out, the examiner should encourage the child to wave to him. The mother will usually see that the child does this if he can, or will at once say: "Oh, he hasn't learned to do that yet", etc. The child must make some attempt to wave to the examiner to pass this item.

B 27. *Gives affection.* (*Eleventh month.*)

The baby, to pass this test, gives affection to the mother or nurse or other member of the family. Earlier the child will have been content to "accept" the expression of affection from others rather passively, now he ***returns*** the embrace or kiss. Many babies, however, at this stage cannot give a true kiss; they put their face to the mother, or their parted lips, or their arms round her, etc. Any of these manifestations that appear to be expressions of affection may be accepted.

This is a valuable item in diagnosis of backward and sometimes maladjusted children, for they accept affection passively, without evincing any desire to return it, much longer than do normal babies, who, before the end of the first year, are definitely giving evidence of affection towards others.

B. 28. *Finger feeds—thumb and forefinger.* (*Eleventh month.*)

The baby begins to show signs of self-help at this stage by his ability to take up small pieces of food, bread, biscuit or small sweetmeats, neatly between thumb and forefinger. He may have been conveying food to his mouth for some time, taking it up awkwardly and messily with the second, third and fourth fingers, but to pass at this stage he must be using the thumb and forefinger neatly, using fine prehension. (See D 23.)

B 29. *Plays with cup, spoon and saucer.* (*End of eleventh month.*)

The child of this age usually likes to manipulate these three familiar objects. They should be placed in a row near him, cup in the middle, and then the examiner observes the child's stage of play. If he puts the spoon into the cup or saucer and then carries it to his mouth as if feeding, or puts the cup into the saucer, etc., he passes this item. He must play constructively, showing that he is aware of the function or use of any of these articles, and should combine two of them in play.

B 30. *Obeys simple requests—"Give me cup", etc.* (*Twelfth month.*)

To pass this test the child's social development must be such that he will on kindly request give up a toy or other object he is manipulating. If he will not give the object up to the examiner, the mother may be requested to ask the child for it. If he gives up the toy to an adult, he passes the test.

B 31. *Pat-a-cake.* (*Twelfth month.*)

This is a simple hand-clapping test. The examiner (or the mother) claps hands when the child is successful at some other test. The child imitates the gesture. The child is more likely to respond to the mother's clapping than to the examiner's, but either scores plus.

B 32. *Puts small objects in and out of cup in play.* (*Twelfth month.*)

Whilst the child is happily playing with cup, spoon and saucer (B 29), the examiner pushes bricks or small toys one by one towards him, and then drops one of these into the cup and watches what happens. To pass this test the child must put at least one object into the cup and take at least one out during play. The test may be taken twice; that is, the examiner may a second time drop a toy into the empty cup and rattle it and observe the child's reactions.

B 33. *Tries to help dressing—coat, etc.* (*Thirteenth month.*)

This item is passed if the child does anything at all towards helping with the dressing process, e.g. putting his arm ready for his coat, fetching his shoes, lifting arms to have jersey pulled off, etc.

B 34. *Can hold cup for drinking.* (*End of thirteenth month.*)

At this stage the child can take the weight of the cup in his hands, but he cannot yet be trusted to manage it. His hands come round the cup and he can drink from it whilst holding it, but mother has to take responsibility or else he will spill the contents. The examiner must judge of this by offering the child the cup to hold with a little water in it and observing his degree of competence. The mother may also be asked about this item by way of a check, but the examiner must base his final judgment on his own observation during the test.

B 35. *Uses spoon himself fairly well—spills some.* (*Fifteenth month.*)

The child is now, by the fifteenth month, able to feed himself with a spoon, but not very efficiently yet. The spoon tends to be lifted and turned over before reaching the mouth, spilling the contents; but the child is learning and likes to feed himself without help for at least part of each meal. The examiner can judge of this to some extent by the manner of handling the spoon shown during earlier items and should also confirm his judgment by asking the mother about the child's feeding habits at home.

B 36. *Shows shoes.* (*Sixteenth or seventeenth month.*)

Little children are very interested in their shoes, and "shoe" is one of their early spoken words. The examiner asks the child: "Where are your shoes?" or "Show me your shoes", etc., coaxingly, and although the child may not at first quite understand, if the request is repeated, presently the average sixteenth-month baby will lift up his foot or point to his shoe. He may not yet be able to say the word "shoe", but he indicates that he understands it and will co-operate in this social situation enough to show his shoe to the examiner.

B 37. *Tries to turn door-knob.* (*Seventeenth month.*)

Most babies are walking by the seventeenth month, and they attempt to open and shut doors in spite of adult precautions. To pass this item the child must take hold of the door-knob, rattle it, etc., but may not yet be quite able to turn the knob to open the door. It is sufficient if by his efforts he indicates that he knows it is the knob that is the functioning agent in the opening of the door.

B 38. *Cleanliness—asks.* (*Eighteenth month.*)

By his eighteenth month the average baby deliberately and habitually indicates by word or sign of some kind that he needs attention.

B 39. *Manages cup well—half full.* (*Eighteenth month.*)

By the eighteenth month the child should be able to manage a cup about half full very well, without spilling or with very little spilling. This can be tested for by offering the child a drink of water in the cup provided, which should be handed to him barely half full.

B 40. *Can take off shoes and socks.* (*Nineteenth month.*)

To pass this item the child must be able to pull off his own shoes (if unfastened for him) and also his socks. To pull off his own shoes involves first placing one hand to the back of the shoe and pushing the shoe down and then off. This is a fairly complex task, not usually passed by average babies before the nineteenth month. Leather walking shoes are intended, not soft slippers.

B 41. *Likes adult to show book.* (*Nineteenth month.*)

At this stage the child not only shows evidence of enjoying a book (see C 40), but also enjoys the social situation involved in *sharing* a book and having the adult explain the pictures or repeat the rhymes in it, etc. The mother may be asked to show the little book provided to the child, or the examiner himself may do this. The child must show some interest in the pictures, animals, etc.

B 42. *Parts of body—I.* (*Nineteenth or twentieth month.*)

For this test the doll is used. Many children at this age are not yet quite ready to interpret a picture, and so the cardboard doll used by Terman and Merrill, although appropriate for older children, does not quite serve the purpose of the test at this early age. The child is given the doll to hold and asked: "Where are dolly's hands?", "Where is her hair?", "Where are her feet?", etc. The six items are: hands, hair, feet, eyes, nose and mouth. Hands and hair appear to be the easiest for most children. Any *one* item at this level scores plus for B 42, if correctly pointed out. (The child is not expected to *name* the part at this stage.)

B 43. *Bowel control complete.* (*Nineteenth or twentieth month.*)

The average child is now usually quite clean and reliable as regards this function, except for an occasional mishap.

B 44. *Uses spoon well.* (*Twentieth month.*)

The average child can now manage the spoon very well and feed himself cleanly.

B 45. *Bladder control by day.* (*Twentieth month.*)

The average child is by the twentieth month usually quite reliable by day in regard to this function, but not necessarily at night for some time to come.

B. 46. *Tries to tell experiences.* (*Twenty-first month.*)

In spite of a not very extensive vocabulary and the presence still of much babble, the average child tries to explain or report experiences to others. The mother may be asked whether the child tries to tell others what he has seen in the street or in the park, etc. Any effort to tell such experiences is sufficient to pass at this stage. This too can sometimes be elicited during the test, or the friendly child of this age may struggle to tell the examiner something on arrival as soon as he is greeted.

B 47. *Asks for things at table.* (*Twenty-second month.*)

For this the child must definitely *name* one or two articles of food appropriately when seated at the table for a meal, e.g. cake, biscuit, juice (orange juice), etc. Babbled nouns will do so long as they are consistently and appropriately applied.

B 48. *Parts of body—II.* (*Twenty-second month.*)

As for B 42, but the average child now knows two of the six parts of the body already named above. If any two of the six are correctly pointed out, he passes the item.

B 49. *Parts of body—III.* (*Twenty-third month.*)

As for B 42, but three parts of the body are now correctly indicated.

B 50. *Parts of body—IV.* (*Twenty-fourth month.*)

As for B 42, but four parts of the body are now correctly indicated. They need not be named by the child.

B 51. *Can open door.* (*Twenty-fourth month.*)

To pass this item the child must be able to *turn the door-knob* and open a door himself. This should be tested for in the clinic. A good time to take this item is at the end of the interview when the child is taking his departure with the mother.

B 52. *Helps actively to dress or undress.* (*Twenty-fourth month.*)

To pass this item the child must be able to help actively to dress or undress himself; for example, he must be able to pull off his blouse or jacket, if it is unfastened for him, or pull on his jersey if it is given to him the right way round.

CHAPTER XIII

ADMINISTERING THE HEARING AND SPEECH SCALE (SCALE C)

In coming now to the Speech Scale, we begin as before with babies in their first month.

Throughout this study of the interesting early development of speech, it has become increasingly clear that in assessing a child's progress in this direction account must be taken of the length of reaction times. There is a time-lag that can be observed between what the child hears and what he later attempts to produce or reproduce. It is important to note the difference between immediate imitation, which cannot be expected in the early stages, and a delayed reaction. Still farther on in this study a similar time-lag can be observed between what the child understands of the speech of others and his later ability to make himself understood verbally. There is also the important question of the function of attention and that of practice over considerable periods in the development of learning and of habit formation in response to heard speech, and the effort to imitate it.

There are thus several important stages in this development, which may be very briefly indicated here:

I. At first the child, confronted with all the complexity of heard adult speech, is quite unable to get into relationship with it. This is also the case with all other aspects of his situation in a complex environment. He therefore appears to take little notice, but is listening and observing nonetheless and from a very early age. There are varying degrees of attention, at first to the voice of the mother and later to the voices of other people as well as to certain other sounds in his environment. The mother instinctively simplifies her speech, using one or two caressing syllables in her vocal soothing of the child and "talking" to him. Quite early, however, the baby begins to vocalise in response to the mother's voice and in other circumstances, and there is evidence, during this phase, of much active listening.

II. Gradually the child builds up a vocabulary of vocalised

sounds which become increasingly complex and also more numerous. He still listens attentively for much of his time and falls into the habit of doing a good deal of his "practising" when lying resting and when the stimulus of heard speech is absent. To what extent the child is at this stage *understanding* the speech of others, or attributing meaning to his own undoubted attempts to imitate, it is not possible in the present stage of knowledge to say. But both of these gradually come into being out of the seeming chaos of infant vocalisation and babble from about the seventh month onwards.

III. The third stage is that difficult one for the child and intriguing one for the psychologist or student of speech development, in which the child undoubtedly understands a great deal of what is said by others around him, but has so little command of the means of verbal expression that he cannot communicate his ideas or converse normally as yet with others. Frequently failing to make himself understood and often exasperated to the point of tears or temper, he yet struggles to imitate the words he hears. Being obliged to work selectively, he gradually builds up a vocabulary intimately related to his personal needs and interests: names of members of his family, the names of pets and toys, articles of food, personal possessions and so on. These develop in type as his social awareness and adjustment also grow.

IV. In the fourth stage the child develops word combinations and then the sentence, the adult unit of thought and communication of ideas, and so gradually begins in early childhood to make more satisfactory and intelligent relations with his immediate milieu and with his general environment.

But throughout all this development there is that lag or gap between his comprehension of what is said around him and his own ability to express himself verbally. Probably it is this gap between what is understood (passive speech) and what can be expressed (active speech) that becomes part of the complex stimulus to progress that is present in all normal subjects from infancy onwards. For even later on, in mastering a foreign language it is possible to follow a conversation or a lecture with a high degree of understanding at a time when facility in reproduction is at a much lower level. Thus many students can get the meaning of a conversation but cannot themselves converse in the foreign tongue. A baby's predicament would appear to be somewhat similar to this.

Where this situation is complicated by a disability that still further delays verbal expression, as in cases of retarded speech development who are of a normal general intelligence level, the gap between what is understood and what can be reproduced becomes even wider and is liable to become associated with a degree of emotional maladjustment. Such a case was described at the end of Chapter VIII.

In building up the verbal scale to be described below, we have tried to keep these stages of development and their implications in mind. In the very earliest phases of this complex development, in the early tests, it will be noticed that there is an emphasis on tests of hearing or rather of active listening. In fact, we may call the first few weeks and months the "listening phase", and careful observers of this aspect of infant development can confirm the frequent presence of the attentive "listening expression" in the very young infant.

Tests of hearing and listening are also important from the beginning because of the desirability of determining whether an unusually silent child is merely retarded in regard to speech or whether his condition may be complicated by hearing loss.

In those older cases where speech development as expressed (active speech) lags behind comprehension of the speech of others (passive or subjective speech), the indirect method, used throughout the second year in some of the language tests, will help to disclose to some extent the degree of comprehension that does exist, even where speech or spoken vocabulary is not yet present. This indirect method can also in such special cases help diagnosis of mental status in serious cases of gross speech disorder among somewhat older subjects.

In the latter part of the second year, the young child has reached a stage of great complexity in his speech development. His comprehension is frequently far ahead of his ability to reproduce speech, and he struggles for verbal means of expression. We therefore find, side by side with one another: (1) a good deal of babble still, long sentences of so-called jargon, full, however, of meaning for the child but not understood by those around him; (2) a small but growing vocabulary of clear words used appropriately and understood by others, of which the child is inordinately proud; (3) a much larger vocabulary of single words, too indistinct or inaccurate in pronunciation to be understood by others but being definite words to the child, having appropriate objective meanings and the pronunciation of which he struggles to bring to a stage such that they can be understood; (4) one or more quite clear word-combinations (see item C 46); and even (5) the use of a few short clear sentences of four or more syllables.

A great deal has yet to be learnt about all these stages of speech development in infancy. (See M. M. Lewis, 1936.) Its implications are far-reaching for the psychologist and also for the student of education. In this chapter we present a new inventory of some of the stages of this complex development that have been observed in the course of this research and standardised as the Hearing and Speech Scale. As before, there are 52 items covering this development from the first to the twenty-fourth month of life. This scale is also approximately of the same difficulty as the other four scales. (See Table V, Chapter V.)

Scale C

DETAILS OF THE HEARING AND SPEECH SCALE (SCALE C)

First Year

Items *First Three Months*

The baby:

1. Is startled by sounds.
2. Is quieted by his mother's voice.
3. (Vocalisation other than crying.) Makes murmured sounds.
4. Listens to a soft bell note near him.
5. Makes definite cooing noises, one syllable.
6. Searches for sounds with eye movements.
7. Listens to music
8. Makes two or more different sounds.

Second Three Months

9. Searches for sound with head movements.
10. Laughs aloud.
11. Turns his head deliberately to the bells.
12. Listens to tuning-fork.
13. Coos or stops crying on hearing music.
14. Talks (babbles) to persons.

15. Manipulates the handbell.
16. Makes four or more different sounds. (Separate single sounds or syllables.)

Third Three Months

17. Responds when called.
18. Uses two-syllable babble.
19. Shouts for attention.
20. Listens to conversations.
21. Uses singing tones.
22. Uses babbled phrases of four or more syllables.
23. Says "Mama", or "Dada", etc. *One* word clear.
24. Listens to a stop-watch.

Fourth Three Months

25. Shakes head for "No!"
26. Now says two clear words. *Two* words clear.
27. Uses short babbled sentences. (Meaningful babble.)
28. Rings the bell.
29. Reacts to music vocally.
30. Babbled monologue when alone.
31. Says *three* clear words.

Second Year

First Three Months

The baby:

32. Tries to sing.
33. Looks at pictures for a short while.
34. Knows his own name.
35. Likes nursery rhymes and jingles.
36. Uses four or five clear words.

Second Three Months

37. *One* object in the box is identified when named by the examiner.
38. Uses six or seven clear words.
39. Makes long babbled conversations, with some words clear.
40. Enjoys a picture-book.
41. Two objects in the box are identified.
42. Uses nine clear words.

Third Three Months

43. Four objects in the box are identified.
44. Vocabulary—twelve clear words.
45. Picture vocabulary—one picture named.
46. Uses word combinations.
47. Picture vocabulary—two pictures named.

Fourth Three Months

48. Listens to stories.
49. Vocabulary—twenty words clear.
50. Identifies eight objects in the box when named by the examiner.
51. *Names* four toys.
52. Uses sentences of four or more syllables.

C 1. *Startled by sounds.* (*First month.*)

The object of this item is to check up straight away on the child's hearing and general reaction to sounds. The examiner does not attempt to create any artificial situation that might frighten the child, by producing or arranging for noises of any kind. (No brick-dropping, tray-banging or door-slamming are allowed!) Instead, the mother should be asked if the child starts at sudden noises in the house or on the street. Also the effect of any unexpected loud sound that may occur during the test may be noted. This item has little relationship to the "startle reflex" so frequently described in the literature. This is not a violent fear reaction, but the slight start that a child of any age might make at a sudden noise.

C 2. *Quieted by voice.* (*First month.*)

At this early stage the child should quieten down, if restless, to the sound of an adult's voice, usually the mother's, and give evidence of *hearing* it and being reassured by the sound, the adult holding him or bending over the cot. (This is quite different from B 12 in the Personal-Social Scale. There the older child accepts the comfort and reassurance of knowing from her voice and speech that mother is near at hand, although she is not holding him, and the child stops crying. At that later stage it involves a degree of self-control.)

C 3. *Vocalisation other than crying.* (*First month.*)

The examiner should listen throughout the examination for any vocalisation produced by the child. It may be a mere open vowel, scarcely voiced: "a—a—a", or a soft gurgle. Any vocal sound other than crying scores plus.

C 4. *Listens to bell.* (*Second month.*)

The examiner should take the small handbell and sound one *small* note on it, the bell being held beyond the child's field of vision and about $1\frac{1}{2}$ feet away from the right ear. The examiner observes the child's expression. If the baby *hears* the sound, he will take on an intent expression of the eyes and keep quite still, listening. Or he may dislike the sound and cry. In either case the examiner knows the child has heard the bell. The test is then repeated on the left side and, if both results are positive, showing that the child *pauses to listen*, the examiner scores it plus. If the child cries at the first sound, the softer note of the bell-ring may be tried for the second side. It is the *listening* quality in the child's reaction that we want to note. (No repeated or loud ringing of the bell is necessary or desirable.)

C 5. *Cooing—one syllable clear.* (*End of second month.*)

This is a continuous or frequent happy sound—the same sound occurring over and over; the earlier vague vocalisations may alternate with this one characteristic sound. This cooing is frequently noticed during the examination, but if the child is quite silent, all hearing items must be taken with great care and the mother questioned about the child's vocalisation at home. Mother may be asked to talk to the baby to get him in a happy mood, when cooing frequently results. Any fairly distinct syllable or open vowel, produced and repeated when the child appears in a happy mood, scores plus. (Examples: "a-a-a", "la-la", "oo-oo" or "goo-oo-oo".)

C 6. *Searches for sound with eyes.* (*End of second month.*)

(See C 4.) There is not yet definite head turning towards the sound of the bell, but the child's *eyes* move rather slowly from side to side in search of the sound. The examiner rings the bell gently as in C 4.

C 7. *Listens to music.* (*Third month.*)

Mother may be asked about the child's reaction to music in the home, e.g. the radio. Does baby appear to listen? If not, does he listen when mother sings to him? The writer often gets a listening reaction by herself singing softly to the child or getting the mother to do so. This item is scored plus if there is evidence that the baby listens actively to music.

C 8. *Makes two + different sounds.* (*End of third month.*)

These are not phonetic sounds of which several might be distinguishable in one vague syllable, but two different noises, syllables or speech sounds made frequently by the child and becoming characteristic, e.g. "goo", "a", "la", etc. See C 5, but now the baby has a vocabulary of *two* such speech elements.

C 9. *Searches for sound with head movements.* (*Fourth month.*)

At this stage, in response to the bell or bell-ring, the child makes small searching movements of head and eyes but does not yet turn his head deliberately in the direction of the sound. Definite *head* movements in any direction in search of the sound are scored plus. (See items C 4 and C 6.)

C 10. *Laughs aloud.* (*Fourth month.*)

Having learnt to smile by six weeks of age, it is not until the fourth month that the average baby produces a laugh. To pass this item he must laugh aloud.

C 11. *Turns head deliberately to bells.* (*Fifth month.*)

During the fifth month the average baby can turn his head deliberately towards the sound of the bell. (See C 4, C 6, C 8.) Both sides must be tested for, and the child must turn his head in each direction towards the sound, deliberately and immediately, to pass the test at this level.

C 12. *Listens to tuning-fork.* (*Fifth month.*)

The tuning-fork gives the note of C (upper C), a sound sometimes interpreted by older babies as a train whistle! At this level, the child should listen intently to the sound of the tuning-fork.

The fork must not be struck noisily on a piece of furniture; this distresses the baby and damages the instrument. The fork must be rung by pressing the prongs together and releasing suddenly. The tuning-fork is held a few inches from the child's ear. Both sides are tested. It is best to approach the child from behind for this test, keeping the fork out of his field of vision as much as possible, for if he catches sight of the bright object he may reach out for it instead of listening. The examiner may steady the child's head with the left hand, and should watch for the listening expression on the child's face and the quietening down of physical movements that accompany interest in the sound. If the child persists in clutching at the instrument instead of listening, he fails in this item.

This is an important item in relation to hearing and speech, but is also complicated by the maturity of the infant for, at a less mature level, the child wants the fork as a toy to play with and carry to the mouth, but the average baby at five months can give his attention more definitely to an interesting sound. Failure in this item must not therefore lead to the assumption that the child may be deaf. This can alone be studied in relation to the entire hearing and speech scale, and the child's level on that sequence in relation to his level on the four other scales. (See Chapter VIII.)

The tuning-fork is a delicate instrument, and should be carefully wrapped after use and placed in the box provided. The baby must not be allowed to play with it.

C 13. *Coos or stops crying on hearing music.* (*Fifth month.*)

The mother may be asked about this, or the examiner may get this reaction as suggested in C 7.

C 14. *Talks* (*babbles*) *to persons.* (*Beginning of sixth month.*)

This item is usually scored on the basis of observation throughout the interview. The examiner must train himself to listen to and note all vocal reactions of the child, no matter what test is being taken, and enter these in the margin provided on the form. They then form the basis for scoring many of the speech items. At this level the baby begins to hold "conversations" with friendly adults; his babble is still vague and formless but persistent, especially to members of the family group. The examiner must himself have observed and noted some degree of babble in response to himself and to the mother during the test to be in a position to credit this item as plus.

C 15. *Manipulates hand-bell.* (*End of sixth month.*)

Attracted by the apparatus because of its interest as a sound-producing object, the child stretches out his hand for it. After the examiner has completed the hearing tests with the bell, he puts it down near the child and observes. If the child takes up the bell and manipulates it, exploring the clapper with his finger, or trying to ring it, he scores plus. The child must show that he is exploring or trying to understand the source of the sound, e.g. a baby who immediately lifts the object to his mouth does not pass this test, but one who in trying to ring it bangs it on the floor or table, does. (See Plate 21.)

C 16. *Makes four + different sounds.* (*Sixth and seventh months.*)

(See C 8.) The child now has a vocabulary of four or more different vague sounds, e.g. "a", "er", "gl", "kkk", "oo", "goo", "la", etc. Any four separate sounds or syllables that he habitually makes pass him at this level. Mother may be questioned about this, and syllables described by her should be entered on the form in the appropriate place, marked "M". The examiner must himself, however, have heard some babble from the child and recorded it in the space marked "E". When the test is finished, these notes will form the basis for his judgment as to whether the child has a vocabulary of at least four such sounds.

C 17. *Responds when called.* (*Seventh month.*)

The examiner calls softly to the child ("Hullo! Hullo!") during the test and notes the baby's response. The child should look or turn his head to the examiner when called. This is sufficient to pass this item. Vocal response is sometimes obtained but is not expected for a pass.

C 18. *Two-syllable babble.* (*Seventh month.*)

Examples of two-syllable babble are: the same syllable repeated to make a word, or two different syllables joined, e.g. "ala", "ama", "oogoo", "looloo", or more advanced ones such as: "mimi", "aja", "aha", "ippi", etc.

The difference between babble and mere vocalisation is in its degree of clearness. The early vocalisations of a child are vague and slurred and extremely difficult to reproduce or write down, whether phonetics are used or not. They are usually monosyllables. Babble begins to approximate nearer to adult speech and become clear enough that it can be definitely reproduced. To pass C 18 any two-syllable remark is a pass if fairly distinct.

C 19. *Shouts for attention.* (*Eighth month.*)

To pass this test the baby must have developed the habit of shouting to his mother or other adult to attract attention. This is not a cry or a yell but a definite shout, or loud vocal sound, made in fun or in annoyance, but having the object of calling attention to himself. The baby will sometimes do this if adults are talking and he feels left out of the conversation or is bored. This reaction is seldom observed during a test; the mother must therefore be questioned about it.

C 20. *Listens to conversations.* (*Eighth month.*)

This item again measures active listening that is so essential if the child is to learn to imitate adult speech. When adults (or older children) are talking, the baby at this age can be observed to grow quiet but very attentive, turning his head from one to the other and occasionally trying to join in the conversation. The examiner frequently has opportunity of observing this during the examination, whenever he refers a question to the mother, and in particular during the note-taking and settling-down period at the beginning of the test.

C 21. *Singing tones.* (*Eighth month.*)

The mother must be asked about this item as the baby seldom has enough confidence to sing during the test, although it is occasionally noticed. At this level the baby merely makes a few essays up the scale whilst happily babbling. Where there is music in the home or the mother sings to her child frequently, the reaction is often heard about the eighth month. The sounds made must be definite singing tones, not just happy squeaks.

C 22. *Babbled phrases: four + syllables.* (*Beginning of ninth month.*)

The child's babble at this age is developing rapidly and phrases of four or more syllables begin to be heard, e.g. "a loolooloo", "dadadada", "babababa", "dub-dub-dubby", and also more complicated ones such as: "jajajajay", "mu-mum-mer", "ah-vwa-vwa-vwa", "oo-wa-wa-wa", "oh-wa-oh-wa", "ah-dee-ah-gang-ee", "gay-yer-gay-yer", etc. These are all from the writer's notes taken during testing. A much larger list could be compiled. If the child uses four or more syllables in one expression, he passes at this level. True speech is very near when expressions such as these are being used. The interesting question of the meaningfulness of such phrases lies beyond the scope of this work at its present stage.

C 23. *Says "Mama" or "Dada", etc. One word clear.* (*Ninth month.*)

Although still producing much babble, the average child by the end of the ninth month has usually also acquired one clear word. To pass this item the child must have a vocabulary of at least one clear word, and this must be used appropriately and consistently for the same object. Thus the child who says "Dad-dad" must use this name for the father and not also for the mother, otherwise there is no means of distinguishing certainly between the meaningful name and the earlier "dadadada", which is definitely babble in preparation for the "Dad-dad" but not quite there yet. Examples of early words are: "Dad-dad", "Mum-mum", "Baba", "Nan-nan", "Lili", "Bow-wow". It will be noted these are all names of people, or of pets, showing the social significance of speech finding early expression in the interest in members of the family group and pets in the home. The names of objects used by the child in his daily life come rapidly after this, e.g. articles of food, utensils, toys, etc.

C 24. *Listens to stop-watch.* (*Ninth month.*)

The examiner sets the watch going and holds it near to the child's right ear. The child's head may be slightly steadied with the left hand, and the examiner can sometimes get the child in a quiet listening mood by whispering the instructions: "Listen—tick-tick." As for earlier tests, the quiet listening expression must be observed. The test is repeated on the left side. The child must show evidence of listening on both occasions to pass the test. Again, the child who does not listen but tries repeatedly to grab the object to manipulate it or carry it to his mouth, fails the test.

C 25. *Shakes head for "No!"* (*Tenth month.*)

This can frequently be observed early in the test situation at this age, tenth month, before a good positive rapport has been built up. It must be a definite shaking of the head by way of refusal, not a mere withdrawing or turning away. The mother may be asked about this item, but the examiner should make every effort to observe it himself during the test.

C 26. *Says two clear words.* (*Tenth month.*)

The child now has a vocabulary of two clear words, each one used consistently and appropriately for the same object. (See C 23.)

C 27. *Short babbled sentences.* (*End of tenth month.*)

The child's babble is now more varied and his essays at conversing more lengthy, and definitely beyond the four-syllable level scored in C 22. The examiner must himself judge of the child's level by his own observations and recordings of the child's attempts at speech during the test, supplemented by the mother's report.

C 28. *Rings bell.* (*Eleventh month.*)

Method: The examiner rings the bell and then places it on the table or floor close to the child. The child should manipulate the bell in exploring it (see C 15), but at this stage he should also take it deliberately by the handle and ring it successfully.

C 29. *Reacts to music vocally.* (*Eleventh month.*)

The mother may be questioned about this item, but the examiner must also make note of any vocal sounds used during the test. These may be elicited by singing to the child or asking the mother to sing some familiar song or rhyme to the child. Any vocal reaction scores plus. This is a definite reaction to music, singing, radio, etc., and is imitative, occurring during the sound or immediately afterwards. It is a big step beyond the mere occasional singing tones produced earlier (C 21) during the child's vocal experimenting. The child who echoes the sound of the tuning-fork (this was occasionally observed) scores plus for this item.

C 30. *Babbled monologue when alone or resting.* (*Twelfth month.*)

Most babies of this age develop a habit of lying in the early mornings, or when happily resting at other times, "talking" to themselves. By this activity they "practise" pre-speech until it gradually approximates to adult speech. Mother may be asked about the child's habits in this regard, but the examiner must also observe the child's babble during the test and use his judgment in regard to this item. Many babies babble away at once when happily manipulating objects or if left on the floor with toys whilst the adults are conversing. These activities score plus, especially if confirmed by the mother as occurring frequently.

C 31. *Says three clear words.* (*End of twelfth month.*)

The child should now have a vocabulary of three words pronounced clearly enough that those around him can understand them, and each one used appropriately and consistently for the same object, etc. (See C 26.)

C 32. *Tries definitely to sing.* (*Thirteenth month.*)

At this stage the child definitely tries to join in when others are singing or when the radio is playing.

C 33. *Looks at pictures briefly.* (*Thirteenth month.*) (See Plate 16.)

The baby at this level is beginning to notice and interpret pictures, but only makes an effort in this direction for very brief periods. The examiner should take up the little picture book and, opening it, give it with encouragement to the child to look at. (Or he may ask the mother to show the book to the child.) The baby must give evidence of a passing interest. Even if it lasts only about ten seconds, he passes at this level. He may then throw the book aside. Definite failure is scored when the child immediately pushes the book aside or manipulates it without looking at the pictures, tries to tear or screw it, or carries it to his mouth.

C 34. *Knows own name.* (*Fourteenth month.*)

At this stage the child should give evidence of knowing his own name, although he does not yet *say* his name. The examiner may ask the mother in a level tone: "Where is Jimmy?", etc., using the child's first name, or when doing the mirror test he may ask: "Where is Jimmy?" If the child looks up at the first question or points to himself in the mirror or gives evidence of regarding the name as his own, he scores plus. Care must be taken to distinguish between a pass at this level and the mere response to being called

(C 17), which is a response to a tone of voice, not necessarily to a meaningful word such as his name should now be. A baby at fourteen months frequently smiles or looks self-conscious when he hears his own name, and this is a significant indication.

C 35. *Likes rhymes or jingles.* (*End of fourteenth month.*)

The mother should be asked to sing or say over to the child a rhyme that he is familiar with, or she may at once say: "Oh! he doesn't listen to rhymes yet", etc. Any response that shows pleasure in the rhyme scores plus. (Familiar rhymes are: any nursery rhyme or song or game such as "Baa-baa, Black Sheep"; "This little pig went to market"; "Round the Mulberry Bush", etc.)

C 36. *Uses four or five clear words.* (*Fifteenth month.*)

As for C 31, except that now the child uses four or five clear words. These are used consistently and appropriately.

C 37. *One object in box identified.* (*End of sixteenth month.*)

For this test the examiner produces the box of small toys and, beginning with the easiest, "cup, spoon, cat", etc., places them one by one *slowly* in front of the child. (Approximate order of difficulty: cup, spoon, cat, baby, dog, car, chair, ball, horse, penny, brick, button.) The bright baby may immediately name one, saying "Spoon" or "Pussy", etc., straightaway, and if so he passes C 37. The test should, however, in any case be continued until all the toys are spread out on the table and the child is happily manipulating them. Any speech items produced, whether relevant to this test item or not, must be noted. When the child has been manipulating the toys and babbling for about a minute or less, the examiner should ask: "Which is the spoon?", "Give me the pussy", etc., and go on until the child has given up those he knows the names of. Great care must be taken not to ask for a toy that the child is actually handling. Sometimes the baby misunderstands and thinks it is a game of handing objects to one another. If he therefore gives up the wrong toy, the examiner should ask, in surprise, e.g. "Oh, is *that* the pussy?", "Where is the pussy?", etc., and do this two or three times to see if the child is capable of indicating the right object, for that is what we want to know. If the child's finger goes to the right toy, even although he does not actually hand it to the examiner, that toy is credited as known. It is not necessary for the child to *name* any of the toys, only to identify the toys correctly when named by the examiner. The examiner must avoid talking very much during this test and merely ask: "Which is the dolly?", "Give me the pussy", etc., or "Car, *please*," is enough. ("Put your finger on the pussy," etc., is too cumbersome and difficult at this early age.)

C 38. *Uses six or seven words.* (*Seventeenth month.*)

The average child now has a vocabulary of six or seven words that he uses clearly, appropriately and consistently.

C 39. *Long babbled conversations, some words clear.* (*Seventeenth month.*)

At this stage the child indulges in long monologues of vague babble or indistinguishable chatter with, however, occasional meaningful words emerging from the rest—sometimes at the *end* of the babbled sentence. This is a further stage of C 30. By "clear" is meant recognisable by the adult.

C 40. *Enjoys picture-book.* (*Eighteenth month.*)

Taken as for C 33, but to pass at this stage the child must show pleasure in the book, e.g. by looking at the pictures or turning the pages, or pointing or smiling or babbling to the pictures. Any of these passes the test. (He must have superseded the stage of using a book merely as an object to manipulate or tear up, although he may still on occasion revert to this.)

C 41. *Two objects in box identified.* (*Eighteenth month.*)

The method of giving this test is as for C 37. The child is *not* expected to *name* the object, but only to identify it when named by the examiner. This is what we have called the "indirect method" of studying a child's comprehension at this early stage. Many older children with speech defects or disorders can pass tests taken by this indirect method at a level beyond their ability to reproduce language, and so give some evidence at least of their level of comprehension of language, even if they are completely lacking in speech.

C 42. *Says nine words.* (*Nineteenth month.*)

The average child of this age has a vocabulary of nine words that he uses clearly, appropriately and consistently.

C 43. *Four objects in box identified.* (*Twentieth month.*)

See C 37 and C 41 for method of taking this test. At this level, four of the objects must be identified when named by the examiner.

C 44. *Vocabulary of twelve words.* (*Twentieth month.*)

The average child of this age has a vocabulary of twelve words that he uses clearly, consistently and appropriately, and that are understood by others in the home. Score twelve words as plus.

C 45. *Picture vocabulary* (1). (*Twentieth month.*)

For this test there is a new set of twenty small pictures of common objects: cat, house, flower, etc. These are shown to the child one by one and he is asked: "What is this?", etc. They must be shown to him in the order of difficulty, as numbered on the back. He is expected to know the name of *one* of these pictures at this level.

If the child fails six cards in succession, there is no need to go further. The child may hold the card whilst looking at it, but must not be allowed to crumple or destroy the apparatus.

C 46. *Word combinations.* (*Beginning of twenty-first month.*)

In studying the child's vocabulary and general verbal facility at this stage, the examiner must note whether the child has begun to combine two or more words together in short phrases. Examples are: "Daddy gone", "More, please", "Wants drink", "Go out", etc. If the child gives evidence of using *one* such word combination, he passes this item.

C 47. *Picture vocabulary* (2). (*Twenty-second month.*)

As for C 45, but now the child should be able to name any *two* of the pictures.

C 48. *Listens to stories.* (*Twenty-third month.*)

To pass this item the child should be able to listen for a short time to an adult telling a story. This is a stage farther on, but in the same series as C 33, C 35 and C 40. Now the child will listen to the mother telling a story that goes beyond what is familiar in a well-known rhyme and even beyond what is pictured in the book. Whilst the examiner (or the mother) is showing the picture-book, some further quite simple imaginative story or explanation should be offered to the child to see if his attention can be held for even a short time by a story about any of the pictures in the little book.

C 49. *Vocabulary—twenty words clear.* (*Twenty-fourth month.*)

Throughout the examination the examiner has been noting and recording the child's vocabulary in the margin provided. He should now peruse and count up the child's vocabulary as listed, and add to it, where indicated; for example, pictures named, toys named, additional words spoken. Mother may be asked to add to the list, but these extra words must be entered in the space marked "M". The examiner must then estimate as exactly as possible the child's total vocabulary of words used clearly, consistently and appropriately. Words mentioned by the mother may be added only if (*a*) they are of similar difficulty to those noted by the examiner, and (*b*) if the mother appears to be a good witness.

The child's general verbal facility, use of word combinations, level of babble, whether babble is left behind, etc., will all help the examiner in forming his estimate.

C 50. *Eight objects in box identified.* (*Twenty-fourth month.*)

By the twenty-fourth month the average child can identify eight of the toys and other small objects in the box (See C 37 and C 41.)

C 51. *Names four toys.* (*Twenty-fourth month.*)

The average child should now be able to *name* correctly at least four of the small toys, as well as identify as many as eight (C 50). This difference between four named and eight identified provides a rough indication of the time-lag between comprehension or "knowing" the name of an object and the much more difficult stage of being able to reproduce the name on seeing the object.

C 52. *Uses sentences of four + syllables.* (*Twenty-fourth month.*)

The average child at two years (twenty-four months) has developed short sentences of four or more syllables. He still probably retains some babbled words or phrases and uses many isolated monosyllables in his speech. If the child shows evidence of using *one* such sentence of four or more syllables, he passes the test at this stage. Examples are: "More pudding, please", "I want dolly", "That's motor-car", etc.

PLATE 16

Note the intent expression of this fourteen-months' boy as he looks at pictures. (See items B 41, Chapter XII, and C 33, Chapter XIII.)

PLATE 17

At sixteen months this little girl is talking well, almost to a two-years' level. Note the intent *listening* expression while she is receiving instructions for the next test. This active listening to and concentration on heard speech is noticed from the first few weeks of life, and is an important factor in speech development. (See introduction to Chapter XIII.)

PLATE 18

At eleven months, this boy plays happily on the floor with toys and can be left alone in his play-pen. He can stand when held and also pull himself up by furniture, but does not yet stand alone. He is seen playing with two objects. He is rattling and listening to both objects at once. The ball rattles and the test box contains bricks.

PLATE 19

He has now abandoned the box and both hands go round the ball. Notice the complete opposition of thumb and fingers. His attention is engaged by watching the little car that is being wound up for him. (The next moment he was across the floor after it.)

CHAPTER XIV

ADMINISTERING THE HAND AND EYE SCALE (SCALE D)

In Scale D we come to a study of Hand and Eye Development and their gradual co-ordination, which is necessary for the growth of manipulative skills. In the last chapter, we found a "listening" phase at first preceding and afterwards accompanying early pre-speech, here in the D Scale there is a period of attentive "looking" or visual examination, by the child, of the immediate spatial environment. Thus the following of a light, looking at objects and at people, following moving objects and persons, precede and later accompany reaching for and grasping and further manipulative activities. Thus the first eight items in this scale are all tests of visual adjustment; they indicate the ability to focus on and fixate objects and keep them in view when they move. The moving object becomes differentiated from the probably only vaguely apprehended background but, out of the baby's active visual exploring of moving objects in his environment, he gradually acquires a sense of the spatial and the spatially continuous.

Presently the child begins to reach after and grasp objects in his immediate neighbourhood, and acquires an increasing skill at this necessary and fundamental manipulative activity. Gesell used a large ring swung before the child to encourage the "reach and grasp" behaviour of his subjects. We follow him in this, using, however, a somewhat smaller ring, brightly coloured, with bells attached. There has been much discussion about this reaching for and grasping activity and its differentiation from the early grasping reflex. It would appear that there is room for more research to be done on this problem. So far as our own observations go, there does not seem to be any discontinuity; the early reflex grasp of the tiny infant becomes modified and extended to the tactual exploring and grasping of any object or material within his reach. Nor does there appear to be any gap or delay in the actual ability to grasp, although the reaching out for an object can only appear when the hand and eye have attained some degree of co-ordination. We find, for example, that the baby will grasp an object put into his hand (E 6), and also take an object given to him (D 9—see Plate 22) some time before he can reach out correctly and grasp the object (D 11). Still later (D 13 and 14), he will clutch at and secure the dangling ring. This development, from the first strong, crude grasping of the young neonate, to the deliberate and persistent reaching after objects, appears progressive and continuous.

Scale D is largely scored on the basis of observation, the examiner merely providing the occasion for the displaying by the child of the various stages of hand development and their association with vision in the general grasping and manipulating of objects in the environment. Later on, the use of a pencil on paper, the building of toys or bricks one upon another, the rolling of a ball, and other natural activities common to every child, find a place in this scale and are tested for in a play way. They provide occasions for observing the stages of hand development: forefinger and thumb in partial opposition (D 22), fine prehension (D 23), thumb opposition (D 27), pointing (D 28), preference for one hand (D 33), and so on.

As already pointed out in Chapter IV and elsewhere (Chapter VIII), children who are handicapped visually or who suffer from a degree of cerebral diplegia may show a degree of failure in this scale (and also in Scale E), due to a defect or defects that hinder the co-operation of hand and eye in the successful manipulation of objects in the environment. To be able to measure the effects of these, in a separate scale such as is offered here, promotes in a further direction the work of diagnosis. (See Chapter IV.)

The educational implications of the D Scale are considerable, for here we have the beginnings of both writing and drawing in the manipulation of pencil on paper, and thus the using of the first formal educational implements and materials. This scale, when extended beyond the second year, will link up very closely with certain types of handwork of other kinds also closely associated with the curricula of nursery and infant schools.

Scale D

DETAILS OF THE HAND AND EYE SCALE (SCALE D)

First Year

Items *First Three Months*

The baby:

1. Follows a moving light with the eyes.
2. Looks at the ring or toy momentarily when it is held up in front of him.
3. Looks steadily at the ring held still.
4. Follows the moving ring when swung horizontally.
5. Follows the ring vertically.
6. Glances from one object to another.
7. Follows the moving object in a circle.
8. Watches an object pulled along on the table surface by a string.

Second Three Months

9. Grasps a ring when given it.
10. Visually explores a new environment.
11. Reaches for ring and grasps when offered.
12. Carries the ring to his mouth.
13. Clutches at the dangling ring.
14. Secures the dangling ring.
15. His hands explore the table surface when he is held sitting near the table.
16. Plays with the ring after he has secured it, waving it or banging on table, etc.

Third Three Months

17. Reaches for and picks up the string tied to the moving object.
18. Looks for a dropped toy.
19. Strikes one object or surface with another.
20. Watches examiner scribble on paper.
21. Secures the ring or toy by means of the string.
22. Forefinger and thumb are partly specialised.

23. Fine prehension.
24. Having secured the ring or toy, he dangles it by the string.

Fourth Three Months

25. Plays pulling the ring or toy along by the string.
26. Throws objects. (This is a deliberate *throw*, not just dropping.)
27. Thumb opposition is complete.
28. Child can point with the index finger.
29. Interested in toy motor-car. Goes after it, picks it up, etc.
30. Can hold a pencil as if to mark on paper.
31. Uses a pencil on paper a little. Makes some kind of mark.

Second Year

First Three Months

The baby:

32. Likes holding little toys continuously in his hands.
33. Shows preference for one hand. Right- or left-handed.
34. Plays rolling a ball.
35. Can hold four cubes at once, two in each hand.
36. Plays pushing little cars around.

Second Three Months

37. Places one lid, box or brick upon another.
38. Scribbles more freely.
39. Pulls paper or cloth to get toy.
40. Enjoys constructive play with boxes, lids and cubes.
41. Builds a tower of three bricks.

Third Three Months

42. Can throw a ball.
43. Builds a tower of four bricks.
44. Enjoys vigorous straight scribble.
45. Can pour water from one cup to another. (No spilling.)
46. Uses a pencil freely, circular scribble. (May be shown this.)
47. Builds a tower of five or more bricks.

Fourth Three Months

48. Makes a perpendicular stroke with the pencil, after shown.
49. Makes a train of three or more bricks.

50. Throws a ball into a basket. (Waste-paper basket, box or bucket.)
51. Makes a brick or toy walk. (Imitation.)
52. Makes a horizontal stroke with the pencil.

D 1. *Follows a moving light with the eyes.* (*First month.*)

For this item the baby may be lying in the dorsal position or held by the mother comfortably in a reclining position, but with his face turned from the main window (or other) light. The examiner takes the torch and holds it about 15 to 18 inches from the child, at right angles to the child's field of vision. Then, beginning from the centre, he moves it slowly a few inches to the right, then slowly back across the centre point to a few inches to the left. The child should be able to fixate and then follow the light a short distance in both directions. The item may be taken again later in the interview if unsuccessful.

D 2. *Looks at ring momentarily.* (*First month.*)

The examiner takes the bell-ring and, making it ring slightly to attract the baby's attention, he holds it about 15 inches from the child, in the centre of the field of vision. The child should fixate the ring for a moment.

D 3. *Looks steadily at ring held still.* (*Second month.*)

Same as D 2, but now the child looks steadily at the ring held still or slightly moving, in the centre of the field of vision.

D 4. *Follows moving ring horizontally.* (*Second month.*)

To swing the ring for this item, as is sometimes suggested, may result in the movement being too rapid at this early age for the child to follow it. The bell-ring should therefore be held in the hand and moved slowly sideways across the child's field of vision and back again. The bells that are attached may be rung slightly to attract the child's attention at the beginning before moving the ring slowly for the test. Go straight on to item D 5.

D 5. *Follows ring vertically.* (*End of second month.*)

As for D 4. When the child has completed D 4, the examiner should continue slowly moving the ring but now in a perpendicular direction, first up about 12 inches, then down, finishing as before in the centre of the field of vision. The ring should be held throughout about 15 inches from the child. (Then on to item D 7.)

D 6. *Glances from one object to another.* (*Third month.*)

For this item the examiner retains the ring, just used for D 7, in one hand and takes up the plastic rattling ball in the other. He then makes a slight sound by shaking the ball, and the child's eyes should go across to the ball and back to the bell-ring with the slightest movement of either object. This item may be taken several times if necessary.

Note.—Too many eye tests must not be taken in succession. If the child ceases to follow after doing one or two tests successfully, the examiner should switch to another scale, e.g. Scale A, and return after a minute or two to the remaining eye tests.

D 7. *Follows moving object in a circle.* (*End of third month.*)

As for D 5. Whilst the examiner is using the bell-ring for item D 5, he just changes the movement to a circular one, keeping it about 15 inches from the baby's eyes and moving the ring slowly round in a circle of about 12 inches in diameter. The child follows the ring right round, to pass this item.

D 8. *Watches object pulled along by string.* (*End of third month.*)

For this item the mother holds baby up near the table and in such a position that the child can see all the table surface clearly. The examiner then draws the ring by the cord across the child's field of vision. The plain ring without bells is the best one for this test. The child must follow this across and back again in a wide sweep across the table, turning his head in doing so. (See Plate 22.)

D 9. *Grasps ring when given.* (*Fourth month.*)

The examiner offers the ring to the child but does not put it into his hand. The ring should not actually touch the palm of the hand to evoke the palmar reflex, but the examiner may very gently touch the child's hand with the ring to draw attention to the object. The child must deliberately take hold of the ring himself.

D 10. *Visually explores new environment.* (*Fourth month.*)

The average baby of this age looks well about him in a new environment. This can usually be observed quite early in the interview, during the note-taking stage (see Chapter X), when the child is noticed to look here and there curiously. This item may be scored at the end of the interview, as by then the examiner will have had ample opportunity to notice if the child looks about him during the interview.

D 11. *Reaches for ring and grasps.* (*Fifth month.*)

The bell-ring is shaken, making the bells ring slightly to attract attention, and is then held a few inches from the child's hands so that he must reach out to secure it. He must securely grasp and retain the ring to pass this test.

D 12. *Carries ring to mouth.* (*Fifth month.*)

Following D 11, the ring is left in the child's hand to see what he will do with it. Most babies of this age immediately carry it to the mouth to explore this new toy with the lips. If so, they pass D 12. Some are sufficiently advanced to wave, shake or bang it also. (See D 16.)

D 13. *Clutches at dangling ring.* (*End of fifth month.*)

The examiner holds the ring by the cord dangling and moving very slightly a few inches (about 10) from the child and slightly above the level of his eyes. He must look up and clutch at the ring. If he does so, he passes item D 13. (If he successfully secures the ring, he also passes D 14.)

D 14. *Secures dangling ring.* (*Sixth month.*)

Following D 13, the child secures the ring after clutching at it. (See also D 16.)

D 15. *Hands explore table surface.* (*End of sixth month.*)

Seated at the table, the child's hands normally begin to fondle the edge of the table, and soon pat or smooth the table surface with the open hand. Any of these reactions scores plus for D 15.

D 16. *Plays with ring.* (*End of sixth month.*)

The child having received or successfully secured the ring, the examiner waits and observes what he does with it. If he plays with it in any way, shaking the bells, banging it on the table or waving it, etc., he passes this item. (*Note.*—Carrying the ring to the mouth does not pass at this level. See D 12.)

D 17. *Reaches for and picks up string—any method.* (*Seventh month.*)

The examiner draws the ring slowly about by the string on the table surface to get the child's attention and to demonstrate the function of the string that is attached. When the child has followed it for a few seconds, the examiner leaves the string 2 or 3 inches from the child's hand and the attached ring far from him. The child should reach after and pick up the string. At this stage the child may not realise that by pulling the cord he can secure the ring, as his interest may be directed towards the cord itself. The test is passed if he manages to pick up the string. Fine prehension is not expected (it should be noted if present), but the test is passed if by whatever method the string is picked up. (See also D 21.)

D 18. *Looks for dropped toy.* (*End of seventh month.*)

Having dropped or thrown a toy or other object to the floor, the child looks after it to see where it has landed. If the occasion for this does not arise naturally during the test, the examiner should take opportunity, when the child is watching the ring on the table, to manœuvre it slowly to the table's edge and let it fall, to see if the child looks down in search of it. If he does so, he passes this item. (Any item may be taken twice, but not more than twice.)

D 19. *Strikes one object with another.* (*Eighth month.*)

The child who bangs a toy about on the table surface, or scrapes it along the table's edge, or bangs the ring (or other object) deliberately on the table (or chair, etc.) passes this item. Opportunity for observing this is readily available during the test, and it is seldom necessary to test for it.

D 20. *Watches the examiner scribble.* (*Eighth month.*)

The examiner takes the red stumpy pencil and a piece of paper and begins to scribble, doing this quite close to the child at the table. He then leaves the pencil handy for the child and observes. If the baby has watched the scribbling with apparent interest, the examiner scores this item plus. The baby is not likely to take up the pencil at this stage, but it is well to leave it near him whilst continuing other tests. (See D 30.)

D 21. *Secures ring by means of string.* (*Eighth month.*)

Following on D 17, if the child has successfully picked up the string, he may pull on it and secure the ring. If he does not do so, the examiner should show him again by pulling the ring about a little by the string and then placing the end of the string near the child again. Sometimes the child gets the idea quite suddenly, and with great joy pulls the ring towards him. He must get the ring himself, pulling it towards him by the string, to pass this item.

D 22. *Forefinger and thumb partly specialised.* (*Ninth month.*)

Throughout this work the examiner will have been noticing the child's hands, how he manipulates, secures, throws, etc. Many of the items of this scale are scored on the basis of close observation of the level of development achieved in the actual manipulation of the specially chosen apparatus. By the ninth month the hands of most babies are learning to grasp objects of varying size and shape with increasing dexterity. At an earlier level, the child could pick up objects by the third, fourth and fifth fingers, with a scooping movement which has been frequently illustrated and described by Gesell (1946a). To pass this item the baby must definitely use the thumb and forefinger in reaching after and grasping objects, although the thumb may not yet be in complete opposition to the fingers. (See Plate 22.)

D 23. *Fine prehension.* (*Tenth month.*)

This is passed when the child picks up small objects (e.g. the tiny sweetmeats or the end of the string), using the thumb and forefinger only, in a pincer position. This should be tested for with a sweetmeat, crumb of bread, etc. (See also B 28.)

D 24. *Dangles ring by string.* (*End of tenth month.*)

The examiner has been swinging and dangling the ring by the cord for several test items. He does so again for this item and then, handing the string to the child, says: "Look, can you dangle it?" To pass this the child must accept the string (about half-way along its length) and enjoy holding the ring dangling from it. Most babies pass this item by the end of the tenth month. If the child drops it immediately, the examiner should return it to him again, to see if he will retain it, but the test must not be taken more than twice.

D 25. *Plays pulling ring or toy by string.* (*Eleventh month.*)

(See D 21.) Having secured the ring by the string, the child should be encouraged to pull it around as the examiner did earlier. If the child does not respond, the little toy on wheels, also with a cord attached, may be used instead, at the table or on the floor. To pass this item the child must pull the toy around a little and show interest in this activity. (This is quite different from item A 42, which can only be taken with a child who is already walking, and it is then more a test of locomotor skill and balance, when attention is directed to the toy.)

D 26. "*Throws*" *objects.* (*Eleventh month.*)

This must be a definite *throw*, not a mere dropping of a toy. Most babies around this age have learnt to send toys, etc., far from them in a definite throw. The sweeping of toys aside or sending them down from the table may be accomplished without a real throwing at all. The object must be in the child's hand and sent by a sudden movement of the wrist in a definite throw, to pass this item. It does not matter how awkward or uncontrolled the movement is, so long as it is an effective throw, at this stage.

D 27. *Thumb opposition complete.* (*Eleventh month.*)

By the eleventh month, thumb opposition should be complete to score plus for this item. (See Plate 19.) The child now grasps objects in an almost adult manner, the thumb being opposite to the fingers in grasping a large object, e.g. the test box, and opposite the forefinger or first two fingers in taking hold of a small object such as a one-inch cube.

D 28. *Can point with index finger.* (*Eleventh month.*)

At this age the majority of babies can point. This item, like D 27, is usually scored on the basis of observation, but if the child does not show this definitely the examiner should put a sweetmeat on the table and say: "Oh! just look at that!" and himself *point* to the sweet. Or a small toy may be used, such as the tiny sitting doll from the box of toys. Then he will observe whether the fore-finger can function apart from the other three fingers, or whether the child points with the whole hand.

D 29. *Interested in motor-car.* (*Eleventh month.*)

The examiner first sends the small car slowly across the child's field of vision on the table or floor. The little brown car that does not wind up is the best one to use. It runs smoothly when pushed on a good surface. The child shows interest or excitement and strives to reach the car and secure it. Sometimes he babbles excitedly or even says "car" or makes car noises. The child should show by his reaction that he has some idea what the object is. He is allowed to handle the toy, and he may now show further interest in the wheels, etc. If the child is not particularly interested, the examiner should wind up the mechanical car and set that going across the floor or table in front of the child. If the child cries or fails to show interest, he fails this item. (See D 36.)

D 30. *Can hold pencil as if to make a mark on paper.* (*Twelfth month.*)

Following on D 20, the child now takes up the pencil and shows that he can hold it, or has some idea of its function, trying to bring it into contact with the paper, etc. The baby who bangs the pencil on the table edge, puts it in his mouth, screws or tears up the paper, etc., fails this item. To pass, he must handle the pencil and make some attempt to bring its point into contact with the paper. (See D 31.) The examiner may hand the pencil to the child and encourage him to take hold of it.

D 31. *Uses pencil on paper a little.* (*End of twelfth month.*)

Following D 30, the child who is successful in making a mark, however slight, upon the paper, but quite unaided, passes this item. His hand must not be held or guided, but the examiner may twice demonstrate, by himself scribbling on the paper to encourage the child.

D 32. *Likes holding little toys.* (*Thirteenth month.*)

This is a definite stage in the manipulation of toys, beyond the throwing-down stage. It shows the beginning of a desire for possession of little objects. The child may hold a small toy closely shut in his hand. A child at this level will sometimes hold on to a toy or other small object all day and even after going to bed. The examiner can observe when a child in handling the small toys keeps one in his hand whilst manipulating others with the other hand. The mother can also be questioned about his holding on to toys for a long time. This phase supersedes the throwing-down phase. Sufficient evidence for the child having reached this stage is readily obtained during the test by careful observation. (See Plate 10.)

D 33. *Preference for one hand.* (*Thirteenth month.*)

This is best observed in the pencil and paper test, but, if this test is refused, the examiner should offer the child the spoon at a time when both the child's hands are free, and, holding it in the middle of his field of vision and within easy and equal reach of either hand, should notice which hand comes out to take the spoon. This test must be taken twice or thrice. If at all ambiguous, the item is scored minus. The mother may be asked in which hand the child holds a spoon at home, but the item should be decided by the examiner's own observation during the test.

D 34. *Plays rolling ball.* (*Fourteenth month.*)

With the child seated on the floor or prone in the crawling position, the examiner rolls the ball towards him and encourages the child to roll it about or crawl after it. If the child is already walking, he may toddle after the ball as the examiner plays is towards him. The item is passed if the child knocks the ball away and goes after it even once.

D 35. *Can hold four cubes at once.* (*Fourteenth month.*)

The examiner takes up two cubes in each hand and holds all four together out to the child. He then *puts* them into the child's hands, encouraging him to grasp two in each hand as the examiner has just done. The object of this item is to see if the hands are developed well enough to manage to hold on to two one-inch cubes in each hand. The test is passed if the child successfully accepts and holds all four cubes even for a moment. The test may be taken a second time, the examiner demonstrating what is wanted by himself again holding the four cubes and showing them to the child before again giving them to him. The second attempt may be deferred and taken later, if necessary. This item is quite different in intention from Gesell's "Accepts the fourth cube".

D 36. *Plays pushing little cars along.* (*Fourteenth month.*)

Following D 29, the child also passes D 36 if he pushes the little brown car along in play, even once or twice. Many babies push the car and then crawl or toddle after it and push it again. The child should not be given the mechanical car to push around, but this may be wound up and set going to get his interest and keep the rapport. All these test items with toys should be taken in a happy play manner and should be enjoyed by the child.

D 37. *Places one lid, box or brick upon another.* (*Fifteenth month.*)

The examiner takes the four yellow bricks just used for D 35 and begins to build a tower of bricks with them. This he lifts down (unless the child has already demolished it) and, placing one cube ready, he offers another to the baby, saying coaxingly: "You make it, put this one on here", indicating where the cube should rest. If the child does this correctly, the examiner hands him another, and so on. The test is passed at this level if a tower of two is made by the child himself, placing just one lid, box or brick on another with intention to build them up. Sometimes the test is passed during play with the brick-boxes, without demonstration or encouragement, and if so it can be scored without having to be specially taken. (See also items D 41, D 43 and D 47.)

D 38. *Scribbles more freely.* (*Sixteenth month.*)

To pass at this stage in the use of the pencil, the child must scribble freely on the paper. Any kind of scribble will do at this stage, but straight scribble, being the easiest, is usually achieved first.

If the child passes D 35, the examiner should go straight on to D 44, D 46, D 48 and D 52, continuing until the child shows he can do no more.

D 39. *Pulls paper or cloth to get toy.* (*Seventeenth month.*)

The examiner arranges the felt on the table and places toy, car, ring or other object that the child has been manipulating on the far end of the strip of felt, away from the child, and then gives the felt (or cloth) a little jerk to encourage the child to see that he can get his treasure again by pulling the cloth. If the child tries repeatedly to climb up after the toy, not pulling the cloth to help him, he fails this item. He must deliberately pull the cloth to secure the toy and pass this item. This is a similar type of test to securing an object by the attached cord, but more difficult. It is not successfully taken on the floor.

D 40. *Constructive play with boxes or other materials.* (*Eighteenth month.*)

This item is scored on the basis of observation of the baby at play with boxes and toys. The item is passed if the child in the course of free manipulation proceeds to combine the pieces of the apparatus, bringing them constructively into relation with one another. He may pile things up. He may fill the little boxes with toys; he may set the doll on the chair or on the box, or the horse on the lid; he may push the car inside as into a garage, etc. Any type of play, however brief, that brings any two pieces of apparatus into such relationship that it suggests a recognition of function, or some form of imaginative construction, passes this item. No help must be given or suggestions made by the examiner.

D 41. *Tower of three.* (*Eighteenth month.*)

As for D 37, except that three bricks are now successfully built up.

D 42. *Can throw a ball.* (*Nineteenth month.*)

The examiner takes up the little rubber ball and tosses it to the mother, inviting her to throw it back. The child watches this play and, when he appears thoroughly interested, the examiner gives the ball to him and says: "Now you throw it to Mummy." This will almost always bring an immediate attempt. The throw must be a definite throw, not a dropping of the ball. There must be a definite movement of the wrist, and the ball should fall some distance from the child. Some babies need a good deal of encouragement before they will attempt this in the presence of the examiner. It should therefore be left until fairly late in the test, at a time when the rapport is at its best, and may be taken until the child has at least twice sent the ball away, so that there is no doubt about his method of sending it. One definite throw of the ball passes this item.

D 43. *Tower of four.* (*Nineteenth month.*)

As for D 37, but the child can now successfully build a tower of four bricks.

D 44. *Enjoys vigorous straight scribble.* (*Twentieth month.*)

To pass this test at this level the child must scribble vigorously, using long straight strokes across the paper and back again continually, and showing evidence of being used to this activity. (See also D 38.) If the child passes D 44, the examiner should go on to D 46 and then to D 48 and D 52.

D 45. *Can pour water from one cup into another.* (*Twenty-second month.*)

For this item the examiner will need the two little plastic beakers. He should put about 1 inch of water into one of the beakers and then approach the child and place the two beakers on the table in front of him, saying: "See what we are going to do now." Then the examiner takes up the beaker containing the water and slowly pours it into the other beaker, then slowly pours it back again, keeping the child's attention meanwhile. Then he hands the beaker with the small quantity of water in it to the child and, placing the other beaker conveniently for the child, he says: "Now you pour the water in here", indicating the empty beaker. The babies like this test. They should be encouraged to do this carefully. It will immediately become evident whether the child has the necessary control to do this item, or any experience of similar situations. To pass the test, he must pour the water from one cup to the other without any spilling. As with all these tests, he may have two trials and need only succeed on one occasion.

D 46. *Circular scribble.* (*Twenty-third month.*)

The examiner takes up the red pencil and, placing a piece of paper near the child, proceeds to draw round and round in a circle, saying: "Round and round, round and round", or even singing "Round the Mulberry Bush" to get the child's interest. Then, handing the child the pencil, the examiner says: "Now you go round and round." To pass this item the child's scribble must form rough circles or ovals. Straight scribble does not pass this item.

D 47. *Tower of five or more.* (*Twenty-third month.*)

As for D 37, but now the child can build a tower of at least five bricks. He should be allowed to continue as far as he can, building a high tower, and be encouraged to go on as long as he can; additional bricks from the test boxes can be utilised, as they are all the same size. Five bricks, built up into a tower, are necessary to pass this item, and the tower must stand when finished.

D 48. *Perpendicular stroke.* (*Twenty-fourth month.*)

With the paper in front of the child, the examiner draws a perpendicular stroke from the top of the paper towards the child as he sits. This should be a very firm, definite line and may be repeated several times to give the child the idea, the examiner saying with emphasis: "Look, I'm making big straight lines." Then, handing the pencil to the child, he says: "Now you make one, a big one like this", etc. If the child makes any one stroke that keeps in general the perpendicular direction from the top of the paper downwards, he passes this item. A straight line is not expected; it is the imitation of the general direction that is important to pass this item.

D 49. *Train of three.* (*Twenty-fourth month.*)

The examiner holds the child's attention by building a bridge with the test boxes. (See Case 3 in Chapter X.) He then makes a train by placing three bricks side by side and makes this go through the tunnel, emerging towards the child as he sits at the low table. The child is then encouraged to send the train back under the bridge. Children of this age enter happily into this game, making train noises, etc. Then the examiner disarranges the train and says: "Can you make that little train again and we'll send it under the bridge?" The child should place the three bricks in a row and send the train along. A perfect result is not expected at this level. If the three bricks are in a row lying in any direction such that by pushing the end one they all go along without the train breaking up, he passes the test. (See Plate 1, Frontispiece, Chapter IX, for the manner of making the bridge and the train going under it.)

D 50. *Throws ball into basket.* (*Twenty-fourth month.*)

At this stage the child should be able to throw a ball with some degree of control of its direction as he sends it. A convenient way of testing for this is to produce a large waste-paper basket or box and, taking up the ball, the examiner should twice throw it into the basket to show the child what is required. Then, giving the child the ball and placing him about 2 feet away from the basket, he says: "Now see if you can throw the ball in there", indicating the basket. Two trials. The child must keep his position a little distance from the basket and be able to get the ball in by throwing it.

D 51. *Making a brick* (*or toy*) *walk.* (*Twenty-fourth month.*)

Taking up a brick (or small animal that the child may have been manipulating), the examiner makes it go along on the table in little jumps or steps, saying: "Can you make it walk along?" The child must make the toy take at least three steps or hops to pass this item.

If the child does not at first do this when asked, the toy should be left lying handy whilst other tests are taken, then the child may spontaneously do this item later, this being his *second* attempt, and he can be scored plus. This method of getting a response is quite permissible with Scale D, especially with very shy or inhibited babies, but two trials only may be permitted.

D 52. *Horizontal stroke.* (*Twenty-fourth month.*)

This is taken as for D 48, except that the strokes are made *across* the paper, the examiner saying: "Can you make a big line *this* way now?" As before, any one stroke made by the child that is roughly horizontal in its direction scores plus.

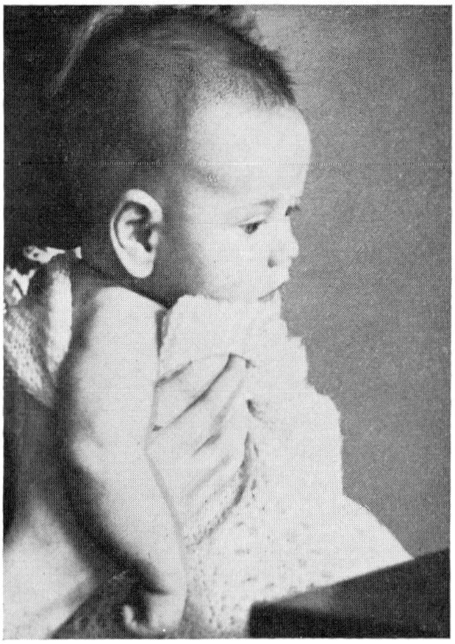

PLATE 20

This three-months' boy is being held up on the mother's knee at the table. He is watching and following with his eyes while small toys are moved slowly about on the table surface. His hands, however, hang limp, for at this young age they are not yet brought into definite relationship with visual activity.

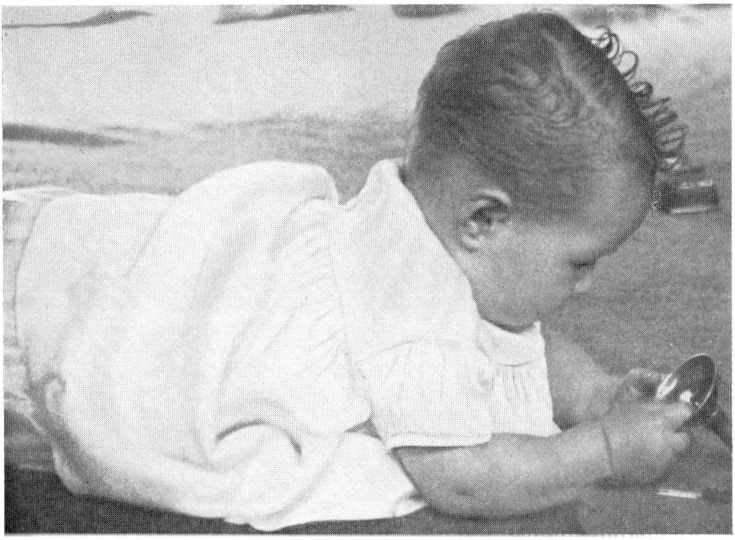

PLATE 21

At seven months, this little girl has herself secured and is manipulating and examining the bell (D 16). The bell was rung and then placed near her on the floor. Note the greater confidence of her attitude at this age; head and chest up, supported on her elbows, her hands are free to satisfy her curiosity by handling objects.

Note. (1) Her posture should be compared with that of the child so much younger in Plate 12; and (2) her facial expression and attentive attitude with that of the child in Plate 20 above, who can observe visually, but does not yet reach after objects, although he can manipulate them when given to him. Development in all directions is very rapid in these early months. (See Chapter II.)

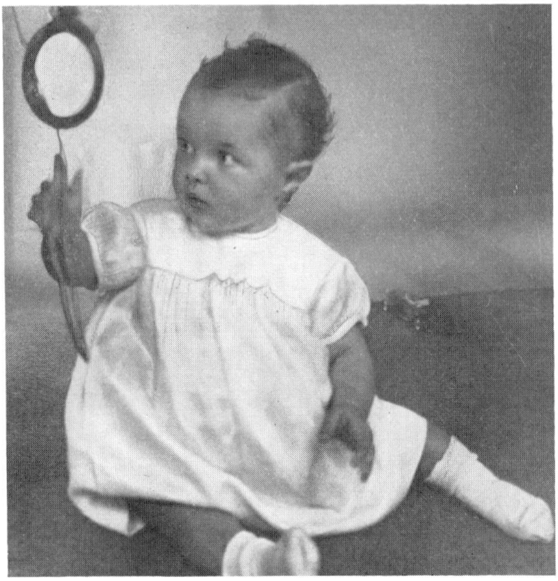

PLATE 22

This little girl is just seven months old, and can sit alone and play with toys on the floor but occasionally overbalances. She is reaching for the ring which is being swung just above the level of her eyes. Her slightly anxious expression is due to her fear of overbalancing while reaching for the ring, although adults are near to prevent this. In her left hand she is still holding the paper tissue she has been playing with. Her finger and thumb are already almost in opposition.

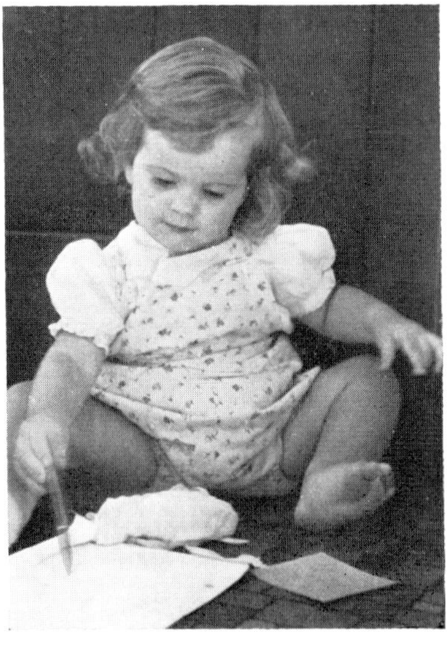

PLATE 23

This little Australian girl, aged twenty months, is seated on the floor "writing a letter." Note her delightful poise as she concentrates on her task.

CHAPTER XV

ADMINISTERING THE PERFORMANCE SCALE (SCALE E)

IN approaching this, the last of our five sub-scales, for testing mental development, we also come to the scale that is in a sense a sequel to the rest and, in a particular sense, to Scale D. Having studied the child's psychological progress in several directions: towards standing and walking with all the detailed associated events, towards social adjustment in the home and beyond, towards development by many gradual stages on the road to adult speech and language, towards the co-ordination of hand and eye in manipulative skills, we now face the child with a number of practical test situations that call upon his ingenuity and readiness to respond.

In some respects this scale is closely similar to Scale D, for it deals entirely with situations that are solved by some manual performance. But here we assume the gradual co-ordination of hand and eye, the maturation of the hand in normal exploring of the environment, and test for the way in which the child applies these skills in novel situations.

At the beginning of the scale, where the baby is still very young, there are several items that are of a preparatory nature, and merely indicate that the ability to explore by hand and arm movements, or the interest in visually perceived objects, is present (E 3, E 4, E 7, etc.). Gradually, as the growing child is capable of performing them, the planned situations become more complex until, in the second year, they are very similar in kind to, although of course much easier than, performance tests offered to older children.

Whereas observation is paramount in all this work, it is in this scale (Scale E) more definitely associated with true experimentation. Thus there are few merely observational items as such. In some respects this is a great advantage for, whilst observing the way a child tackles these simple practical tasks, the examiner is also closely noting the result for the sake of scoring his tests in Scale E; but at one and the same time he also has ample opportunity for observing thumb opposition, left-handedness and other such clinical and developmental items of Scale D. In practice, therefore, after the first three or four months of the tests, Scales D and E may be very largely taken together, although they measure different aspects of the total field.

After these early months, also, the E scale consists almost entirely of two major sequences. These are:

(1) the series of tests for which the Test Boxes or Brick Boxes were invented, and
(2) the new set of Form Boards.

These Brick Boxes are a development of Froebel's Gift III, but each box contains only two small cubes.

The Brick Boxes are taken quite definitely in a play way, although the items must, as always, be very exactly scored, the examiner carefully observing precisely what the child does with the apparatus, even for those items in which he is given freedom to manipulate the pieces as he likes. A set of boxes containing bricks is a fascinating toy for babies of these ages and, in the course of free manipulation, bright babies frequently carry out the tests without any instruction being needed. The boxes were planned for this purpose and to be used in this way. The Form Boards, on the other hand, do not lend themselves to this freedom of usage, and require a certain maturity of attitude on the part of the young examinee. For this reason the Form Board series of items begins much later in the scale than do the Brick Box items, except for the more difficult items that are done with the boxes (E 49, 50). Both these sets of tests continue into the third year, but throughout this work we are obliged to end strictly with the twenty-fourth month.

As with Scale D, visual disabilities or physical awkwardness that may be due to spasticity will be reflected in Scale E, but with these differences: in the earliest months a partially sighted baby fails on Scale D because he cannot do the eye tests, but he may do fairly well at those early items of Scale E that are preliminary to any definite co-ordination of hand and eye; in the case of a young baby with a visual defect the score for the D scale will tend to be low compared with other scales (see Fig. 17, Case 34, Chapter VIII); in the case of the spastic child where the paralysis affects manual skill there will tend to be failure on both D and E scales, or in one of them, according to the type and degree of the disability. For profiles of children suffering from different degrees of cerebral diplegia, see Fig. 16, Chapter VIII.

The items listed below are described, together with the method of administering them, in the order of their difficulty and as they appear on the printed form. However, in actually taking the items it is not possible to keep to this order, as explained elsewhere; but, whilst the child is manipulating the little bricks and boxes, *all* those items that he can pass (and beyond) must be taken as far as possible. Then, when these are completed, the Form Board series, beginning with E 33, should also be taken as a complete test series. Here, too, all that is required with *each separate board* should be taken whilst that particular piece of apparatus is in place, as is suggested in the notes.

Scale E

DETAILS OF THE PERFORMANCE SCALE (SCALE E)

First Year

Items *First Three Months*

The baby:

1. Grasps examiner's finger and holds on for a short time.
2. Reacts to paper on face—I: Generalised physical movements.
3. Hand goes to mouth, sucks fingers, etc.
4. Waves arms energetically.
5. Reacts to paper on face—II: Vigorous head turning.
6. Holds doll.
7. Plays with own fingers.
8. Looks at box on table.

Second Three Months

9. Resists examiner who tries gently to take the doll away.
10. Clasps a cube that is put into his hand, and holds on to it.
11. Drops the first cube when a second one is offered.
12. Reacts to paper on face—III: Pulls it away.
13. Shows interest in box, tries to take hold of it, etc. (Test box.)
14. Picks up a toy from the table.
15. Holds two objects, one in each hand.
16. Grasps the box when given. (Test box.)

Third Three Months

17. Manipulates cube or toy, puts in mouth, etc.
18. Reacts to paper—IV : Reaches for paper held out in front of him, and secures it.
19. Passes toy from one hand to the other.
20. Drops one cube or toy when a third one is offered.
21. Manipulates two objects at once—two toys, one in each hand.
22. Plays with paper—V : Observed by examiner.
23. Lifts inverted box in search of toy.
24. Rattles the box.

Fourth Three Months

25. Clicks two bricks together. (Imitation.)
26. Takes the lid off the box.
27. Finds the toy under the box.
28. Tries to take the cubes out of the box.
29. Takes the third cube, when offered, without dropping the others.
30. Removes both cubes from the box. (Second one shown if necessary.)
31. Manipulates the box, lid and cubes.

Second Year

First Three Months

The baby:

32. Unwraps and finds toy.
33. Puts one circle into circle board. Two trials allowed.
34. Opens two boxes
35. Puts two cubes back into the box when encouraged to do so.
36. Two-circle board. One circle in. Two trials.
37. Puts cubes in and out of boxes in play.

Second Three Months

38. Puts square into the square board. Two trials.
39. Two-circle board. Puts both circles in. Two trials.
40. Can put the lid back on the test box.
41. Three-hole board. One inset placed correctly. Two trials.
42. Puts two cubes into any one test box, lid on, all complete.

Third Three Months

43. Does circle and square board together. Two trials.

44. Three-hole board. Two insets correctly placed. Two trials.
45. Three-hole board. Three in. Two trials.
46. Two-circle board, rotated. Two trials.

Fourth Three Months

47, 48. Circle and square boards rotated. (Credit 2 points.)
49, 50. Assembles three boxes, lids on, all complete, but not yet for colour. (Credit 2 points.)
51, 52. Can open screw-toy. (Credit 2 points.)

E 1. *Grasps examiner's finger.* (*First month.*)

With the child lying quietly in the mother's arms, the examiner gently inserts his little finger into the child's palm. (See Fig. 1, Chapter II.) The small hand closes tightly on the adult's finger. The examiner then moves his hand from side to side gently and, if the child still hangs on, he passes the item. Most babies pass this item in the first month.

E 2. *Reacts to paper—I. Generalised physical movements.* (*First month.*)

With the baby lying comfortably on the mother's knee or on the divan in the dorsal position, the examiner takes a soft paper tissue and lays this gently over the baby's face. This is the first definite performance test. The child struggles to free his face from the paper. The examiner looks under the paper to watch the child. Many babies show facial movements, opening mouth, screwing up eyes, etc. These are quite ineffectual. The test is passed if the baby shows generalised physical movements of the whole body. The arms may move and the child kicks a little. He may not succeed in dislodging the paper, but is making effort towards this end. Score this reaction plus at this level. (See Plate 7.)

E 3. *Hand goes to mouth.* (*First month.*)

Sometimes during the test the young baby lifts his hand to his mouth and sucks vigorously at his fingers or the back of his hand. If he does not do so, the mother may be asked about this item. This is one of the preparatory items already mentioned. If there is evidence that he has found his way to his mouth, he scores plus.

E 4. *Shows energetic arm movements.* (*Second month.*)

The arm waving of the baby of this age is readily observed, being present fairly constantly whilst the child lies and kicks.

The feeble arm movements of the young neonate must have given place to strong energetic movements to pass this item.

E 5. *Reacts to paper—II. Vigorous head turning.* (*Third month.*)

This test is taken as for E 2, but now there is vigorous head turning from side to side. This may also be accompanied by generalised physical movements, but it is the head turning (Bühler's "head movement of flight") that frequently dislodges the paper. Whether the paper (which should lie very lightly on the child's face) is dislodged or not, the test is passed if the child moves his head vigorously from side to side in the attempt to dislodge it.

This reaction appears to be definitely purposive and not a mere turning away or avoidance of an unpleasant situation. (*Now take or score E* 12.)

E 6. *Holds doll.* (*Third month.*)

The small smooth (2-inch) plastic doll is used for this test. The examiner puts the doll into the child's hand, and the baby's fingers must close over the doll, and he must retain it for a few seconds to pass this test. (See also E 9.)

E 7. *Plays with own fingers.* (*Third month.*)

When lying resting, babies of this age frequently bring the hands together and play with their own fingers. They also lie and look at their fingers, which appear to be a great source of interest to them, and indulge in finger fanning, etc. This item is important as showing the child's need to handle objects and his readiness to do so whenever he has the opportunity. If playing with fingers is not noticed during the interview, the mother may be asked about this.

E 8. *Looks at box on table.* (*Fourth month.*)

The mother holds the child up near the table so that the whole of the table surface is visible to him. The examiner moves toys about on its surface. (See D 8.) He then takes the bright yellow box and, clicking it against the table to attract the child's attention, he places it about 12 inches from the child, and in a position such that it is far from other objects and can be clearly seen by the child. The baby looks steadily with interest at the object. (See Plate 20.) (*Now take E* 10.)

E 9. *Resists doll withdrawal.* (*Fourth month.*)

Following E 6, after the child has held the doll for a few seconds the examiner tries gently to take the doll away. The test is passed if the child tightens his grip and resists the withdrawal of the doll.

E 10. *Clasps cube put in hand and holds it.* (*Fourth month.*)

Following E 8, whilst the child is looking steadily at a cube on the table, the examiner takes it up and gives it to the child. The cube usually has to be put into the child's hand. To pass this item, the child retains the cube for a few seconds. (*Now take E* 11.)

E 11. *Drops first cube for second.* (*Fifth month.*)

Following E 10 and whilst the child is holding the first cube, the examiner offers another. The child passes this item if he accepts the second cube, taking it with his free hand, and drops the first cube. (At this age there is a very narrow span of attention.) (See also E 15.)

E 12. *Reacts to paper—III. Pulls it away.* (*Sixth month.*)

Following E 5, when the paper is lying on the child's face, the baby may in his generalised movements touch the paper and pull it away from his face. If he manages to do this, he passes E 12 and also scores plus for the easier items E 2 and E 5.

E 13. *Shows interest in box.* (*Sixth month.*)

The examiner takes up the closed yellow box with the two bricks inside it and gives it a little shake, immediately placing it on the table clearly visible to the child. The baby passes this item if he shows interest in the box. At this level it is more than merely *looking* at the object, as in E.8, that is required. The child now not only looks intently but may purse lips, vocalise, make hand movements towards the box, lean towards it struggling to reach it, or try to pick it up, etc. Any of these reactions passes this item. (*Now take or score E* 16.)

E 14. *Takes toy from table.* (*Sixth month.*)

Following E 8, while the box and other small toys are on the table, the child reaches out and actually takes one object from the table. Score this reaction plus for E 14.

E 15. *Holds two small objects.* (*Sixth month.*)

Following E 11, when a second toy is offered to the child, he accepts it without dropping the first one and holds both for a few seconds. (If he does this, he also scores plus for E 11.) (*Now take E* 20.)

E 16. *Grasps box.* (*Seventh month.*)

Following E 13, if the child actually grasps the box, whether he can lift it successfully or not, he passes item E 16.

E 17. *Manipulates cube or toy.* (*Seventh month.*)

To pass this item the child plays with a toy, manipulating it in any of the following ways: carries it to his mouth, bangs it on the table, looks more closely at it in his hand, etc. (If he passes the toy from one hand to the other, he also passes E 19.)

E 18. *Reacts to paper—IV. Reaches for and takes.* (*Seventh month.*)

For this item the examiner holds up a paper tissue in front of the child, about 6 inches from his face. The child reaches for it and takes it from the examiner's hands, to pass this item. (*Go straight on to item E 22.* If the child tears or crumples or otherwise manipulates the paper, he passes E 22 also.)

E 19. *Passes toy from hand to hand.* (*Seventh month.*)

When manipulating the cube or any other toy or object during the test, if the child passes it from one hand to the other he passes this item.

E 20. *Drops one cube or toy for third.* (*Seventh month.*)

Following E 15, and whilst the child is holding two cubes (or small toys), one in each hand, the examiner offers him a third. Most babies at this age immediately drop one of those that are held in order to accept the third. *This* passes at this level. (If, however, the child accepts the third cube or toy and also retains the other two as well, he passes E 29 as well as E 20.)

E 21. *Manipulates two objects at once.* (*Eighth month.*)

The child of this age should not only accept toys freely from the examiner, but play happily with a toy in each hand. To test for this, the examiner takes the two large red embroidery rings and offers them to the child, one for each hand. The child accepts them joyfully and proceeds to wave both or strike them against each other. The item is, however, passed if the child acts similarly with two other objects; for example, the cup and saucer, the ring and the box, the box and its lid, or the box and the ball, etc. (See, for example, Plate 18.)

E 22. *Plays with paper—V.* (*Eighth month.*)

Following E 18, the child tears, crumples or otherwise manipulates the paper to pass this item. The child may, however, be credited with E 22 if he shows evidence of playing with paper in another connection; for example, if he tears up writing-paper, etc., during the test.

E 23. *Lifts inverted box in search of toy.* (*Ninth month.*)

(See E 27.) This is an item similar to one from Gesell, but here it is divided it into two stages. The examiner places a small toy such as the tiny sitting doll from the box of toys on the table (or a cube if the child has been happily manipulating the cubes) and, just as the child's hand comes out to take up the toy, the examiner places the box (or cup) inverted over it and asks: "Where is it now?" The child must *lift the box* (*or cup*) in search of the toy to pass E 23. He may, however, fail to secure the toy, turning his attention to the box (*or cup*). This does not fail him at this level; the test is scored plus if the child *lifts up the box* (*or cup*).

E 24. *Rattles box.* (*Tenth month.*)

The examiner takes up one of the brick boxes with two bricks in it and rattles it merrily, then places the box near the child. The child must imitate by deliberately taking up the box and similarly rattling it. The child must manage the box well to achieve this, keeping it right way up. If he tips the box, the lid may fall off and the bricks drop out. This cannot be credited plus. The test may be repeated if unsuccessful or left handy for a delayed reaction or taken again later, but must not in any case be taken more than twice. (If the child is successful, *go straight on to E* 26.)

E 25. *Clicks two bricks together* (*imitation*). (*Tenth month.*)

The examiner takes up two bricks, one in each hand, and clicks them together four times in a quick, steady rhythm. Then he gives the bricks to the baby, one in each hand. Next the examiner takes up two more bricks and again clicks these together, saying: "Can *you* do that?" The child must click his two bricks together *at least once* to pass this test. The test may be repeated later if unsuccessful. Most babies enjoy this item, and some tend to keep up the game if not distracted to the next item.

E 26. *Takes or lifts lid off box.* (*Eleventh month.*)

Following E 24, having handled and rattled the box, the examiner places it near the child, and should then go on writing or scoring for a short time while he observes what the child will do with the box of bricks. Most babies immediately begin to explore after shaking the box, and deliberately lift the lid off, which scores plus for E 26. The examiner allows the child to retain the box and continue to explore it—see E 28, E 30, etc.)

E 27. *Finds toy under box* (*or cup*). (*Eleventh month.*)

Following E 23, if after lifting the box (or cup) the child takes up the toy, he passes E 27 as well as E 23.

E 28. *Tries to take cubes out of box.* (*Eleventh month.*)

(See E 26.) Continuing the series of items with the box of bricks, the examiner watches and scores any other items spontaneously passed by the baby in play. Many babies at this stage, having taken the lid off or had it taken off for them, begin to poke a finger at the contents. The box is so planned that the top brick is easily lifted out by the child, but he must *tip the box up* to get the second one out. If the child *lifts the top brick out or tries to do this*, he passes E 28. If the child does not attempt this, the examiner scores minus for E 28 but goes on to E 30.

E 29. *Accepts third cube without dropping.* (*Eleventh month.*)

Following E 20, the average child at this age successfully accepts from the examiner the third cube or toy without dropping either of the others, and holds all three. This reaction scores plus for E 29.

E 30. *Removes both cubes from box* (*shown*). (*Twelfth month.*)

If the baby lifts out the top brick unaided and then tips up the box, thus removing the second brick, he scores plus for E 30. But to do this without being shown is a most advanced reaction at this level. The child usually has to be shown. Having taken and scored E 28, the examiner lifts out the top brick and then very slowly tips up the box, letting the second brick drop out. He then returns *both* bricks to the box and hands it to the baby, saying: "Now you get them out." The child must get both bricks out, either by the method shown or by tipping both out together after the lid has been removed, to score plus for E 30.

E 31. *Manipulates box, lid and cubes.* (*Twelfth month.*)

Having taken E 30, the examiner again leaves the child to play freely with the apparatus. The child passes E 31 if he handles all the pieces, box, lid and cubes, in exploratory play or uses them in any way at all; but he must make contact with each of the four pieces in the process.

E 32. *Unwraps and finds toy or cube.* (*Thirteenth month.*)

For this item the examiner attracts the child's attention and then, taking up a cube or any small toy that the child has been manipulating, he wraps it up in a paper tissue while the child watches. The corners of the paper are drawn together and given a slight twist, and held in the hand like a little bag. The examiner holds this out to the child, asking: "Where is it?" To pass this item, the child must take the packet and unwrap the toy. The item may be taken a second time either straightaway or later in the test, if the child is not interested.

E 33. *Form boards—I. One-circle board. Two trials.* (*Thirteenth month.*)

We now come to the series of ten finely graded items with the form boards. There are four boards and four insets.

For E 33, the examiner takes up the circle board, containing one large circular hole, and the large circular inset. He places the board in front of the child and puts the round inset in the round hole. He waits a moment and then takes the inset out and places it near the child on the table between the child and the form board, saying: "Can you put it in again?" The child must take up the inset and manipulate it into the hole. One of two tries passes E 33. (If the child passes E 33, *go right on to E* 36, *E* 39, *etc.*)

E 34. *Opens two boxes.* (*Fourteenth month.*)

This is a stage in persistence. For E 34 the child is given two boxes of bricks, the yellow and the red, both together, and the examiner watches what happens. If the child appears competent and is about fourteen months old, it is quite suitable to begin with two boxes instead of one, and several of the earlier items can then be readily scored as the child passes them during free play.

If the baby opens both the boxes, taking the lids off unaided, he passes E 34.

E 35. *Puts two cubes back into box when encouraged to do so.* (*Fourteenth month.*)

To pass E 35, the child must return two bricks to one of the boxes. After the child has satisfied his desire to handle the apparatus for a short time, the examiner says: "Can you put these bricks in again?" and points, saying: "Put one in here", etc. He may encourage the child until he has put two cubes into the box, but must not otherwise help him. If the child refuses or has not understood, the item should be left and taken again later. (If the child succeeds at E 35, *go right on to E* 40.)

E 36. *Form boards—II. Two-circle board. One in.* (*Fifteenth month.*)

The examiner places the board that contains two circles in front of the child and then, with the child watching, he places first the large circle and then the smaller one in their appropriate holes. He then lifts each out in turn and places it near its hole between the child and the form board. The baby must get *one* of the circles into its appropriate hole to pass E 36. Two trials are allowed. (If the baby gets *both* circles in, he passes item E 39 also.)

E 37. *Puts cubes in and out of boxes in play.* (*Fifteenth month.*)

E 37 is passed during free manipulation of the apparatus. The child must put at least one cube into one of the boxes, and take at least one out, quite freely during play, to pass this item.

E 38. *Form boards—III. Square board. Two trials* (*Sixteenth month.*)

The examiner places the square board that has a large square hole in it in front of the child and then, with the child watching, he puts the square inset into the board. He then lifts the inset out and places it between the child and the board as before. Two trials. The child must successfully manipulate the inset into its hole to pass E 38. (*Go right on to E* 39 *and other Form Board items.*)

E 39. *Form boards—IV. Two-circle board. Two in.* (*Seventeenth month.*)

As for E 36, but the child successfully places both insets in the board to pass E 39. Two trials. Leave the board in position. (*Go right on to E* 46.)

E 40. *Can put lid back on box.* (*Seventeenth month.*)

The child having been successfully encouraged (E 35) to put the two cubes into the box, the examiner hands him the lid and asks: "Now can you put the lid on?", and as before encourages the child to try to put on the lid. He must not *help*, but only verbally encourage the child to get the lid back on. This is quite a difficult task, to return a square lid to a box, but is passed by about half the babies of this age. E 40 follows easily upon E 35, but may also be taken separately if E 35 was failed. In that case the examiner will himself return the bricks to the box before taking E 40.

E 41. *Form boards—V. Three-hole board. One in.* (*Seventeenth month.*)

The three-hole board is placed in front of the child *with all three insets in place.* The examiner then proceeds to lift out the circle, the triangle and the square, in that order, and place them opposite their appropriate holes on the table between the child and the form board.

To pass this item the baby must place *one* of the insets in its correct hole. Two trials are allowed. For the second trial the pieces must be placed on the table between the child and the form board as before. If the child places two insets correctly, he scores plus for E 44; if he places three insets correctly, he scores plus for E 45.

E 42. *Puts two cubes in, lid on, all complete.* (*Eighteenth month.*)

The child who has passed both E 35 and E 40 in succession has also passed E 42. This item must be done entirely by the child, the examiner offering encouragement only to help him to persist in the task.

E 43. *Form boards—VI. Circle and square board together.* (*Eighteenth month.*)

For E 43 the examiner takes up the one-circle board and the square board as used in E 33 and E 38. He places these together as if they formed one board, with the circle and square in place in their holes. Then, as before, he takes the insets out and places them between the child and the board, opposite their appropriate holes. To pass E 43 *both* insets must be correctly placed. (Two trials.) If the child successfully passes E 43, *go straight on to item E* 47 while the boards are in place.

E 44. *Form boards—VII. Three-hole board. Two in.* (*Twentieth month.*)

As for E 41, but now the child places two insets in the board correctly. Any two insets placed is a pass at this level.

E 45. *Form boards—VIII. Three-hole board. Three in.* (*Twenty-first month.*)

As for E 41, but now the child places all three insets correctly to pass E 45. (See Plate 10.)

E 46. *Form boards—IX. Two-circle board rotated.* (*Twenty-second month.*)

Following E 39, the child having placed both insets correctly, the examiner shows pleasure at this and encourages the child, saying: "Now see what we will do." Then he lifts the board very slowly, leaving the two circles on the table, turns the board slowly round and places it behind the circles, so that the large circle is in front of the small hole and the small circle in front of the large hole. The apparatus must be moved near enough for the child to reach it easily. The child is then invited to put the circles back into the board. He must get both circles in to pass this test. (Two trials allowed.) For the second trial the board must be rotated as before, after the insets are returned to their holes.

E 47 and 48. *Form boards—X. Circle and square boards rotated.* (*Twenty-third month.*) (*Credit 2 points.*)

Following E 43, when the child has placed the two insets correctly, thus passing E 43, the examiner says: "Now see what we are going to do", and he carefully lifts the boards, leaving the insets on the table, and then with the child watching, he changes the boards over and places the square board behind the circle and the circle board behind the square. The apparatus must be moved near to the child so that he can handle the pieces easily. The child is then asked to replace the insets: "Can you put them in now?" Both pieces must be correctly placed to pass this item. (Two trials.) For the second trial the pieces must be in their holes before the boards are lifted and rotated as before.

This is a very difficult test, not passed until the twenty-third month by about half the babies. It scores two points on the form.

E 49 and 50. *Assembles three boxes.* (*Twenty-third month.*) (*Credit 2 points.*)

At this stage the child is given all three boxes to play with. A child who appears competent, and who is about eighteen months old or older, may be given all three boxes together. He may then in play pass the earlier tests in the brick-boxes series very rapidly. When he has satisfied his desire to play with these boxes for a short time, the examiner should, as before, encourage him to return the bricks and lids to the boxes. If the child can persist long enough to get two bricks into *each* box and a lid on *each* box, he passes E 49 and 50. Two points are credited for this item. It does not matter whether he matches up the apparatus for colour or not; if the apparatus is assembled otherwise correctly, he passes E 49 and 50.

This series of items with the boxes is quickly given and measures the child's manipulative ability over a wide range of delicate tasks. It will also continue into the third year, when the colour factor will also be taken into consideration, but that goes beyond what is expected for babies up to two years of age.

E 51 and 52. *Can open screw-toy.* (*Twenty-fourth month.*)

The examiner takes up the small screw barrel and, opening it, places a sweetmeat or a small toy inside. Then, offering the closed barrel to the child, he says: "Can you get the sweet?" or "Where is the doggy? Can you get it?", etc. The child must successfully twist the barrel and open it by unscrewing it to pass items E 51 and 52. Two points are credited for this item.

The method of getting a complete assessment (G.Q. only), in the case of those babies who are capable of passing tests beyond the twenty-fourth month level, is fully explained in *Appendix I.—"Transition to Third Year"*.

APPENDIX I

SCORING THE TESTS AND ASSESSING RESULTS

In several places in this work we have referred to the method of scoring and arriving at quotients, and also to the building of Profiles. It seems advisable here to draw together in one place the full details for reference by the reader.

Scoring.—The details for scoring each separate item of the scale have been given in full in Chapters XI to XV. To get the final score the number of items passed in each scale is counted up, and the totals are entered on the printed form in the places provided. A complete inventory of the items as arranged on the printed form will be found in Appendix II.

Assessing results for tests taken in the first year, for babies under one year old.

1. Count up the total items passed in each scale and enter the results in the appropriate places.

2. Sum these totals across to get the total score.

3. Divide this total by 3 to get the Mental Age (M.A.), because there are three items for each week of life in the first year of tests. This gives the child's Mental Age in weeks.

Thus: $\text{Mental Age} = \dfrac{\text{Total Score}}{3}$ weeks.

Mental Age is expressed in weeks and thirds of a week.

4. Work out the Chronological Age (C.A.) by the calendar, counting across from the child's date of birth the number of complete weeks old he is at test, and deal with any extra days as follows: 1 day over should be ignored, 2 or 3 days over count as one-third of a week, 4 or 5 days over count as two-thirds of a week, and 6 days over as a whole extra week.

5. Obtain the General Quotient (General Intelligence Quotient or Total Quotient) by dividing the Mental Age by the Chronological Age as usual. Thus: $\text{G.Q.} = \dfrac{\text{M.A.} \times 100}{\text{C.A.}}$

Example 1.—A baby of 7 weeks and 5 days of age has the following scores: A, 4; B, 6; C, 5; D, 5; E, 4. Then the total score is 24, and the Mental Age is $\dfrac{24}{3} = 8$ weeks.

But as this child is under eight months of age the correction described in Chapter VI must be applied. That is, the examiner must add 8 weeks to both C.A. and M.A. *before* working out the quotient. (This applies only to babies under eight months of age.)

$$\text{Then, G.Q.} = \frac{\text{M.A.} \times 100}{\text{C.A.}} \text{ or } \frac{8 + 8 \text{ weeks} \times 100}{7\tfrac{2}{3} + 8 \text{ weeks}} = 102.$$

Example 2.—A child of $41\frac{1}{3}$ weeks has the following scores: A, 24; B, 23; C, 23; D, 24; E, 25. Thus the total score is 119, and the M.A. = $\frac{119}{3} = 39\frac{2}{3}$; C.A. = $41\frac{1}{3}$ weeks.

(As this baby is over eight months of age, no correction is applied.)

$$\text{G.Q.} = \frac{39\tfrac{2}{3} \times 100}{41\tfrac{1}{3}} = 96.$$

Transition between First and Second Years

In testing babies who are *approaching the end of their first year* and who pass some second-year items as well as most of the first-year items, failing some of the latter, the scores for the two years must at first be kept separate as they are weighted differently and carry different M.A. credits, there being three items for each week in the first year and only two items for each week in the second year. Thus any first-year item is worth one-third of a week of Mental Age, but any second-year item is worth one-half of a week of Mental Age. Care must therefore be taken, and the totals for the first year entered as before at the base of the first-year columns in the places provided, ignoring for the moment any second-year items that may have been passed.

First-year Items.—As before, add the first-year totals across, and divide by 3 to get the *Mental Age* credit for the first year.

Second-year Items.—Then similarly count up any second-year items passed, putting the second-year totals at the end of the second year in the places provided. Add these across and divide the second-year total by 2 to get the Mental Age credit for the second year. Now add together the Mental Age credit for the first and second years to get the M.A.

$$\text{Then as before G.Q.} = \frac{\text{M.A.} \times 100}{\text{C.A.}}$$

Example 3.—This baby is 50 weeks old. The scores, that is the number of items passed for the first year, are A, 30; B, 29; C, 31; D, 30; and E, 31. But he also passes 2 items of the second year in the A Scale and 1 each in D and E. No others. His result is therefore worked up as follows:

M.A. credit for first year will be the total of first-year items passed divided by 3:

$$30 + 29 + 31 + 30 + 31 = \frac{151}{3} = 50\tfrac{1}{3} \text{ weeks.}$$

Extra credit for second-year items will be 4 items passed divided by 2, that is 2 extra weeks.

Then M.A. = $52\frac{1}{3}$ weeks.

$$\text{Then G.Q.} = \frac{\text{M.A.} \times 100}{\text{C.A.}} = \frac{52\frac{1}{3} \times 100}{50} = 105.$$

Testing Older Second-year Babies

If C.A. and M.A. are both more than 52 weeks, the credits for the two years must still be kept separate, and the result worked up as above *unless* the child has passed *all* the items for the first year. If he has passed all the first-year items, the quotient is very quickly arrived at as follows: Count up the second-year items passed *only* and enter the scores in the places provided; then add these across to get the total *second*-year score. Divide this by 2 to get the second-year Mental Age credit. Then add on the 52 weeks for the first year to get the total Mental Age.

Chronological ages of babies *over* 52 *weeks old* are worked out in weeks and half-weeks because there are two items for each week of age. As before, count across the calendar from the child's birthday, add on 52 weeks for the first year, and deal with any additional days as follows: 1 day over the completed weeks is ignored, 2, 3, 4 or 5 days are counted as half of a week, 6 days as an additional week as before. Then the G.Q. is obtained as before: $\frac{\text{M.A.} \times 100}{\text{C.A.}}$

Example 4.—This baby is $78\frac{1}{2}$ weeks old. It was not necessary actually to take any first-year items, as he was well above that level in every scale. Second-year items passed are: A, 12; B, 10; C, 15; D, 11; E, 12. Then the total second-year items passed are 60. Dividing by 2, we get 30 weeks for the second-year Mental Age credit. Adding the 52 weeks of the first year, the Mental Age is 82 weeks. Then G.Q. = $\frac{82}{78\frac{1}{2}} \times 100 = 104{\cdot}4$ or $\underline{104}$.

After some practice, the working out of these General Quotients is found to be extremely simple. The sub-quotients at different levels are slightly more complicated.

Profiles.—As has been explained in several places, profiles can very well be drawn on the child's *scores* alone. The five scales are all very nearly equal in difficulty at each level, as we have seen, and the general shape of a child's results is all that is usually needed. This can of course be seen from the figures, and differential diagnosis can be based straightaway on the *scores* without turning them all into quotients. It is for this reason that items are numbered right through to 52, and to facilitate counting. Thus in Example 4 just quoted the total scores, if first- and second-year items had been counted right through, would be A, 12 + 31; B, 10 + 32; C, 15 + 31; D, 11 + 31; and E, 12 + 31, adding in each case the first-year total scores. (It will be noted at this point that there are 32 first-year items in Scale B, there being 1 extra item there and 1 less in that scale in the second year. This keeps the 3 items required in each week of the first year (total 156) and also the 2 items for each week in the second year (total 104) accurate. This cannot be avoided.) These totals therefore are: A, 43; B, 42; C, 46; D, 42; and E, 43. A graph could be drawn to illustrate the tendencies suggestive of ability type in this case. The comparatively high score on "C" suggests a good verbal child, the rest of the results being very even at an average level. This way of studying the results would in general be quite sufficient if only one test were to be given and no particular comparison with other cases required. The general quotient in itself is the most indicative piece of information that emerges, and the quotient of 104 shows this child to be of good average ability.

But where it is required to compare one child with another in regard to particular trends or differences on the separate scales, or to compare children of different age levels, or as may be required in clinics to compare tests on the same child taken at different times, as for example before and after treatment, then it is very useful to work up a profile from separate sub-quotients. The advantages of such a method where indicated, either for clinical or research purposes, have been illustrated in Chapters VII and VIII. The method of arriving at the sub-quotients is as follows. Profiles drawn on separate quotients are very seldom needed for very young babies. However, we will now illustrate the method of arriving at the several quotients by using two of the same cases as quoted above.

Example 1.—As there are five scales all equally weighted in relation at one another, the separate scores must be multiplied by 5 before they are divided by 3 to get the Mental Ages. In the case of our $7\frac{2}{3}$ weeks' old baby we shall also have to add 8 weeks to the Chronological Age and also to each of the sub-mental ages before working out the quotients. The sub-mental ages and quotients will then be:

A Scale: M.A. $\dfrac{4 \times 5}{3} = 6\frac{2}{3}$.

$$\text{Q.A.} = \frac{6\frac{2}{3} + 8}{7\frac{2}{3} + 8} \times 100 = \frac{14\frac{2}{3}}{15\frac{2}{3}} \times 100$$

$$= 93{\cdot}6 \text{ or } \underline{94}.$$

B Scale: M.A. $\dfrac{6 \times 5}{3} = 10$.

$$\text{Q.B.} = \frac{10 + 8}{7\frac{2}{3} + 8} \times 100 = 114{\cdot}6 \text{ or } \underline{115}.$$

C Scale: M.A. $\frac{5 \times 5}{3} = 8\frac{1}{3}$.

$$\text{Q.C.} = \frac{8\frac{1}{3} + 8}{7\frac{2}{3} + 8} \times 100 = 103{\cdot}8 \text{ or } \underline{104}.$$

D Scale: Same score as for scale C.

So M.A. (D) is $8\frac{1}{3}$ weeks and Q.D. is $\underline{104}$.

E Scale: Same score as for Scale A.

So M.A. (E) is $6\frac{2}{3}$ weeks and Q.D. is $\underline{94}$.

If required, a graph can then be drawn as in Chapter VII on these quotients: Q.A. = 94; Q.B. = 115; Q.C. = 104; Q.D. = 104; and Q.E. = 94.

(*Note.*—A check of the figures is obtained by taking the average of the five quotients, which should equal (within a few decimal points) the general intelligence quotient, G.Q., which in this case is 102.)

At the transition between the first and second year the items must be dealt with separately, and the Mental Age credits for the second year added as in working out the G.Q., remembering to multiply in each case by 5. As will be noticed, the items for the second year are divided by 2 to obtain the second-year Mental Age credit on the sub-scales.

We will now work up the Profile for Example 4. C.A. = $78\frac{1}{2}$ weeks.

A Scale: M.A. $= 52 + \frac{12 \times 5}{2} = 82$ weeks.

$$\text{Q.A.} = \frac{82}{78\frac{1}{2}} \times 100 = \underline{104}.$$

B Scale: M.A. $= 52 + \frac{10 \times 5}{2} = 77$ weeks.

$$\text{Q.B.} = \frac{77}{78\frac{1}{2}} \times 100 = \underline{98}.$$

C Scale: M.A. $= 52 + \frac{15 \times 5}{2} = 89\frac{1}{2}$ weeks.

$$\text{Q.C.} = \frac{89\frac{1}{2}}{78\frac{1}{2}} \times 100 = \underline{114}.$$

D Scale: M.A. $= 52 + \frac{11 \times 5}{2} = 79\frac{1}{2}$ weeks.

$$\text{Q.D.} = \frac{79\frac{1}{2}}{78\frac{1}{2}} \times 100 = \underline{101}.$$

E Scale: M.A. $= 52 + \frac{12 \times 5}{2} = 82$ weeks.

$$\text{Q.E.} = \frac{82}{78\frac{1}{2}} \times 100 = \underline{104}.$$

General Quotient (G.Q.) = $\underline{104}$.

This profile confirms the impression of a child doing well on the verbal side, but with average results elsewhere.

Transition to Third Year

As has been explained in several places, we have been obliged to limit the discussion of this research at its present stage to testing children under two years of age. We may, however, indicate how the transition to other tests to complete a child's test result might best be done. Some of the older babies within the two-year range will of course be able to take tests beyond the twenty-four months' limit. In fact, a few children from eighteen months onwards need more tests than this scale alone provides. The examiner will therefore need to go on to another scale, using whichever Revision of the Binet Scale is preferred. If the Terman Merrill Revision is used, the examiner should complete the Griffiths Scale to the end of the second year, and then, omitting the first six tests of the Terman Merrill Scale, which are for the latter part of the second-year period, he should go on to the tests for two and a half years. Credit must then be added to the total Mental Age as indicated for the Terman Merrill Scale (one month, or, if working in weeks, $4\frac{1}{3}$ weeks, for each test passed), before the quotient is worked out. In the case of those Revisions of the Binet Scale that begin at the third year and have only six tests for each year, the tests for the second year (Griffiths Scale) should be completed and then the Binet Tests for the third year taken from the beginning. Appropriate Mental Age credits (two months, or, if working in weeks, $8\frac{1}{2}$ weeks) are added for each test passed at the third-year level.

In regard to profiles, it is not possible at present to draw accurate profiles for children who pass tests beyond two years, where other scales not classified in the same way are used. It will, however, be one of the writer's early endeavours to continue the work on the new scale beyond the second year, and this will then make differential diagnosis as outlined in this book available for testing children over two years of age.

APPENDIX II

THE GRIFFITHS MENTAL DEVELOPMENT SCALE
COMPLETE INVENTORY OF TEST ITEMS

Months of Age	*A* *Locomotor*		*B* *Personal-Social*		*C* *Hearing and Speech*		*D* *Eye and Hand*		*E* *Performance*	
1	Lifts chin when prone.	1	Regards person—momentarily.	1	Startled by sounds.	1	Follows a moving light with the eyes.	1	Grasps examiner's finger.	1
	Pushes with feet against examiner's hands.	2	Quieted when picked up.	2	Quieted by voice.	2	Looks at ring or toy momentarily.	2	Reacts to paper. I—Generalised physical movements.	2
	Holds head erect for a few seconds.	3	Enjoys bath.	3	Vocalisation other than crying.	3	Looks steadily at bell-ring held still.	3	Hand goes to mouth.	3
2	Lifts head up when prone.	4	Smiling.	4	Listens to bell.	4	Follows moving bell-ring horizontally.	4	Shows energetic arm movements.	4
	Kicks vigorously.	5	Visually recognises mother.	5	Cooing—one syllable.	5	Follows ring vertically.	5	Reacts to paper. II—Vigorous head turning.	5
3	Active in bath—kicks.	6	Vocalises when talked to.	6	Searches for sound with eyes.	6	Glances from ring to bell or other object.	6	Holds doll.	6
	Lifts head when in *dorsal* position.	7	Follows moving persons with eyes.	7	Listens to music.	7	Follows moving bell-ring in a circle.	7	Plays with own fingers.	7
	Rolls from side to back.	8	Returns examiner's glance with smiling or cooing.	8	Makes 2 + different sounds.	8	Watches object pulled along by string.	8	Looks at box on table.	8
4	Back firm when held in sitting position.	9	Friendly to strangers.	9	Searches for sound with head movements.	9	Grasps ring when given.	9	Resists doll withdrawal.	9
	Lifts head and chest when prone.	10	Resists adult who tries playfully to take toy.	10	Laughs aloud.	10	Visually explores new environment.	10	Clasps cube put in hand and holds it.	10
	Holds head erect continuously.	11	Frolics when played with.	11	Turns head deliberately to bell.	11	Reaches for ring and grasps.	11	Drops first cube for second	11
5	Lifts head and shoulders, *dorsal*.	12	Stops crying when talked to.	12	Listens to tuning-fork.	12	Carries ring to mouth.	12	Reacts to paper. III—Pulls it away.	12
	Rolls from side to side.	13	Turns head to person talking or singing.	13	Coos or stops crying on hearing music.	13	Clutches at dangling ring.	13	Shows interest in box.	13
6	Plays with own toes.	14	Anticipatory movements when about to be lifted.	14	Talks (babbles) to persons.	14	Secures dangling ring.	14	Takes toy or other object from table.	14
	Crawling Reaction (I). Draws up knees, etc.	15	Holds a spoon.	15	Manipulates bell.	15	Hands explore table surface.	15	Holds two cubes.	15
	Sits with slight support.	16	Stretches to be taken.	16	Makes 4 + different sounds.	16	Plays with ring—shaking bells, etc.	16	Grasps box.	16
7	Can roll from back to stomach, etc.	17	Drinks from a cup.	17	Responds when called.	17	Reaches for and picks up string—any method.	17	Manipulates cube or toy	17
	Stepping reaction (*a*): Dancing movements.	18	Manipulates cup or spoon in play.	18	Two-syllable babble.	18	Looks for dropped toy.	18	Reacts to paper. IV—Reaches for and takes.	18
8	*Crawling (II)*. Tries vigorously to crawl.	19	Reacts to mirror image —I. Looks at.	19	Shouts for attention.	19	Strikes one object with another.	19	Passes toy from hand to hand.	19
	Sits alone for a short time.	20	Knows strangers from familiar friends.	20	Listens to conversations.	20	Watches examiner scribble.	20	Drops one cube for third.	20
	Stepping reaction (*b*): One foot in front of the other.	21	Prompt reaction to situations, e.g. at table.	21	Singing tones.	21	Secures ring by means of string.	21	Manipulates 2 objects at once.	21
9	*Crawling (III)*. Can turn around when left on floor.	22	Displeased if toy is taken away.	22	Babbled phrases: 4 + syllables.	22	Forefinger and thumb partly specialised.	22	Reacts to paper. V—Plays with, crumples, etc.	22
	Can be left sitting on floor.	23	Helps to hold cup for drinking.	23	Says Mama or Dada, etc. (one word clear).	23	Fine prehension.	23	Lifts inverted box or cup in search of toy.	23
	Crawling (IV). Makes some progress forwards or backwards.	24	Pulls off hat.	24	Listens to stop watch.	24	Dangles ring by string.	24	Rattles box.	24
10	Stands when held up.	25	Reacts to mirror image —II. Smiles at, or plays with.	25	Shakes head for "No!"	25	Plays pulling ring or toy by string.	25	Clicks two bricks together. (Imitation.)	25
	Sits well—in a chair.	26	Waves bye-bye.	26	Says two clear words.	26	*Throws* objects.	26	Lifts lid off box.	26
11	Pulls self up by furniture.	27	Gives affection.	27	Short babbled sentences.	27	Thumb opposition complete.	27	Finds toy under box or cup.	27
	Can stand holding to furniture.	28	Finger feeds (thumb and forefinger).	28	Rings bell.	28	Can point with index finger.	28	Tries to take cubes out of box.	28
12	*Crawling (V)*. Creeps on hands and knees, etc.	29	Plays with cup, spoon, and saucer.	29	Reacts to music vocally.	29	Interested in motor-car.	29	Accepts third cube without dropping.	29
	Side-steps round inside cot or play-pen holding rails.	30	Obeys simple requests: "Give me cup", etc.	30	Babbled monologue when alone.	30	Can hold pencil as if to mark on paper.	30	Removes both cubes from box (shown).	30
	Can walk when led.	31	Plays "Pat-a-cake" (claps hands).	31	Says three clear words.	31	Uses pencil on paper a little.	31	Manipulates box, lid and cubes.	31
			Puts small objects in and out of cup in play. •	32						
	Total Items Passed: A..................		Total B		Total C		Total D............		Total E	

Second Year	*A* *Locomotor*		*B* *Personal-Social*		*C* *Hearing and Speech*		*D* *Eye and Hand*		*E* *Performance*	
13	Climbs on a low ledge or step.	32	• See Ch. XII, Introduction.		Tries definitely to sing.	32	Likes holding little toys.	32	Unwraps and finds toy or cube.	32
	Stands alone.	33	Tries to help dressing —arms into coat, etc.	33	Looks at pictures for a few seconds.	33	Preference for one hand.	33	One-circle board—two trials.	33
14	Walks alone.	34	Can hold cup for drinking.	34	Knows own name.	34	Plays rolling ball.	34	Opens two boxes.	34
	Kneels on floor or chair.	35	Uses spoon himself—spills some.	35	Likes rhymes and jingles.	35	Can hold 4 cubes in hands at once.	35	Puts two cubes back into box when encouraged to do so.	35
15	Climbs stairs (up).	36	Shows shoes.	36	Uses 4 or 5 clear words.	36	Plays pushing little cars along.	36	Two-circle board—one in.	36
	Likes pushing pram, toy horse, etc.	37	Tries to turn door-knob.	37	One object in box identified.	37	Places one lid, box or brick upon another.	37	Puts cubes in and out of boxes in play.	37
16	Trots about well.	38	Cleanliness—asks.	38	Uses 6 or 7 clear words.	38	Scribbles more freely.	38	Square board—two trials.	38
17	Stoops.	39	Manages cup well—half-full.	39	Long babbled conversations—some words clear.	39	Pulls paper or cloth to get toy.	39	Two-circle board—two in.	39
	Climbs on a low chair.	40	Can take off shoes and socks.	40	Enjoys picture-book.	40	Constructive play with boxes or other materials (E).	40	Can put lid back on box.	40
18	Can walk backwards.	41	Likes adult to show book.	41	Two objects in box identified.	41	Tower of three.	41	Three-hole board—one in, two trials.	41
19	Walks pulling toy on string.	42	Parts of body—1.	42	Uses 9 words.	42	Can *throw* a ball.	42	Puts two cubes into box, lid on, all complete.	42
	Climbs stairs (up and down).	43	Bowel control complete.	43	Four objects in box identified.	43	Tower of four.	43	Circle and square board together.	43
20	Jumps.	44	Uses spoon well.	44	Vocabulary 12 words.	44	Enjoys vigorous straight scribble.	44	Three-hole board—two in.	44
	Runs	45	Bladder control by day.	45	Picture vocabulary (1).	45	Can pour water from one cup to another.	45	Three-hole board—three in.	45
21	*Walks* upstairs.	46	Tries to tell experiences.	46	Word combinations.	46	Circular scribble (imitation).	46	Two-circle board rotated.	46
22	Climbs to stand on a chair.	47	Asks for things at table by name.	47	Picture vocabulary (2).	47	Tower of five or more.	47	Circle and square boards rotated. }	47
	Can jump off a step.	48	Parts of body—2.	48	Listens to stories.	48	Perpendicular stroke.	48	(Credit two points). }	48
23	Can seat himself at table.	49	Parts of body—3.	49	Vocabulary 20 words clear.	49	Train of three.	49	Assembles three boxes. }	49
	Walks up and *down* stairs.	50	Parts of body—4 +.	50	Eight objects in box identified.	50	Throws ball into basket.	50	(Credit two points.) }	50
24	Can kick a ball.	51	Can open a door.	51	*Names* 4 toys.	51	Making a brick or toy walk.	51	Can open screw-toy. Can reassemble screw-toy. }	51
	Can be trusted on stairs alone.	52	Helps actively to dress or undress	52	Uses sentences of 4 + syllables.	52	Horizontal stroke.	52	(Credit two points). }	52
	Total Items Passed: A..................		Total B		Total C............		Total D............		Total E	

BIBLIOGRAPHY

AINSWORTH, M. D., and BOSTON, M. (1952): "Psychodiagnostic Assessments of a Child after Prolonged Separation in Early Childhood", *Brit. Jour. Med. Psych.*, **25,** 169–201.

ALDRICH, C. G., and DOLL, E. A. (1931): "Comparative Intelligence of Idiots and of Normal Infants", *Jour. Genet. Psychol.*, **39,** 227–57.

AMES, L. B. (1937): "The Sequential Patterning of Prone Progression in the Human Infant", *Genet. Psychol. Monogr.*, **19,** 409–60.

ANDERSON, J. E. (1939): "The Limitations of Infant and Pre-School Tests in the Measurement of Intelligence", *Jour. Psychol.*, **8,** 351–79.

ARLITT, A. H. (1928): *Psychology of Infancy and Early Childhood* (New York: McGraw Hill).

ARLITT, A. H. (1930): *The Child from One to Six* (New York: McGraw Hill).

BAKWIN, R. M., and BAKWIN, H. (1942): *Psychologic Care During Infancy and Childhood* (D. Appleton Century Coy., New York and London).

BARKER, R. G., KOUNIN, J. S., WRIGHT, H. F. (1943): *Child Behaviour and Development* (New York: McGraw Hill).

BAYLEY, N. (1933): "Mental Growth during the First Three Years. A Developmental Study of Sixty-one Children by Repeated Tests", *Genet. Psychol. Monogr.*, **14,** 1–92.

BAYLEY, N. (1940): "Mental Growth in Young Children", *Year-book Nat. Soc. Stud. Educ.*, **39** (II), 11–47.

BERNFELD, S. (1929): *Psychology of the Infant* (London).

BERNFELD, S. (1935): "The Psycho-Analytic Study of the Young Child", *Psycho-anal. Quart.*, 1935, **3,** 3–14.

BIEBER, I., and FULTON, J. F. (1938): "Relation of the Cerebral Cortex to the Grasp Reflex and to Postural and Righting Reflexes", *Arch. Neurol. & Psychiat.*, **39,** 433–54.

BILTO, E. W. (1941): "A Comparative Study of Certain Physical Abilities of Children with Speech Defects and Children with Normal Speech", *Jour. Sp. Disord.*, **6,** 187–203.

BINET, A. (1903): *L'Étude Expérimentale de l'Intelligence.*

BINET, A. (1911): "Nouvelles Recherches sur la Mesure du Niveau intellectuel chez les Enfants d'École", *Année psychologique*, Vol. 17, pp. 145–201.

BINET, A., and SIMON, T. (1908): "Le Développement de l'Intelligence chez les Enfants", *Année Psychologique*, Vol. 14, pp. 1–94.

BINET, A., and SIMON, T. (1914): *Mentally Defective Children* (trans.) (New York: Longmans, Green).

BINET, A., and SIMON, T. (1915): *A Method of Measuring the Development of Intelligence in Young Children* (Chicago Medical Book Coy.).

BLATZ, W. E., and MILLICHAMP, D. A. (1935): *The Development of Emotion in the Infant* (Univ. Toronto Stud. Child Developm. Ser., No. 4).

BOWLBY, J. (1949): *Forty-four Juvenile Thieves: Their Character and Home Life* (Baillère, Tindall & Cox).

BOWLEY, A. H. (1944): *The Natural Development of the Child* (Livingstone, Edinburgh).

BRIDGES, K. M. B. (1931): *The Social and Emotional Development of the Pre-School Child* (London: Kegan Paul).

BRIDGES, K. M. B. (1932): "Emotional Development in Early Infancy", *Child Development*, **3**, 324–41.

BÜHLER, C. (1930): *The First Year of Life* (New York: Day).

BÜHLER, C. (1932): "The Child and its Activity with Practical Material", *Brit. Jour. Educ. Psychol.*, **2**, 27–41.

BÜHLER, C. (1935): *From Birth to Maturity* (London: Kegan Paul).

BÜHLER, C., and HETZER, H. (1935): *Testing Children's Development from Birth to School Age* (New York: Farrar & Rinehart).

BÜHLER, C., with five collaborators (1940): *The Child and His Family* (London: Kegan Paul).

BÜHLER, K. (1930): *The Mental Development of the Child. A Summary of Modern Psychological Theory* (London: Routledge and Kegan Paul).

BURT, C. (1909): "Experimental Tests of General Intelligence", *Brit. Jour. Psychol.*, **3**, 94.

BURT, C. (1910): "General and Special Abilities in School Children", *Brit. Ass. Ann. Report*, pp. 804 f.

BURT, C. (1921): *Mental and Scholastic Tests* (P. S. King & Sons).

BURT, C. (1925): *The Young Delinquent* (P. S. King & Sons); (1944), 4th ed. (revised) (University of London Press).

BURT, C. (1937): *The Subnormal Mind* (Oxford University Press).

BURT, C. (1937): *The Backward Child* (Univ. London Press).

BURT, C., and JOHN, E. (1942): "The Factorial Analysis of the Terman-Binet Tests", *Brit. Jour. Educ. Psychol.*, 12.

Care of Children Committee, Report of the (Myra Curtis, Chairman), 1946) (H.M. Stationery Office).

CARMICHAEL, L. (1936): "A Revaluation of the Concepts of Maturation and Learning as Applied to the Early Development of Behaviour", *Psychol. Rev.*, **43**, 450–70.

CARMICHAEL, L. (1946): (Ed.), *Manual of Child Psychology* (Chapman & Hall, London; John Wiley, New York).

CATTELL, P. (1940): *The Measurement of Intelligence of Infants and Young Children* (New York: The Psychological Corporation, Lancaster Pa. Sc. Press).

CATTELL, R. B. (1936): *A Guide to Mental Testing* (London: Methuen).

CHAMBERS, E. G. (1940): *Statistical Calculation for Beginners* (Cambridge University Press).

CHAMPNEYS, F. H. (1881): "Notes on an Infant", *Mind*, **6**, 104–7.

CROSSE, V. M. (1945): *The Premature Baby* (London: J. & A. Churchill).

CUNNINGHAM, K. S. (1927): "The Measurement of Early Levels of Intelligence", *Teach. Coll. Contr. Educ.*, No. 259.

DARWIN, C. (1877): "A Biographical Sketch of an Infant", *Mind*, **2**, 285–94.

DEARBORN, C. V. N. (1910): *Moto-sensory Development: Observations on the First Three Years of Childhood* (Baltimore: Warwick & York).

DENNIS, W. (1936): "A Bibliography of Baby Biographies", *Child Development*, **7**, 71–3.

DEWEY, E. (1935): *Infant Behaviour* (New York: Columbia Univ. Press).

DRUMMOND, M. (1921): *The Dawn of Mind: An Introduction to Child Psychology* (London: Arnold).

DUNSDON, M. I. (1952): *The Educability of Cerebral Palsied Children* (Newnes, London).

EICHHOLZ, A. (1932): *A Study of the Deaf in England and Wales* (H.M. Stationery Office).

EWING, A. W. G. (1930): *Aphasia in Children* (Oxford Univ. Press).

EWING, I. R. (1943): "Deafness in Infancy and Early Childhood", *Jour. Laryng. Oto.*, **58**, 4.

EWING, I. R., and EWING, A. W. G. (1938): *Handicap of Deafness* (London: Longmans, Green).

EWING, I. R., and EWING, A. W. G. (1944): "Ascertainment of Deafness in Infancy and Early Childhood", *Jour. Laryng. Oto.*, **59**, 9.

EWING, I. R., and EWING, A. W. G. (1947): *Opportunity and the Deaf Child* (Univ. London Press).

FENTON, J. (1925): *A Practical Psychology of Babyhood* (Boston: Houghton Mifflin).

FIRTH, J. R. (1930): *Speech* (London: Benn).

FISHER, M. S. (1934): "Language Patterns of Pre-School Children", *Child Devel. Monogr.*, No. 15, p. 88.

FLÜGEL, J. C. (1921): *The Psychoanalytic Study of the Family* (London: Hogarth Press).

FREUD, ANNA (1934): "The Training of the Infant from the Psychoanalytic View-point", *Z. psychanal. Pädag.*, 1934, **8**, 17–25.

FREUD, ANNA (1946): *The Psychoanalytic Treatment of Children.*

GARDNER, D. E. M. (1937): *The Children's Play Centre* (London: Methuen).

GESELL, A. (1925): *The Mental Growth of the Pre-School Child* (New York: Macmillan).

GESELL, A. (1928): *Infancy and Human Growth* (New York: Macmillan).

GESELL, A. (1939): "Reciprocal Interweaving in Neuro-muscular Development: A Principle of Spiral Organisation shown in the Patterning of Infant Behaviour", *Jour. Comp. Neurol.*, **70**, 161–80.

GESELL, A. (1942): *The First Five Years of Life* (London: Methuen).

GESELL, A. (1946a): "The Ontogenesis of Infant Behaviour", in L. Carmichael (Ed.), *Manual of Child Psychology* (New York: John Wiley).

GESELL, A. (1946b): *How a Baby Grows* (Hamish Hamilton Medical Books, London).

GESELL, A., and AMATRUDA, C. S. (1941): *Developmental Diagnosis: Normal and Abnormal Child Development* (New York: Hoeber).

GESELL, A., and AMATRUDA, C. S. (1945): *The Embryology of Behaviour: The Beginnings of the Human Mind* (New York: Harper).

GESELL, A., and THOMPSON, H. (1929): "Learning and Growth in Identical Infant Twins (Co-Twin Control)", *Genet. Psychol. Monogr.*, **6**, 1–24.

GIBBENS, J. (1946): *The Care of Young Babies* (2nd ed.) (London: J. & A. Churchill).

GIBBENS, J. (1947): *The Care of Children from One to Five.* (3rd ed.) (London: J. & A. Churchill).

GODDARD, H. H. (1911): "The Binet-Simon Measuring Scale for Intelligence, Revised", *Training School Bulletin*, **8**, 56–62.

GOODENOUGH, F. L. (1946): "The Measurement of Mental Growth in Childhood", in L. Carmichael (Ed.), *Manual of Child Psychology*, pp. 450 et seq.

GOODENOUGH, F. L., and ANDERSON, J. E. (1931): *Experimental Child Study* (New York: Century).

GOODENOUGH, F. L., and MAURER, K. (1942): *The Mental Growth of Children from Two to Fourteen Years* (Univ. of Minnesota Press).

GRAHAM, M. (1919): "Intra-Uterine Crying", *Brit. Med. Jour.*, **1**, 675.

GRIFFITHS, R. (1933): "Children's Phantasies", *Australian Journal of Psychology.*

GRIFFITHS, R. (1935): *Imagination in Early Childhood* (London: Kegan Paul, Trench, Trubner & Co.).

GROOS, K. (1896): *The Play of Animals.*

GROOS, K. (1899): *The Play of Man.*

HALLER, M. W. (1932): "The Reactions of Infants to Changes in the Intensity and Pitch of Pure Tone", *Jour. Genet. Psychol.*, **40**, 162–80.

HALVERSON, H. M. (1931): "An Experimental Study of Prehension in Infants by means of Systematic Cinema Records", *Genet. Psychol. Monogr.*, **10**, 107–286.

HALVERSON, H. M. (1937): "Studies of the Grasping Reflexes of Early Infancy", I, II, III., *Jour. Genet. Psychol.*, **51**, 371–449.

HAZLITT, V. (1931): "Modern Trends in Infant Psychology", *Brit. Jour. Educ. Psychol.*, **1**, 120–9.

HAZLITT, V. (1933): *The Psychology of Infancy* (New York: Dutton).

HEIDER, F. K., and HEIDER, G. M. (1940a): "A Study of Phonetic Symbolism of Deaf Children", *Psychol. Monogr.*, **52**, No. 1, 23–41.

HEIDER, F. K., and HEIDER, G. M. (1940b): "A Comparative Study of Sentence Structure of Deaf and Hearing Children", *Psychol. Monogr.*, **52**, No. 1, 42–103.

HESS, J. H. Y., MOHR, G. J., and BARTELME, P. E. (1934): *The Physical and Mental Growth of Prematurely Born Children* (Chicago: Univ. of Chicago Press).

IRWIN, O. C. (1941): "Research on Speech Sounds for the First Six Months of Life", *Psychol. Bull.*, **38**, 277–85.

ISAACS, S. (1929): *The Nursery Years* (London: Routledge).

ISAACS, S. (1930): *Intellectual Growth in Young Children* (London: Routledge).

ISAACS, S. (1932): *The Children We Teach* (Univ. of London Press).

ISAACS, S. (1933): *Social Development in Young Children* (London: Routledge and Kegan Paul).

ISAACS, S. (1948): *Childhood and After* (London: Routledge and Kegan Paul).

JAMES, W. (1890): *Principles of Psychology*, 2 vols. (London).

JEWELL, A. A. (1933): "Birth Injury in Relation to Mental Deficiency", *Proc. In. Acad. Sci.*, **40**, 191.

KEIR, G. (1952): "A History of Child Guidance. Symposium on Psychologists and Psychiatrists in the Child Guidance Service", III, *Brit. Jour. Educ. Psychol.*, **22**, (I), 5–29.

KELLOGG, W. N., and KELLOGG, L. A. (1933): *The Ape and the Child* (New York: McGraw Hill).

KIRKPATRICK, E. A. (1923): *Fundamentals of Child Study* (New York: Macmillan).

KLEIN, M. (1932): *The Psychoanalysis of Children* (London: Hogarth Press).

KNIGHT, R. (1933): *Intelligence and Intelligence Testing* (London: Methuen).

KOEHLER, W. (1924): *The Mentality of Apes* (London: Kegan Paul).

KOFFKA, K. (1928): *The Growth of the Mind* (London: Kegan Paul).

KOFFKA, K. (1935): "Psychology of Learning, with reference to the Acquisition of Language", *Engl. Jour.* (coll. ed.), **24**, 388–96.

KOUPERNIK, C. (Ed.) (1951): *Psychiatrie Sociale de l'Enfant*. Conférences, publiées sous la direction de C. Koupernik. Travaux et Documents du Centre international de l'Enfance, Paris.

KOUPERNIK, C. (1952): "Les tests de Gesell, leurs limites, leur intégration à une clinique du premier âge", *Presse médicale*, 60e année, **21,** 449–50.

LANGAN, I. W. (1945): *Instruction Booklet for a Special Adaptation for the Blind of the 1937 Revision of the Stanford-Binet Tests* (Bristol: Stoke Park Colony).

LEWIS, M. M. (1936): *Infant Speech: A Study of the Beginnings of Language* (London: Kegan Paul).

LEWIS, M. M. (1937): "The Beginning of Reference to Past and Future in a Child's Speech", *Brit. Jour. Educ. Psychol.*, **7,** 39–56.

LEWIS, M. M. (1938): "The Beginning and Early Functioning of Questions in a Child's Speech", *Brit. Jour. Educ. Psychol.*, **8,** 150–71.

LIEBERMAN, S. S. (1952): "Notes on the Clinical Use of Achievement Testing", *Brit. Jour. Med. Psychol.*, **25,** 169–268.

LOCKE, J. (1690): *Essay Concerning Human Understanding.*

LOWENFELD, M. (1935): *Play in Childhood* (London: Gollancz).

MCCARTHY, D. (1929): "The Vocalisation of Infants", *Psychol. Bull.*, **26,** 625–51.

MCCARTHY, D. (1930): *The Language Development of the Pre-School Child* (Inst. Child Welfare Monogr. Ser., No. 4) (Minneapolis: Univ. of Minnesota Press).

MCCARTHY, D. (1946): "Language Development in Children", in L. Carmichael (Ed.), *Manual of Child Psychology*, Ch. 10.

MCDOUGALL, W. (1908): *An Introduction to Social Psychology* (London: Methuen).

MCGRAW, M. B. (1942): *The Neuromuscular Maturation of the Human Infant* (New York: Columbia Univ. Press).

MACMEEKEN, A. M. (1939): *The Intelligence of a Representative Group of Scottish Children* (London: Univ. of London Press).

MCMILLAN, M. (1930): *The Nursery School* (2nd ed.).

MCNEMAR, Q. (1942): *The Revision of the Stanford-Binet Scale: An Analysis of the Standardisation Data* (Boston: Houghton Mifflin).

MAJOR, D. R. (1906): *First Steps in Mental Growth: A Series of Studies in the Psychology of Infancy* (New York: Macmillan).

MELCHER, R. T. (1934): "Children's Motor Learning with and without Vision", *Child Development*, **5,** 315–50.

Mental Deficiency Committee, Report of (1929) (H.M. Stationery Office, London).

MURCHISON, C. (Ed.) (1933): *A Handbook of Child Psychology* (2nd ed. revised) (Worcester: Clark Univ. Press).

NISSEN, H. W. (1931): "A Field Study of the Chimpanzee", *Comp. Psych. Monogr.*, **8,** No. 36.

PAVLOV, I. P. (1927): *Conditioned Reflexes: An Investigation of the Physiological Activity of the Cerebral Cortex* (trans. by C. V. Anrep) (London: Oxford Univ. Press).

PENROSE, L. S. (1933): *Mental Defect* (London: Sidgwick & Jackson).

PREYER, W. (1882): *Die Seele des Kindes* (Leipzig). Translated as *The Mind of the Child*, Pts. I and II (New York: Appleton (1888, 1889)).

ROBERTS, J. A. F., NORMAN, R. M., and GRIFFITHS, R. (1935): "Studies on a Child Population, I. Definition of the Sample, etc", *Annals of Eugenics*, **6**, 319–38.

ROBERTS, J. A. F., and GRIFFITHS, R. (1937): "Studies on a Child Population, II. Retests on the Advanced Otis and Stanford-Binet Scales, etc", *Annals of Eugenics*, **8** (I), 15–45.

ROBERTS, J. A. F., NORMAN, R. M., and GRIFFITHS, R. (1938a): "Studies on a Child Population, III. Intelligence and Family Size", *Annals of Eugenics*, **8** (II), 178–215.

ROBERTS, J. A. F., NORMAN, R. M., and GRIFFITHS, R. (1938b): "Studies on a Child Population, IV. The Form of the Lower End of the Frequency Distribution, etc", *Annals of Eugenics*, **8** (IV), 319–36.

ROBERTS, J. A. F., GORDON, R. G., and GRIFFITHS, R. (1939): "Does Poliomyelitis Affect Intellectual Capacity?", *Brit. Med. Jour.*

Scottish Council for Research in Education (1933): *The Intelligence of Scottish Children* (Univ. of London Press).

SETH, G., and GUTHRIE, D. (1935): *Speech in Childhood: Its Development and Disorders* (London: Oxford Univ. Press).

SHELDON, W. (1936): *Diseases of Infancy and Childhood* (London: J. & A. Churchill).

SHERRINGTON, C. S. (1906): *The Integrative Action of the Nervous System.*

SHINN, M. W. (1893–99): *Notes on the Development of a Child* (Univ. Calif. Publ., **1**, 1–178, 179–424).

SHINN, M. W. (1900): *Biography of a Baby* (Boston: Houghton Mifflin).

SHIRLEY, M. M. (1933): *The First Two Years: A Study of Twenty-five Babies*, Vols. I to III (Minneapolis: Univ. of Minnesota Press).

SPEARMAN, C. (1904): "General Intelligence Objectively Determined and Measured", *Amer. Jour. Psychol.*, **15**, 201–92.

SPEARMAN, C. (1923): *The Nature of Intelligence and the Principles of Cognition* (London: Macmillan).

SPEARMAN, C. (1927): *The Abilities of Man: Their Nature and Measurement* (London: Macmillan).

STERN, W. (1930): *Psychology of Early Childhood* (trans. by A. Barwell) (New York: Holt; London: Allen).

STINCHFIELD, S. M., and YOUNG, E. H. (1938), *Children with Delayed or Defective Speech: Motor-kinesthetic Factors in their Training* (Stanford Univ. Press, Calif.).

STUTSMAN, R. (1931): *Mental Measurement of Pre-School Children* (Yonkers: World Book).

SULLY, J. (1896, 1908): *Studies of Childhood* (London and New York: Appleton).

SYKES, J. (1940): "A Study of the Spontaneous Vocalisations of Young Deaf Children", *Psychol. Monogr.*, **52**, No. 1, 104–23.

TERMAN, L. M. (1916): *The Measurement of Intelligence* (Boston: Houghton Mifflin).

TERMAN, L. M., and MERRILL, M. A. (1937): *Measuring Intelligence: A Guide to the Administration of the New Revised Stanford-Binet Tests of Intelligence* (Boston: Houghton Mifflin).

THOMSON, G. H. (1939): *The Factorial Analysis of Human Ability* (Univ. of London Press).

THOMSON, G. H. (1940): *An Analysis of the Performance Test Scores of a Representative Group of Scottish Children* (Scottish Council for Educ. Research) (Univ. of London Press).

THORNDIKE, E. L. (1931): *Human Learning* (New York: Century).

THURSTONE, L. L., and THURSTONE, T. G. (1941): "Factorial Studies of Intelligence", *Psychometr. Monogr.*, No. 2.

TREDGOLD, A. F. (1929): *Mental Deficiency* (*Amentia*), 5th ed. revised.

VALENTINE, C. W. (1942): *The Psychology of Early Childhood* (London: Methuen).

VALENTINE, C. W. (1945): *Intelligence Tests for Children* (London: Methuen).

VERNON, P. E. (1940): *The Measurement of Abilities* (London: Univ. of London Press).

VERNON, P. E. (1950): *The Structure of Human Abilities* (London: Methuen).

WALLIN, J. E. W. (1949): *Children with Mental and Physical Handicaps* (New York: Prentice-Hall).

WEST, R. (1937): *The Rehabilitation of Speech* (London and New York: Harper).

WOODWORTH, R. S. (1922): *Experimental Psychology* (London: Methuen).

WOOLF, L. I., GRIFFITHS, R., and MONCRIEFF, A. (1955): "Treatment of Phenylketonuria with a Diet low in Phenylalanine." *Brit. Med. Jour.*, Jan. 8th, 1955, **1**, 57.

WOOLF, L. I., GRIFFITHS, R., MONCRIEFF, A., COATES, S., and DILLISTONE, F. (1958): "The Dietary Treatment of Phenylketonuria." *Archives of Disease in Childhood*, Feb. 1958, **33**, No. 167.

YERKES, R. M., and YERKES, A. W. (1929): *The Great Apes: A Study of Anthropoid Life* (New Haven: Yale Univ. Press).

YULE, G. U., and KENDALL, M. G. (1937): *An Introduction to the Theory of Statistics* (London: Charles Griffin).

INDEX